D1067522

ON

INTERNAL

WAR

320.91724
Od 50

ON

INTERNAL

WAR

· ·

American

and Soviet

Approaches

to Third World

Clients

and Insurgents

William E. Odom

Duke University Press

Durham & London

1992

© 1992 William E. Odom
All rights reserved
Printed in the United States of America
on acid-free paper ∞
Library of Congress Cataloging-in-Publication Data
appear on the last printed page of this book.

Contents

· ·

CAT Apr 12 '93

2-17-93 MLS 28.27

ALLEGHENY COLLEGE LIBRARY

To my West Point roommate,
Andre C. Lucas,
Congressional Medal of Honor winner,
who was killed leading his battalion
off Firebase Ripcord in Vietnam,
23 July 1970.

Acknowledgments

This book was made possible by the Hudson Institute, which supported the research; the former president of Hudson, Mitchell Daniels, Jr., deserves credit for encouraging me to write it. The navy provided funding for an earlier version, and Admiral William Smith of the navy staff in particular showed encouraging interest in the initial results.

Naturally I bear the responsibility for choosing the focus of the analysis. It attempts to meld together a variety of perspectives on a subject that has been fairly significant over the past four decades, not only for U.S. national security policy but also for political science as an academic discipline—both "governing" and "war" fall into its domain. Having served in Vietnam on the planning staff of the U.S. Military Assistance Command I bring some biases to the subject, but not necessarily the ones readers may expect. That laboratory experience, shortly after graduate study at Columbia University where I was first introduced to political development theory, allowed me to witness the degree to which theory both informed and misinformed practice as well as where theory played no role at all.

More recently, U.S. involvement in internal wars in Central America and elsewhere and the renewed attention in government circles to "low intensity conflict" suggest that the topic needs a fundamental rethinking. The end of the Cold War may also mark the end of the U.S.-Soviet competition in these wars, but continued U.S. involvement in global politics makes it unlikely that the United States will wholly ignore all such conflicts. By attempting to cover so much ground and open so many issues I will surely frustrate some readers. Where I am wrong in the analysis or have overlooked some of the growing body of political and economic development theory, I am anxious to learn from my critics.

John Tsagronis, my research assistant at Hudson, deserves a special word of gratitude. His unflagging energy and keen intelligence have contributed enormously to the effort. No less important has been his willingness to take a critical view and force me to rethink the analysis from time to time.

Finally, I am indebted to Carol Lynch, my secretary. She kept the study on a much faster schedule than I believed possible. Her extraordinary skills and diligence are difficult to exaggerate.

I

Introduction

· ·

Over the past four decades, the Third World has been a vast theater of warfare. While the trilateral regions of North America, Europe, and Northeast Asia have enjoyed an unprecedented period of peace, the remainder of the world has endured unprecedented violence and military strife. The Middle East, South and Southwest Asia, Southeast Asia, Africa, and Latin America have been the scene of small wars, large wars, wars between states, wars among tribes, civil wars, ethnic wars, race conflicts, religious wars, peasant-based insurgencies, coups, countercoups, and perhaps other kinds of violence. The level of military technology in these wars has risen as arms transfers and military assistance from the advanced industrial states have become steadily more abundant.

Over this panoply of diverse strife, political and military, has been imposed a global competition between the Soviet-led forces of communism and the American-led forces of liberal democracy. Although the West has not always been disposed to see itself as a "camp" in a great two-sided struggle, Soviet leaders imposed that definition on it and cast the world as divided into two camps—a socialist camp and an imperialist camp locked in an irreconcilable conflict. The ensuing competition, of course, took the Cold War as its name.

The U.S. policy of "containment" was rather successful in creating alliances in the trilateral region that checked the Soviet bloc. The Third World, however, proved to be a far more intractable problem, not only for Washington but also for Moscow. While Washington's alliances in Southwest Asia and Southeast Asia proved more often to be form than substance, Moscow found its leadership of the socialist camp challenged in Yugoslavia and China, creating what was called "polycentrism." Client states and political movements in the Third World have not always been willing to see things as a two-camp struggle, and they have sometimes changed camps, tried to remain neutral, and formed nonaligned groupings.

In the detente era of the 1970s, many believed that the Cold War was ending, but by the end of the decade, competition in the Third World proved this a false hope. The U.S. failure in Vietnam convinced many opinion makers and political leaders that the United States simply could not compete effectively in these Third World conflicts and that it should withdraw completely. Too often the United States seemed to be supporting dictatorships rather than expanding democracy. Moscow had its own problems with bourgeois nationalists who were not willing to introduce the Soviet version of socialism.

By the end of the 1970s, however, the Soviet Union was making notable gains in Southwest Asia, Southeast Asia, Africa, and even Central America. And by the early 1980s, the United States was deeply engaged in conflicts in Central America, Southwest Asia, and Africa. Soviet policy in the Gorbachev era has shown strong signs of retrenching, drawing back from the Third World. The dramatic ideological revisions by Gorbachev, the collapse of the Soviet position in Central Europe, and the increasing anarchy within the Soviet borders have been hailed in the West as the end of the Cold War. These events may well mark Soviet withdrawal from the Third World competition. They have already had a visible impact in several regions. In light of the dramatic change in the Soviet Union, does it make sense to proceed with this study? The answer is yes for several reasons.

First, such a study has value as historical perspective on East-West competition in internal wars. The actual cases provide a rich body of material for understanding more about the dynamics of these wars and the patrons of the competing sides. If, indeed, the Soviet Union abandoned all of its clients in the Third World today or in the near future, the policy relevance of this study might be reduced—but not its analytical relevance for political science.

Second, even if the Soviet Union drops out of the competition entirely, a few other Marxist-Leninist states have not—notably Cuba, China, North Korea, and Vietnam. Although they may be forced to follow the Soviet example in the near future, some of them may not.

Third, radical insurgencies carrying banners ranging from Marxism and Leninism to Maoism are active in a number of places—for example, the Philippines, Peru, and Central America. The Shining Path or Sendero Luminoso in Peru and the New People's Army in the Philippines may be affected by Soviet policy, but they are unlikely to give up in the near future. The same is true for radical insurgent factions in Cambodia. Winding down support for the "international class struggle" has not been easy for Gorbachev in the Soviet Union, and it could take even longer in some of the radical movements abroad.

Fourth, Leninism and Maoism in their organizational concepts, strategy, and tactics offer a body of well-articulated guidance for any radical group in the world which wants to draw on them for attacking a Third World government. The failure of socialism in the Soviet Union after seven decades of strenuous effort to make it succeed may mean much less to angry radicals anxious to take power away from a local regime than the success of socialism as a formula for mobilizing a revolutionary party and army. The failure of the Soviet economy today does not discredit Lenin's strategy and tactics for seizing and holding power in a backward country.

Fifth, a number of non-Marxist-Leninist states in the world today encourage and support radical political and insurgent movements. Libya is an example. Iran is another. Yet others may arise. While they are inspired by different ideologies, their methods and techniques have parallels with the Soviet approach.

Finally, the Soviet Union cannot be counted out of the Third World entirely. During 1990, significant Soviet assistance was still flowing to client states and insurgents. Moreover, the turbulent political change in the Soviet Union could eventually produce a regime not as willing to drop out of the competition as Gorbachev's government. Whatever happens, internal wars will not disappear from the Third World in the 1990s. Some of them are bound to affect U.S. interests, raising the issues of U.S. involvement. The probability that the Soviet Union or some other Marxist-Leninist state will be supporting at least one side in those wars, although lower than in the past, is hardly zero. At the same time, other sources of material support for left radicalism already exist, are not likely to disappear, and could increase. The end of the Cold War, therefore, does not remove the relevance of this study for the decade ahead.[1]

Critics of the U.S. policy of competing in the Third World have long insisted that the conflicts there have indigenous dimensions and causes which wholly transcend the East-West competition. It is certainly true that misjudgments have afflicted U.S. strategy in coping with Third World conflicts, and it is true that U.S.–Soviet competition is much less important for determining the outcome of some of these conflicts than are the indigenous factors. No U.S. strategy for Third World security problems has much chance of success unless it is better informed about political and economic development factors in the countries that become the focus of a security problem. This will remain true with or without Soviet efforts to influence their development.

The critics often imply, or say explicitly, that the United States can and should simply walk away from Third World conflicts and leave them to the Soviet Union or some other interested power. Precisely what this would produce, however, is not always made clear. It is probably true that the United States can ignore many such conflicts without serious danger to its own security and other interests. Criteria for selecting those to ignore and those to take seriously, however, are seldom spelled out.

Even if they were, another challenge arises: how should the United States be involved where its interests are at stake? The techniques of involvement in the 1950s and 1960s have, in the minds of many Americans, been wholly discredited by our experience in Vietnam. Numerous books and articles have been written on our mistakes in Vietnam, on what went wrong, and on how to avoid such failure again.

In some ways, this study, although not about Vietnam, falls into that category of analysis, but it is different in more ways than it is similar. It has been inspired by what seems to be a failure to conceptualize adequately not only the full dimensions of the U.S.–Soviet competition in the Third World but more particularly the nature of insurgent wars and the politics of patron-client relations. American officials have learned a lot, but they have not put it together so that they can take advantage of much available scholarship and analysis of the manifold aspects of the problem.

For example, students of Third World political development have made much progress in understanding why Third World states face instability and why some of them cope effectively while others do not. Their understanding has improved considerably since the 1950s. The same is true for students of economic development. Students of Soviet strategy for the two-camp struggle have uncovered much about

Soviet tactics, strengths, and weaknesses. Students of military affairs have written much about insurgency and counterinsurgency, and in the 1980s a new slogan, "low intensity conflict," has become popular. Presumably it is inspiring innovative and promising new approaches to the military dimensions of Third World conflicts.

A look at much of what is going on under the "low intensity conflict" banner, however, does not inspire confidence that progress is being made on the military front. Precisely what the term "low intensity conflict" means is not clear. Depending on where one is and what role one plays, a "low intensity conflict" may seem extremely intense. Furthermore, while proponents of low intensity conflict forces and doctrine acknowledge the importance of the political and economic aspects of such wars, they seldom spell them out in specific cases so that their relevance to the proposed military doctrine can be judged. Too often these theorists appear to take for granted old and patently wrong ideas about what begets political stability and democratic development in Third World states. The U.S. involvement in Central America has given added impetus to the low intensity conflict school, and while it offers new technologies and some new ideas about how to structure appropriate U.S. forces for participation, it carries a lot of the old baggage from the counterinsurgency doctrine of the 1960s.

Two things seem to be missing from the various lines of study of the problem that the Third World poses for U.S. security. First, there is seldom an effort to stand back and view the U.S.–Soviet competition in its broadest context, to examine the assumptions and political values on both sides, to reexamine the record on both sides, and to relate the competition to the indigenous factors that cause wars in the Third World. Second, there has been little effective effort to integrate the military dimension of wars in the Third World with two other dimensions—external influences and indigenous politics. Mention of their importance and urgings that they be seen as important are numerous, but how they interrelate and how they affect U.S. strategy are integrating issues that are largely neglected.

The purpose of this study is to provide those two missing perspectives. It ranges widely and brings together several dimensions of internal wars in the Third World, showing some causal relationships that are important to U.S. strategy but are poorly understood or that operate in the opposite direction of that we most often assume—to the detriment of our goals and the client state.

This study begins with a critical review of U.S. and Soviet approaches to the competition in the Third World, including the political ideologies and aims both sides bring to the competition. It attempts to highlight some of the advantages and constraints that both sides face, and it assesses the record to date of successes and failures for both sides. Next it examines indigenous political developments in the Third World, drawing heavily on political development theory to underscore critical determinants of change, stability, and prospects for democracy.

Against this broad analysis of the Third World in general, this study offers a judgment about where wars in the Third World actually affect U.S. interests adversely—that is, which areas the United States cannot responsibly ignore in light of its own interests and security. If some readers disagree with the areas selected, the analysis should force them to think rigorously about the problem of selection and proper criteria for making other choices. American resources are limited. We cannot compete equally everywhere.

Next the study offers three case studies of wars in Central America and Southeast Asia, regions of significant U.S. interest, wars where the U.S. is heavily engaged in one case, little engaged in another, and drifting toward heavy engagement in yet another. In each of the cases, a common analytic approach is taken to assess the results. First, this approach brings together the indigenous political and economic development in each case with external influences—including those of the United States—showing how all parties are engaged and permitting some judgments about the criticality of each of these factors to the way the war is going. Second, it allows us to look at the military strategy and tactics on both sides as well as understand that the "order of battle" extends far beyond the boundaries of the country in which the war is occurring. Third, it facilitates cross-case comparisons, helping to identify causal relationships. In addition to the case studies, it offers a review of political and military developments in the Middle East, a region of great strategic importance to the United States where the character of internal wars is quite different from its character in the case studies, thus clarifying the ways in which the United States has been and is likely to become militarily engaged. The appropriate U.S. military capabilities are, accordingly, also quite different.

The case studies provide a basis for some analytical excursions on alternative strategies that the United States might pursue, strategies that promise more effective prosecution of the wars in each. The excursions also examine the political consequences that could result as well as note the political feasibility for such changes in U.S. strategy.

Finally, some conclusions are drawn about what kinds of military means the United States needs to engage effectively in these conflicts. These conclusions are seriously at odds with the present Defense Department emphasis on building large special operations forces for extensive counterinsurgency campaigns. On the contrary, they suggest that such forces are needed only in very limited numbers. Furthermore, they suggest that the redundant creation of paramilitary capabilities by the CIA does not make much sense and that the Director of Central Intelligence would be wiser to borrow such capabilities from the Department of Defense.

The study's conclusions are not limited to military force structure implications. In the course of the case studies, it became clear that U.S. economic assistance policy is not only ineffective; it seems to be counterproductive. Economic development and local government seem to suffer rather than profit from such fiscal assistance. Private sector capital has much more to offer. Students of economic development theory will not be surprised at this finding as it concerns economics, but the fact that direct fiscal aid seems to hurt more than help the government in genuinely winning the war against an insurgency is not the conventional wisdom.

It also became clear in the case studies that democracy in these countries has little enduring prospect until land reform essentially removes the oligarchy of large landowners from their powerful political position. Democratic elections and rule may take place, but broadly inclusive democratic institutions have little chance of developing as long as a large landless peasantry persists. This may be the greatest obstacle facing U.S. strategy in these states. It not only makes democracy improbable but also makes the war unwinnable. For political development theorists, this is not a new insight. Nor has it gone unappreciated in U.S. policy since the 1950s. It does, however, tend to be pushed aside and ignored when U.S. political and military leaders find it difficult to make progress in getting the assisted government to implement land reforms. For that reason, therefore, it deserves special emphasis in our findings.

An overarching theme in this study is the American tendency to become confused about internal wars and external wars, to make this analytical distinction too much an operational constraint in how our military develops a strategy for such conflicts. The transnational dimensions of internal wars are noted in principle in the counterinsurgency literature, but in determining military tactics and strategy for counterinsurgency campaigns, the focus is almost wholly internal. In some regards this focus is imposed by our political leadership's disposition to see these wars in this way. Politically we may have to treat them as purely internal wars, but in determining the adversary's "order of battle," the forces that it brings to bear in the conflict, it is imperative to include the external dimensions. They are difficult to find in many cases, and they are not only military in nature. Yet they contribute to the insurgent's military strength, and they can play a very large role at different times and stages of a conflict.

Over two decades ago, Harry Eckstein edited a study of "internal war."[2] It went quite far in defining the concept, and even today it stands as an excellent departure point for analysis. Unfortunately, little of what has been written about civil war and lesser kinds of violence since then has built on the work of Eckstein and his coauthors. As one of them, Karl Deutsch, recognized, it is not enough to deal with internal war only as a domestic affair. Internal wars are certainly in a different class from external wars, but that does not mean they are always devoid of external involvement. History is filled with examples of transnational participation in internal wars. Deutsch noted the Continental Congress's efforts to subvert Canada's loyalty to Britain. The ideological struggle in Europe during the French Revolution, he observed, involved the spreading of cheap translations of Rousseau's works throughout Europe. Britain and the conservative powers responded with translations of Edmund Burke and Joseph de Maistre. Much earlier, he pointed out, France and Spain got Sweden and Austria to fight as their respective proxies in an "internal war" in Germany, the Thirty Years War.

The connection between internal war and external war is as important as either category by itself if we are to understand the true nature of modern internal wars. While this is true enough for purely academic understanding, it is equally true and perhaps more urgent for American policy-making. External war in its traditional form has virtually disappeared among the modern industrial states, certainly among the liberal democracies.[3] Nuclear weapons have made it most unattractive between the old Soviet bloc and the opposing Western alliances in Europe and East Asia. At the same time, both internal and external wars have been numerous and frequent in the Third World, and there is little prospect that the number will abate more than temporarily in the decades ahead.

The transnational character of so many contemporary internal wars is a major strategic reality which gives them a central place in American national security concerns. How we view those conflicts, how we judge what is at stake, how others, particularly the Soviet Union, participate in them, and how we decide whether to become involved in them—these are major strategic choices.

We do not have to compete within the constraints that seeing these wars as wholly internal imposes. However, to a large degree, international law has developed in a way that reinforces our disposition to overlook the external dimensions or to leave those dimensions free from attack.

This study makes no pretense of advancing theories of political and economic development. Rather it tries to take advantage of the growing body of scholarship available in those areas by applying it selectively— and to the best of our understanding, appropriately—in order to gain a comprehensive appreciation of the complex array of variables that affect U.S. strategy in competing with the Soviet Union and its allies in the Third World. Nor does it attempt a microanalysis of the effectiveness of various counterinsurgency tactics that U.S. military advisors bring to internal wars. Rather it tries to show the larger battlefield of political, economic, and military elements and what they portend for likely success or failure in the overall campaign. Clever tactics cannot compensate for poorly conceived strategy. We must get the strategy right first of all.

The major findings of this study are that the present U.S. strategy for dealing with counterinsurgencies has very low prospects for success and that some rather counterintuitive policies, such as cutting almost all direct aid to the client state and giving its military very little advice, would not be less effective and in some cases would be more effective for U.S. aims. Our present strategy amounts essentially to "colonialism by ventriloquy." Actual colonialism would be more effective, not only for our military aims of defeating the insurgents but also for developing a stable democracy. Given the political unacceptability of that alternative, we could leave some of our clients to defeat and allow our interests to be so damaged that a quite different political consensus emerges in the United States for a quite different strategy. In between these two extremes, there are things we can do to focus more military and

political attention on the external dimensions of these internal wars—
an approach that promises better results than our present emphasis
primarily on the internal dimensions.

Soviet strategy has its own problems, but Marxist-Leninist institutions, once installed in Third World states, do not show a propensity to
evolve into democracy. At least there have been no examples to date.
Although not Third World states, Poland and Hungary and perhaps
other East European states are making progress that may prove the exception. In any event, Soviet-type regimes have proven both highly
durable and highly repressive.[4] The political attitude in the United
States that supports abandonment of besieged client states to Marxist-
Leninist takeovers may prevail. That course may alleviate the United
States of responsibility for shoring up antidemocratic regimes and the
moral discomfort that comes with such support, but it also amounts to
abandonment of support for democracy. We cannot have it both ways.
Expanding democracy in areas of strategic significance to us will sometimes require much greater U.S. involvement, militarily and politically.
There is no technical military way around this dilemma, certainly not
in the arsenal of "low intensity conflict" doctrine and forces. As Samuel
Huntington has observed, "A significant correlation exists between the
rise and fall of American power in the world and the rise and fall of
liberty and democracy in the world."[5] The burden of the argument in
this study is not to compel a choice for one or the other horn of the
dilemma; rather the aim is to clarify the consequences of the choice we
make as a country and the policies we follow.

II

The Two-Camp Struggle:

Competing Approaches

●●

In this postwar era, there have been two competing visions of historical development and politics. The American vision is more ambiguous and variously understood when projected to the Third World, yet it is based on sound general ideas about justice, democracy, and economics. The Soviet vision is more explicitly articulated in its ideological assumptions, and its strategy and tactics are more integrated in their components, but the vision is based on flawed notions of justice, democratic politics, and economic development. Let us review the theoretical and philosophical foundations of each approach to the competition. This is important for understanding their historical records even if the Cold War has ended. Moreover, the diffusion of Soviet tactics to other states and radical movements means that its relevance in the post–Cold War period will persist for some time to come.

The American Approach

Two lines of thought have guided most of our policies in this East-West struggle. The first is found in the academic world, largely in two disciplines—political science and economics. It focuses on political and economic development of the nonindustrial states. It began with some fairly simplistic notions of how democracy and economic prosperity could arise in the Late Developing Countries (LDCs). In its crudest form, this approach projected the American experience onto the LDCs. Economic growth would create a middle class which in turn would create stability and encourage liberal democratic politics. Many distinguished scholars come to mind if we trace this theory of development to its more textured and insightful analysis of politics and economics in the Third World. Almond, Powell, Lipset, Apter, Rustow, Deutsch, Lerner, Black, Shils, La Palombara, and Huntington are a few of the more illustrious political development theorists.[1] Gerschenkron, Kuznets, Hirschman, Olson, Hoselitz, and Hagen are among the economists.[2] These short lists do injustice to a large number of other names whose contributions are equally rich and prolific.

All of these scholars proceed on the assumption that the international system is properly composed of sovereign states. "Nation states" is a more commonly used term. While they recognize that many new states are hardly nations in the traditional sense, they devote their studies to learning how nation states develop—how they come to be— and they seek formulas that might guide policies for building democratic institutions in such states. Their assumptions, implicit and explicit, do not challenge the concept of international law that has grown up in Europe since the time of Grotius. On the contrary, they favor a Third World development along this European path—one that will bring the LDCs into this North American–European community of modern states.

American policymakers have been greatly influenced by these political scientists, both directly and indirectly; and, although government officials have generally understood their theories poorly, they have drawn on them to develop and justify diplomacy and economic assistance policies.

The second line of thought concerns the use of military capabilities to support assistance policies. The first major contribution to this field of thought came from General Maxwell Taylor. In his book, *The Uncertain Trumpet,* he challenged our excessive reliance on nuclear deterrence and insisted that we must have military forces capable of limited operations, able to fight wars without nuclear weapons and within a limited geographical area. He was concerned primarily with war in the conventional sense, and Korea was his paradigm. Under President Kennedy, he got his chance to put the theory into practice; and, at the same time, some of the scholars—most notably, W. W. Rostow—were given the same opportunity. On the military side, the JFK School at Fort Bragg was founded to teach officers how to combine military capabilities with civil efforts in nation building.

Early in 1962, within the National Security Council (NSC), the special group Counterinsurgency was formed with General Taylor as its chairman. Its task was to coordinate all government agencies that have a role in internal wars, and it included the attorney general, the under secretary of state for political affairs, the chairman of the Joint Chiefs of Staff (JCS), the special assistant to the president for national security affairs (i.e., the national security advisor), the head of the Agency for International Development (AID), and the director of the United States Information Agency (USIA).[3] Its composition recognized that such conflicts involved more than military actions and required a coordinated strategy. President Kennedy, speaking to the graduating class at West Point in June 1962, declared that America faced a new kind of war: "This is another kind of war, new in its intensity, ancient in its origins—war by guerrillas, subversives, insurgents, assassins. . . . It requires . . . a wholly new kind of strategy." Although General Taylor's NSC special group never really managed to resolve the coordination problem, and no lead agency was selected to give it a solid foundation in the bureaucracy, a whirlwind of activity did follow. The Special Warfare School (later named the JFK School) began to call on the academic world. In March 1962, a symposium of 350 social and behavioral scientists was held to help the army define a proper approach for the strategy the president demanded.[4] While they all insisted that new military training and tactics were required, no clear view of a new strategy emerged.

The development of military theory was more disjointed than the growth of political development theory. Scholars like Thomas Schelling, Bernard Brodie, Robert Osgood, Herman Kahn, and Albert Wohlstetter had already inserted their theories of limited war, nuclear deterrence, game theory, and escalation concepts into the thinking about strategy by the uniformed military. When President Kennedy emphasized internal war, the military, primarily the army, tried to adapt the forces it had developed for more traditional forms of warfare. The Special Forces grew out of the residue of World War II special operations left in the army by the Offices of Strategic Services (OSS). The CIA, meanwhile, broke away from the army and took an independent organizational form, mixing traditional intelligence collection with covert action and paramilitary operations. While the CIA was authorized to continue the OSS tradition in peacetime, conducting actual operations in such places as Guatemala and Iran, the Special Forces were reduced to training for the event of another conventional war. They prepared to assist and train insurgents within the territories of enemy states in wartime. Their early field manuals were dedicated to the techniques and tactics of unconventional operations using indigenous insurgent forces.

In the early 1960s, as the United States became involved more deeply in Vietnam, the Special Forces found themselves turned on their heads. They would set aside the insurgency mission and become "counterinsurgents." Instead of exploiting political contradictions in an enemy state, they would have to help an American client state prevent insurgents from exploiting its own political conditions.

It takes little imagination to realize that this reversal of roles would not easily be accomplished. The necessary skills and equipment for insurgency and counterinsurgency are only partially overlapping, and the most important ones are in the nonoverlapping areas. That, however, is not the most critical difference for our analysis here. In their original role, the Special Forces were to create civil war in another state. They would recruit and assist allies for the U.S. side within the populace of the adversary state. In their new role, it was just the opposite. They would prevent this kind of transnational interference, stop civil war, and help the local government defeat such politically directed violence.

The distinction is apparent in the name for the earlier mission: unconventional warfare. It implicitly recognized that this was not really "cricket" in the European tradition of interstate war where regular armies met in battle to decide the struggle. In this context, this form of warfare violated the rules; thus the name "unconventional warfare."

While Special Forces have kept the original mission for wartime contingencies, they have been unable to shed the new mission—counterinsurgency and military assistance. The new mission, however, is more in line with the traditional concept of interstate warfare. It is based on the assumption that terrorism and insurgency are violations of international law and the international system. States have a right to ask for assistance in putting down such paramilitary actions, and the United States has a right to lend that assistance if U.S. leaders judge the incumbent government worthy and a contributor to American interests.

In the past decade, a new concept, "low intensity conflict," has emerged to guide military force development for such conflicts. Precisely how it is to take operational form is far from clear, but it seems to include more than Special Forces. Air and naval forces also seem to have a place in the new scheme.[5]

Many conclusions and observations could be made about this mix of military developments related to nation building and competition with the Soviet Union in the Third World, but one is especially important: U.S. policy-makers proceed on the assumption that the conflict is primarily an interstate conflict. The legitimate actors are states and incumbent governments. The insurgents are illegimate actors. They differ from ordinary criminals only in that they are de facto forces of other governments, cadres which mobilize dissident forces within a foreign state to unseat its incumbent government.

In assessing this American approach to the competition, many observers have commented on the American preference for political stability and the status quo. That is indeed the case in military affairs. While the United States is not wedded to the political status quo and even insists on changing it in some cases, the United States has yet to develop a legal theory for the use of military force that transcends traditional international law. Admittedly some attempts have been made to look back at the Vietnam War from the viewpoint of international law and determine whether a legal case for American military actions can be established. Louis Henkin concluded in such an analysis that "Vietnam epitomizes the obstacles to a rule of law in regard to military interventions in internal wars in an age of ideological conflict. The traditional law is extant but too often disregarded, and there is no consensus between East and West or even between North and South that would support new law against such intervention."[6] Britain, France, and other European colonial powers had such a legal theory in their territorial sovereignty over colonies. The United States has found itself in the predicament of trying to play the old colonial role by ventriloquy, advising local sovereign governments and armies rather than taking direct control.

Nation states based on territorial sovereignty are relatively new in the world.[7] In feudal Europe, the modern idea of territorial sovereignty was unknown. The Catholic church and Christendom did not recognize such secular authority. Nor did noble families and intermarried feudal dynasties. Many institutions moved freely across territorial, ethnic, and language boundaries. Institutional obligations between individuals and the organization tended to transcend territories. The history

ALLEGHENY COLLEGE LIBRARY

of modern Europe is the story of breakdown of these trans-state institutions and the emergence of a new set of institutions based on the sovereignty of a state over a precisely defined territory. The sovereign was bound by very little. In Britain, a constitutional tradition developed but only through years of war and dispute. Machiavelli developed new ideas about the reasons for state power. Jean Bodin and Thomas Hobbes provided early theories of sovereignty. They placed the source of sovereignty in the ruler. Later, Locke and Rousseau would place it in the people. American theorists followed the later tradition.

Parallel with these theories of the states, theories of relations among states also had to develop. What obligations to other states were incumbent upon a sovereign state? How did war fit into the law among the nations? For a time, jurists struggled to articulate practical distinctions between just and unjust wars. According to J. L. Brierly, Grotius's attempt became popular even though it was never practical in real cases. Eventually the distinction between just and unjust wars disappeared. War was treated as a normal relationship among states although not a desirable one. With the Covenant of the League of Nations and the UN Charter, however, the distinction has reappeared with all the old difficulties of applications to cases. In fact, the UN Charter disallows war except for self-defense. In earlier times, the law recognized it for a number of circumstances such as reprisals and civil wars that entangled other states.

In the American political tradition, war has been treated as an anathema, particularly the Clausewitzian notion of war as an instrument of policy. By and large America has accepted the traditions of international law, seeing war as an interstate affair. It has built its military forces almost wholly for that kind of war. While it rejected the Covenant of the League, it enthusiastically supported the UN Charter and its reintroduction of the legal problem of deciding between just and unjust wars. International jurists in earlier times had recognized justice in international relations as secondary to peace. The Charter comes close to making peace more important than justice. While the United States has endorsed that legal tendency in the Charter, it has pursued a foreign policy more concerned with justice. Yet the legal basis for our military forces remains wedded very much to the ideas of international law, seeing peace among nations as the higher priority. We are thus afflicted with a serious disjuncture between our foreign policy and other ideas about the legal use of military forces.

This ambiguity has deep historical roots. America's very foundation as a nation required a war, a war justified on the theories of English political philosophy and law, a tradition based on "natural law." A revolution, a resort to armed force, is justified when certain inalienable rights of man are denied. Sovereignty is just only when it resides in the people. A sovereign tyrant, in the American view, is not justly sovereign. Tyranny over individual rights is a justification for civil war. But is it a justification for war among states? Are Americans obliged by this doctrine to declare war on all tyrants in other states? Here Americans are deeply ambivalent. In principle most would answer yes, but they would also agree that it is impractical given the limits of our military power.

This ambivalence puts the United States at odds with the very restrictive international law of today concerning when a resort to war is justified. Only a war in self-defense is legal under the Charter. Going to war to liberate a people in another state from a tyrant is illegal. The problem is further compounded when the United States finds itself allied with a state where individual freedoms are restricted. If the United States agrees to help it defeat a Soviet-backed insurgency, it is violating its own constitutional concept of just war. At the same time, one can argue that the United States is helping "keep the peace" internationally against Soviet policies aimed at subverting the peace through irregular warfare.

An argument has been made that these legal difficulties can be transcended by giving the word "doctrine" a legal status. Citing the "Brezhnev doctrine" and the "Reagan doctrine" as relevant cases, Michael Reisman insists that "critical defense zone claims made by the United States and the Soviet Union are lawful, precisely because they are indispensable to the avoidance of serious conflict." The Reagan doctrine, when it applies to a zone critical to U.S. national security, does, in Reisman's argument, carry the status of international law, allowing the United States to intervene to prevent Soviet infringement in the zone. It can be deemed lawful, however, insofar as it relates "directly and plausibly to superpower defense, no further." [8] While Reisman's development of the law solves some of the problems for U.S. policy, it holds with the basic twentieth-century assumption that peace is the primary goal, not necessarily justice. It does not deal adequately with the American traditional interest in justice in other states and in the interest in spreading democracy. On the contrary, it implicitly emphasizes the problem that international law creates for the pursuit of justice that has characterized many aspects of American foreign policy.

Eugene V. Rostow has put the crux of the American approach to internal war with external sources of support and supply more sharply than most: "One of the most poignant manifestations of the unresolved contradiction between morality and pragmatism in the American approach to the problem of world order is the long and passionate crusade for the compulsory arbitration of international disputes as a way to achieve peace—and a just peace—without war."[9] In Rostow's view, Article 2(4) of the Charter of the United Nations, which obliges states not to resort to war except in accordance with Article 51, self-defense, has been violated so often through support to insurgents across state borders that it is probably no longer a norm of international law. Such actions have always been considered as casus belli, and, therefore, Security Council approval is not actually required for action against parties assisting insurgents. Michael Reisman and James Baker show that the General Assembly's reformulation of the Charter in various declarations actually tends to justify insurgencies against regimes when they are aimed at "self-determination" and "independence." Moreover, "Third states are obliged to help the struggling groups, but cannot be held legally responsible by the targeted state."[10] In other words, not only is self-defense under Article 2(4) no longer the norm of international law; the law has suffered an "inversion" in the judgment of Reisman and Baker. The inversion, of course, exploits the ambiguity toward peace in the American mind when it reflects on the American Declaration of Independence. It seems, however, that Americans have so internalized the priority of peace above justice in such cases that it is difficult for political leaders to build a consensus for using whatever discretion international law may be made to yield in this regard. Americans cling to the image of war as an interstate phenomenon, not a transnational affair, when it comes to the direct use of military force.[11]

Our analysis thus far may seem like an intellectual trip through legal niceties that have little practical significance, but it is not. It helps explain a basic predicament we have in building military forces and fitting them to support political objectives selected by our elected leadership.

We build our forces for interstate war, war that is "declared" in the tradition of international law. Yet the United States has not "declared" war since 1941, although it has fought several wars since that time. The president cannot use much of his military forces without a declaration of war or its equivalent in some forms of congressional consent. When a president did use military force with ambiguous Congressional support, as in Vietnam, he caused a domestic political backlash that makes a repetition of that scale and kind of use impractical to contemplate seriously. Now, once again the Department of Defense is trying to build large special operations forces that cannot be used legally, short of a declaration of war or at the request of another government under attack.

The combination of this legal predicament and the commitment to man's inalienable rights makes it difficult, to say the least, to design military forces for unconventional warfare, either for insurgency or for counterinsurgency. Legal conventions and political sentiments both work to complicate if not make impossible the development of useful special operations forces.

"Low intensity conflict" as a new concept for building such forces does not evade this predicament. It is impaled by the predicament unless it envisions military actions only in declared wars. Yet that is not what its proponents seem to have in mind.

It can rightly be objected that the legal dilemma for U.S. strategy merely reflects the lack of a domestic consensus over the aims of U.S. strategy and foreign policy in both the East-West competition as a whole and in the Third World in particular. That is indeed true. John Lewis Gaddis has traced the dichotomy between the ideas of realists and idealists, between those who see the East-West competition more in terms of a balance of power and those who see it as an irreconcilable clash of political values.[12] He clearly sides with George Kennan and Henry Kissinger in favor of a less ideological approach, one that does not seek to "contain" Soviet power everywhere. Others, such as Paul Nitze, W. W. Rostow, and Zbigniew Brzezinski, have viewed the competition as a more fundamental struggle for the primacy of political values. The legal issue, nonetheless, has been a constraint troublesome to both sets of American strategists.

There is, however, a difference over the aims of American foreign policy that must be highlighted. It cuts differently through American foreign policymakers, the Congress, and the public. Throughout the nineteenth century, Americans followed George Washington's advice to avoid "foreign entangling alliances." This attitude underpinned American isolationism. Americans believed that their democracy was unique, a special endowment, the envy of others but not something Americans ought to carry to them or impose on them. While isolationist sentiment has not disappeared in the twentieth century, it has taken a back seat since World War II to the conviction that democracy can be taken to foreign states and implanted there.

George Kennan found himself isolated in the 1950s in advocating the realist approach at the expense of spreading democracy. American liberals showed great enthusiasm for the foreign crusade until the Vietnam War. In its final years, President Nixon and Secretary Kissinger captured considerable liberal support for a time for attempting a less ideological, more realistic approach, but it soon lost an adequate constituency. President Carter's administration brought the liberals once again to office, but they had become divided—some holding with the old fervor for spreading democracy, others willing to seek a balance of power with the Soviet Union. The Reagan administration once again managed to gain fairly broad public support for an activist policy of spreading democracy abroad, but its client regimes in Latin America created a serious and unresolved dilemma. It simply was not possible to find regimes or insurgents who were qualified in the eyes of the American public to be called democrats.

The dilemma leaves Americans with a serious problem of setting a clear goal for foreign policy and military strategy. Is it democracy? Or is it national self-interest and a balance of power? We cannot resolve that dilemma, but for this analysis we shall assume that it is spreading democracy—but not everywhere. In practice, American policymakers have never wholly followed one aim. United States policy tolerates a wide range of political systems among the Third World states with which it has good relations. Where the United States becomes involved in internal wars, especially on the side of the incumbent regime, questions soon arise in Congress and the media about the democratic character of the client state. A sustained commitment to a client, therefore, is likely to prove impossible unless U.S. policy is clearly aimed at creating democracy in that country. I personally favor the public and congressional constraints that make this true. Others may not. They must agree, however, that it is a political reality with which American policymakers must contend. Some might argue that it will become less a reality in the post–Cold War period. Perhaps it will, but to date it has constrained American support for dictatorships of any stripe, left or right. To the extent the United States continues to be involved in foreign internal wars, the pressure to promote democracy is likely to remain a reality with which policymakers must reckon.

The Soviet Approach

The Marxist-Leninist theory of internal war escapes the American predicament by essentially rejecting both the international order with its legal traditions and the domestic order of nation states based either on the sovereignty of a ruler or sovereignty vested in the people. In 1917 historical realities thrust upon the new Bolshevik regime another kind of predicament. World revolution did not follow as predicted. That left the young socialist state in a world of states it defined as hostile. Lenin, the agile theorist, quickly developed a doctrinal innovation to deal with the predicament, but before we examine it, let us review Marx's theory of war and further Soviet development of it.

The source of man's alienation from man, according to Marx, is private property. He developed this idea in his *Economic and Philosophic Manuscripts of 1844* and jointly with Engels spelled out its political implications in *The German Ideology* in 1845.[13] This assumption underpins all the later writings of Marx and Engels. Property divides men into classes—exploiting and exploited classes. War and revolution grow out of this alienation between classes. War, therefore, is a manifestation of class struggle—exploited against exploiting class. Engels applied this theoretical assumption to a study of the Peasant Wars in Germany in 1525–26 and the revolutionary events of 1848 in Germany.[14] They were class wars based on a struggle over property in his interpretation. Feudal regimes were being attacked by an incipient capitalist class, a class that rejected feudal concepts of rights and authority over property. Of more current interest to Marx, however, was the emerging working class as Europe industrialized. Because it was a propertyless class, it held the prospect of carrying through a revolution on an international basis which would destroy the concept of private property altogether. A new classless society devoid of private property should, in principle, remove the very source of warfare.

In Marx's view this would not happen in a purely mechanical fashion. Contrary to much popularization of Marxism as raw determinism, Marx himself believed that the transition depended on a political awakening of the working class, a recognition by workers that property indeed was the source of struggle. This "consciousness" on the part of workers would lead them to build a new economic order in which property relations would not alienate man from man. Moreover, this new consciousness would be required to inspire the working class to revolt.[15] The duty of all Social Democrats belonging to the First and Second Socialist Internationals was to propagate this scientific finding so that it would create the necessary new class consciousness.

After the failure of the revolution of 1848, Marx had to wait until the French civil war in 1871 to find new empirical evidence for his theoretical proposition. Bismarck's Germany invaded France but did not fully occupy Paris. While the German army sat in the outskirts, civil war broke out within the city. The Paris Commune, a provisional government of Parisian working-class elements, took shape and resisted the government's efforts to disarm its members who had been formed into the National Guard for the defense of France. The Germans stood by while the government eventually defeated the insurgents. In the Paris Commune Marx saw a preview of what a working-class revolution would be. Its failure, in his estimate, was due to the imperfect understanding by its leaders, Blanquists and Proudhonists, of "scientific socialism" and how to apply its doctrine to awaken working-class consciousness. But in part they had succeeded. The Blanquists and the Proudhonists of the International Working Man's Association saw their interests not in supporting the bourgeois French government any longer against the Germans but rather in taking power in their own right and calling on workingmen in other countries to do the same.[16]

Soviet theorists, until most recently, leaned heavily on Marx's interpretation of the Paris Commune. It was a clear rejection of the European nation-state system, its theories of sovereignty and laws of war for interstate conflict, by an incipient working class that believed its allies were workers in all the states of Europe. It foreshadowed the coming of transnational groupings—exploited classes—allied in war against other transnational groupings—exploiting classes.

Revolution for Marx and Engels was warfare. The age of interstate wars was coming to a close. It would be ended by a great transnational war in which the international working class would destroy the ruling capitalist regimes and establish a dictatorship of the proletariat to carry to completion the abolition of private property, a new economic order, and permanent peace.

Marxism in its essence, therefore, is a theory of class war, transnational war, war to end war. It rejects out of hand all the legal baggage developed in modern Europe and America to legitimize sovereign governments of nation states and to regulate relations among states.

Lenin's contribution was primarily twofold. First, his theory of a vanguard political party of the working class provided what the French Commune lacked: a political and military general staff fully educated in scientific socialism, leadership that could awaken class consciousness and guide its actions effectively to ensure the birth of a world socialist revolution. The squabbling among the socialist leaders in Europe and Russia struck Lenin as bound to cause failure when the opportunity for revolution arrived. Militarylike discipline, "democratic centralism," and professional revolutionaries welded into a clandestine revolutionary party—these were the prerequisites Marx and Engels had not fully explicated.[17]

Second, Lenin's theory of imperialism conceived the structure of capitalism as including the colonies of the European empires. Interlocked as a global economic system, capitalism had to be vulnerable to revolution not only at home in the most industrialized states of Europe but also in its colonies. All Russian socialists had long believed that Russia was a feudal system which would soon fall to a bourgeois revolution led by the new commercial class. A socialist revolution could occur only in industrial Europe. Lenin's theory of imperialism allowed him to reject that assumption and to believe that a world socialist revolution could start in Russia. Russian socialists, therefore, could go ahead and seize power, ignoring the role of a bourgeois class development in Russia.[18]

In practice this required a two-class alliance. The peasants in Russia showed strong signs of revolutionary zeal. As a property-minded class that wanted to own land, they were prepared to take it away from the landowners. Lenin's Bolsheviks would ally the Russian workers temporarily with the peasants and thereby create adequate revolutionary forces to carry the day. As revolution spread to Western Europe, the Russian workers could ally with German, French, and British workers to contain the property-owning, and thus alien, class of peasants.[19]

The point of importance for our analysis here is that Lenin from the beginning saw warfare as a transnational class-based phenomenon. The nation state was a creation of the bourgeois epoch. With a socialist revolution it would disappear.[20] By 1921, however, it was clear to Lenin that it would not disappear quickly. The socialist revolution did not expand beyond Russia with the alacrity he had anticipated. The practical problem he faced, therefore, was how to protect this small socialist bastion and at the same time work to propagate revolution elsewhere.

"Peaceful coexistence," as the strategy would much later be called, was his solution.[21] It required acknowledging the persistence of the bourgeois state and the old international system. It even required that the new Soviet state seek proper diplomatic relations with the states of that system and make peace with them. At the same time, it also required another level of international cooperation. The Comintern, or Third International of working-class parties, would maintain party-to-party relations, clandestine relations where necessary, and help these parties advance the cause of the working classes everywhere.[22]

An additional facet of "peaceful coexistence" was its emphasis on the colonial regions of the world. The working class there was infinitesimal or nonexistent, but that did not mean there were no prospects for revolution. By making alliances with other classes against the imperial states of Europe, the Bolsheviks might destroy imperialism at its weaker points, points where bourgeois nationalist groups were willing and strong enough to throw out the colonial rulers. In essence this was merely the projection of Lenin's tactic in Russia, an alliance with the peasant class, onto the Third World. If one could not find working classes, one must look for other classes with hostility for imperialism.

Another view of this theoretical development can be seen in Lenin's fascination with Clausewitz. Clausewitz's view of war as an instrument of state policy rested on the emerging system of nation states in Europe. War for him was an interstate phenomenon. The "nation," its people, provide the passion for war, the willingness to fight. The cabinet and the general staff provide rational and purposeful direction of this national energy, harnessing it to a strategy for imposing the state's will on its opponent. Clausewitz rejected the mechanistic ideas of Jomini and others who sought to devise principles of tactics that would ensure victory if applied. Cause and effect were not so predictable in Clausewitz's view. The "fog of war" made it impossible to calculate so easily. Battle, therefore, was a highly problematic affair. Intellect and strategic vision could provide direction toward the state's political objective, but chance and probability also come into play.

Lenin accepted Clausewitz's idea of the relationship between war and politics as well as his view of the "fog of war" and the problematic nature of conflict. In place of the cabinet and general staff as the "brain" that imposes strategy and purpose onto war, Lenin could easily substitute the central committee of the Bolshevik party. In place of the nation, he substituted "class." Thus he transformed the Clausewitzian paradigm into one appropriate for interclass war, transnational war, war aimed to destroy the nation-state system.

This Leninist adaptation of Clausewitz has become virtually holy writ in Soviet military and political circles.[23] It fits their needs nicely. While "peaceful coexistence" leaves them with an incomplete world socialist revolution, a world in which they must still deal with the old international system, it also provides them with a general set of categories for continuing international class struggle. If one keeps this in mind, one is not surprised at the curious alliances the Soviets have struck in the world—the groups they have supported, the international groups and organizations they have tried to use, and their mix of traditional international diplomacy with transnational subversion of the interstate system. Any group that is willing to fight is first to be assessed for its "progressive" or "reactionary" character. If it opposes the interests of Western capitalist states—that is, if it is objectively anti-imperialist—it is "progressive." If it fights against what Moscow sees as its interests, it is "reactionary." The fighting need not be military action. Political struggle, propaganda, agitation, diversion, and so forth by any group may be objectively "progressive" in the Soviet interpretation. If so, that action may deserve Soviet support—material, rhetorical, clandestine, or other. "Peaceful coexistence" has been traditionally defined in the Soviet Union as a specific form of the international class struggle. Thus it commits Moscow to develop transnational coalitions, fronts, insurgencies, and other organizational forms and to provide strategic guidance in the commitment of these "progressive" forces against imperialism.[24]

While Lenin's concept of peaceful coexistence neatly deals with the Soviet predicament of holding power while also needing to foster world socialist revolution, it also has fundamental problems. The first is old. The second is newer.

Nationalism is the first problem. In the Soviet Union national political sentiment has never been eradicated. The same is true in East Europe, Yugoslavia, China, and Vietnam. Again and again, Soviet policy has come up against nationalism as an obstacle to international communism. Where it has succeeded against it, it has been by force—police and military means. Where those means are short, it has generally failed.

The second is economic performance. In the first couple of postwar decades, Moscow was able to peddle its economic system as a solution for LDCs. In the past couple of decades, its credibility has fallen dramatically.

Why has Moscow succeeded in some cases in spite of these obstacles? Many factors can be cited, and the appeal of the ideology, particularly Lenin's theory of imperialism, certainly has captured the minds of many Third World intellectuals. It provides a pseudoscientific rationale for doing what they want to do anyway: forcibly resist colonial rule and Western influence on their societies. Probably the most significant factor is the Bolshevik state bureaucratic system. While it began to develop under Lenin, Stalin perfected it. A single-cadre party; a secret police; a state-controlled economy to include a collective farm system to control the peasantry; mass organizations; and other collective mechanisms for social, economic, and political control—these organizational schemes allow a ruling elite to hold power in highly fragmented societies, to repress centrifugal political forces, and to mobilize economic and human resources for purposes pleasing to the elites.

The American approach—pressing for an elective political system and a plural party and social structure—is not very attractive to the ruler of a highly fragmented state with tribal and ethnic rivalries, with disaffected classes and groups, and with an economy that performs poorly. The Soviet alternative may be oppressive, but it is stable and secure for the ruling elite. The Soviet approach is also attractive to a political counterelite which wants to oust the incumbent elite. Particularly in states where there are no electoral systems or ones that are rigged, the Soviet recipe for organizing revolutionary forces, forcing a civil war, and seizing power is attractive. Thus the Soviet approach is basic and practical for both counterelites and ruling elites in many parts of the world. These short-term practical considerations can easily blind political elites to the longer term drawbacks: poor economic performance and repression of basic national and cultural sentiments.

Finally, the Leninist formula deals admirably with a problem the American approach has failed miserably to solve: the integration of a theory of political development with a theory of military development. Leninism recognizes the identity of politics and war in the pure Clausewitzian sense. Americanism rejects the identity except in the cases of insurrection against tyranny and in self-defense as defined by the UN Charter. When American policy has tried to integrate the political and the military, the political analysis is usually highly ethnocentric. It often confuses fragmentation in a developing society with pluralism. It de-emphasizes the concentration of power in the hands of an elite with a common political program. At the same time, it tries to build unity and cohesion in the state's own military. These two disparate tactics work against an effective political-military coupling.

The Leninist approach starts by trying to militarize the ethos and organization of a single political party. It teaches how to penetrate and weaken opposition parties and organizations. It cultivates a fusion of the political and military leadership, and it focuses sharply on the loyalty and reliability of the military as its ranks expand. It places the highest priority on intelligence, clandestinity, subversion, diversion, covert action, and other aspects of intelligence operations. The first line of combat is the intelligence war, a war that knows no territorial or organizational boundaries.

Only after an adequate intelligence infrastructure is built can political structures be developed. Intelligence is required to assess contradictions and antagonisms in the society, to find potential class allies among non-working-class groups and social strata. Upon this knowledge, the clandestine party must design its tactics for penetration and effective control of objectively "progressive" groups and organizations; that is, organizations whose subjective and conscious purposes are not Marxist-Leninist, but whose objective consequences aid revolutionary purposes. With that tactic must come an overall political program capable of appealing to many levels of comprehension. It must tell people what they want to hear, yet combine those promises with a unified program for political action that may eventually alienate allied groups and organizations.

Moving to military organizations and action should come only after the political program, tactics, and organization are sufficiently developed. This is the theory. Soviet practice has not always been so tidy, but the theory truly does integrate military struggle with political objectives and organization.

Most important for our analysis is the transnational character of the approach, its rejection of the Western concept of interstate warfare, its different concept of true peace—that is, the abolition of private property—its military ethos imposed on a united political elite organized in a political party.

In the course of 1987 a remarkable revision of the Soviet approach to the East-West competition began to appear. Gorbachev's own book, *Perestroika*, set forth a bold new interpretation of "peaceful coexistence." The international class struggle practically fell out of the definition. Gorbachev identified a new kind of "interests." "Humankind interests," as he called them, transcend class struggle and class interests. In pursuit of them, socialist states must cooperate with all states, particularly imperialist states, pushing class struggle into the background. Examples of humankind interests are preventing nuclear war and protecting the global environment. Their pursuit gives new urgency to cooperation with the United States.

Gorbachev did not reject wholly class interests and class struggle,[25] but the new definition of peaceful coexistence promulgated at the Twenty-seventh Party Congress puts the highest priority on proper interstate relations, international institutions, and cooperation with capitalist states—while virtually ignoring class struggle. Taken at face value, this revision essentially eradicates all features of the Soviet approach to the competition that have characterized its theory—and to a lesser degree its practice—since 1921.

As the old Russian proverb goes, "paper will put up with anything written on it." Merely publishing the revisionist formula on paper does not mean that the entire Soviet foreign policy, KGB, military establishment, and Communist party have done an abrupt about face and accepted the change. Clearly a lot of change has occurred, and many of Gorbachev's collaborators have achieved a great deal in undermining and neutralizing the old institutions and policies. At the same time, conservative elements within the institutions have resisted. But even if they eventually succeed in rejecting the revision of the ideology, they will not be able to revert to the old policies with ease. The political struggle within the Soviet Union is likely to continue for several years, and it may well lead the Soviet Union—or residual parts of it—to withdraw entirely from the Third World competition. Or it could lead to a reduced effort, strategic withdrawal, and consolidation of client relations in a smaller number of Third World States. In the process, the Soviet position in the Third World could collapse entirely.

The important conclusion for our analysis here is twofold. First, it is too early to judge how things will turn out in the Soviet Union. The future reality will probably surprise both the optimists and pessimists in the West. It is safest, therefore, to assume that some kind of eventual stabilization will occur in the Soviet Union. Residual pretensions of being a superpower could well keep Moscow in the Third World competition at some level. Second, the ideology, tactics, and organizational techniques of Leninism have become widely known and internalized in many Third World radical groups. In their own contexts, Third World revolutionaries are at an early historical stage where winning power is the most critical concern—not economic stagnation from economic central planning. Traditional Marxist-Leninist strategy and tactics, therefore, retain considerable relevance and attraction for some political groups—not only for gaining power but also for holding onto it and consolidating it. The issue of effective economic development is less urgent for insurgent groups. These realities make it likely that Marxist-Leninist ideology and organization will remain a significant factor in Third World internal wars for some time.

Two Competing Views of Political Development

Let us now step back and look at the symmetries and asymmetries in the Soviet and American world views on global developments.

The Soviet vision is capitalist states and international state systems giving way to socialist revolution and the emergence of communist societies which live peacefully because the basic cause of war, private property, has been abolished. Admittedly, in the Soviet assessment, this ultimate state of affairs would come about slowly, by fits and starts, with setbacks and advances, according to the law of uneven historical development. But the Soviet road map has not been very clear, especially concerning the relationship between communist societies. Will there be interstate relations? Perhaps, but not in the same form as that of interstate relations in the capitalist era. The nation state has been viewed as a vestige of the bourgeois epoch, eventually to be destroyed. That has been the task of the dictatorship of the proletariat as it arises through revolutions. It has also been the task of the present socialist camp, in the name of socialist international solidarity, as it has sought to bring the international correlation of forces to favor the socialist camp overwhelmingly.

An important tactic in shifting the correlation of forces has been to encourage nationalism where it conflicts with imperialism.[26] The origin of this tactic can be traced to Lenin's nationality policy in 1917. In addition to promising the land to the peasantry in Russia to cement the working-class–peasant alliance, he also promised the national minorities within the Russian Empire the right to self-determination. The aim was to unite all potential antitsarist forces in a battle to bring down the provisional government because it showed no tolerance toward the national movements within the old empire's boundaries.

The same tactical rationale, of course, was equally applicable to the colonial regions in the Third World once the Bolsheviks held power in Russia. The Baku Conference of Eastern Peoples, held in 1919, was one of the first steps in implementing this policy on a global scale. In practice it meant that nonruling communist parties in the colonial regions could and should ally with bourgeois nationalist forces to break the colonialist hold on those countries. The story of Soviet policy in China in the interwar period is precisely the saga of this political strategy. This strategy also prevailed in the Spanish civil war.[27] It has remained a tactic with mixed results right up until the present.

The American view in the nineteenth century was to ignore the world. America was special. Special endowments made America possible. The rest of the world could envy us. It should try to be like us, but we seriously doubted that our model could be emulated successfully. At the end of World War I, however, our viewpoint changed. President Wilson, in his Fourteen Points, called for self-determination of nations in the reshaping of Europe. In principle, he implied that the rest of the world could follow the American example. Henceforth, American foreign policy would support anticolonialism and self-determination. The final goal, however, was not a stateless community of societies. Rather it was an international family of nation states in which the people retain the sovereignty, where liberal democratic government prevails and market economies based on private property thrive.

In the ashes of the empires of Central and Eastern Europe, nationalist movements sought to implement the principle of self-determination. The East European succession states were the result. Although America retreated from the world in 1919, the Wilsonian concept did not die. It remained dormant until after 1945 when America became actively engaged in international politics. President Roosevelt committed the United States to the decolonization struggle and pressed our European allies to divest themselves of their colonies.

The symmetries in American and Soviet policy are striking. Both made a bid to lead the decolonization process. Both offered a rationale, a justification. Both appealed to eschatological principles of historical development. And both actively worked to help history proceed on its predestined course.

The asymmetries lie in the clash between eschatological visions. Moscow held a "social democratic" vision of historical development. Washington insisted on a "liberal democratic" image of the course history should take. Both were convinced that voluntarism and choice by leaders would affect the course of history, but Moscow also believed in economic determinism to the degree that Marx had defined such historical determinism in his "scientific" analysis.

In a sense, American scholarly analysis of the developing region also began with a determinist tendency. Economic development would beget a middle class which would insist on liberal democratic government and political stability.[28] Economic liberalism, in its early conceptualization, was indeed deterministic. The "invisible hand in the marketplace" would guide development. Government and political leaders should let the invisible hand have its way. Their duty was to keep the peace and protect property and the marketplace. In the 1940s and 1950s, as scholars began to explore the politics of the Third World, they did so not as political activists but as detached observers. They were trying to learn to predict what would happen, not dictate what would happen. W. W. Rostow's classic, *Stages of Economic Growth*, is an outstanding example of such scholarship.

Soviet theorists studied the Third World from a determinist Marxist perspective, but they did so as Leninist political activists. They wanted to know how to dictate historical development. Here again, we have curious symmetries and asymmetries.

Already in the Greek civil war and in the Philippines during the Huk rebellion, American policymakers were trying to learn from scholars about how to take an active role in guiding political and economic development. A similar shift also occurred in our policy toward Latin America. It was Vietnam, however, where America belatedly tried to integrate an academic understanding of political and economic development with foreign and military policies. After an initial excitement at being invited to join the activist ranks, the theorists from the academy became disillusioned and retreated to their previous detached isolation as observers. The post-Vietnam syndrome was nowhere stronger than in the political science and economic faculties of the universities.

From their detached position, they began to learn a great deal more about political development. Case studies and theories multiplied, and they continue today. Some provide remarkable insight into the development process in particular states. Some are useful cross-national generalizations. Others, such as "dependency theory," essentially offer the Leninist theory of imperialism couched in American political science jargon.

Soviet analysis, too, has undergone change. Class analysis has frequently been a poor guide for Soviet policy. Some Soviet specialists look at social institutions and structures as more important for tactical policy guidance. Alliances with Third World military establishments have been popular. Military sales and advisory assistance have bulked large in Soviet policy. Tactical approaches to religion and churches have also appeared in the Soviet pattern. Liberation theology in Latin America and the Philippines is an example. Soviet Banking and trade have also been used to provide a local presence and resources in support of Soviet policy. These techniques, of course, are in addition to the old ones—clandestine parties, national fronts, popular fronts, and other organizational schemes.

In the 1970s we witnessed some significant shifts in Soviet policy. Direct military intervention appeared—sometimes with surrogate forces, sometimes with Soviet forces. Economic assistance became exceptional, as did direct grants of military equipment. Military sales expanded. Many other techniques have changed.

In American policy the labor unions have played a large role in combatting Soviet-backed labor groups. The AFL-CIO has contributed enormously to our competition with the Soviet Union, not only in the Third World but in the industrial states as well. Military assistance, arms sales, and covert action by the CIA all play a role in American tactics in the competition. To be sure, American business has been a transnational factor, most significantly in Latin America and in the Middle East. The American private sector, including the media and the consumer culture it spreads, has also been a large factor in East-West competition.

Both sides have tended to converge in some of their instrumentalities, but they remain fundamentally opposed on the basic political issues: liberal democracy versus communism. At the same time, both have stumbled against nationalism in the Third World, and both have misjudged the requirements for economic development.

Finally there are symmetries and asymmetries in the efforts by both sides to bring the Cold War competition to an end. Gorbachev's radical new policies, of course, are aimed precisely at ending the competition, or at least introducing a very long strategic pause. The socialist camp is exhausted. It has lost confidence in its ideology and institutions. Quite a different attitude is expressed by some in the West as they accept the end of the East-West competition as a reality. Frank Fukuyama's "end of history" thesis is the most succinct statement of Western optimism.[29] Taking Hegel's theory of history as the "actualization" of "idea" in reality, Fukuyama suggests that the Western "idea," the theory of liberal democracy, has triumphed. Its practice has proven the most effective way to organize a polity and its economy. Ideological surrender in the socialist camp and in leftist circles elsewhere reflects a broad recognition that alternative political and economic systems are illusions, not effective solutions.

At the same time, a pessimism somewhat symmetrical to Soviet pessimism has been articulated, most notably by Paul Kennedy.[30] In this view the United States is overextended and in danger of serious setbacks unless it retracts its global involvement in a timely fashion. The economic powers of East Asia and Western Europe are beginning to push the United States out of its dominant position. The economic "base" for American power is no longer adequate to the "superstructure" of its global military alliances and commitments. "Base" and "superstructure," of course, are not Kennedy's terms or the terms of other Western prophets of American decline. They are Marxist terms. Marx argued that as the economic "base" changes, it creates new political forces which eventually destroy the ruling political institutions— that is, the "superstructure." There is, curiously, an implicit symmetry between this Western declinist view and the original Marxist theory of scientific socialism. To be sure, the declinist view has its Western critics. Fukayama's thesis on the ultimate triumph of liberalism leads the list of optimists about the future of the West, and Joseph Nye has addressed Kennedy directly, offering a less ideological and more pragmatic assessment of the case for Western optimism.[31]

The messy realities of the international politics of the future are likely to prove both the optimists and the pessimists somewhat off the mark. Both America and the Soviet Union have deeply rooted eschatological views of their purposes in the world. Although the Soviet

Union appears to be entering another one of Russia's periodic "time of troubles," it remains a large geographical entity with several vigorous and creative ethnic populations. Its inherent power and its enormous self-pride cannot be simply dismissed as a major factor in world politics, including those of the Third World.

III

The Political and Economic Context

for Internal War

••

The East-West competition, in both its military and nonmilitary aspects, has not taken place on a tabula rasa in the Third World. Yet one American critic of U.S. Third World policy insists that precisely this misconception is at the root of the American problem.[1] We have viewed the Third World as universally vulnerable to Soviet influence, an influence exercised by means of a universal tactic. Our answer has been a universal countertactic. Its prescriptions are (1) win the hearts and minds, (2) maintain unity principle for a coordinated effort, and (3) apply a cost-benefit approach to assessing counterinsurgency results. While this critic makes many telling points, he offers no solutions other than, by implication, to abandon the competition, to refuse to assist client governments. He does, however, remind us that the competition takes place in a highly differentiated and complex environment: many different states and regions with quite different cultures, political traditions, and historical experiences. Although his analysis purports to deal with political development theory as it has emerged in American academe and has been applied in policy, it tends to stumble on contradictions in testing theory against U.S. experience, and it fails to recognize the growth and maturity of such studies.

Since so-called low-intensity conflict doctrine is an effort to generalize about internal war in the Third World, we must examine the generalizations that the academicians are making about Third World political and economic development. The 1950s and early 1960s witnessed an initial surge of studies of political development. The late 1960s and early 1970s saw considerable diversity beset this branch of political science, a diversity based as much on reactions to the American involvement in Vietnam as on new empirically based findings. In the late 1970s and early 1980s, a maturity and texture has emerged in political development theory that offers somewhat greater detachment and objectivity. The normative bias, of course, has been and remains the focus on democracy, how political development can produce democratic systems.

One exception has been "dependency theory," initially inspired by the works of Fernando Henrique Cardoso, Andre Gunder Frank, Osvaldo Sunkel, and Theotonio dos Santos in the late 1960s. The focus of dependency theory has been on the autonomy of developing states, how foreign capital undercuts political autonomy and leads to dependency on the advanced industrial economies. Upon close examination, it looks like a dressed up but less sophisticated version of Lenin's theory of imperialism, and Gabriel Almond has called it an "intellectual ambush" of the general field of political development theory—one that has not stood up to further empirical study and that has not left a significant impact on the field except to draw attention to the role of the state and its sovereignty in the Third World.[2] This may be too harsh a judgment. Another way to see it is simply as a recognition of global economic interdependency. Certainly many Third World states become dependent on economic relations with advanced industrial states, but it is a two-way, even if highly unbalanced, dependency. The advanced industrial states are dependent on each other as well. "Dependency theory," therefore, may not be entirely wrong but rather highly incomplete. Its incompleteness, however, can be used for very parochial political purposes in affecting the relations between Third World states and the industrially advanced states. There may be some justice in that parochialism, but there also may be considerable injustice.

For our purposes here we must first review the political development literature for what it shows us about the prospects for democracy, because that is the goal of American involvement in internal war in the Third World. Second, we must examine it for the light it throws on the conditions and causes of internal wars and the degree to which they are truly "internal" and how they may also be "external" in character. The best insights in this regard are found in the nature of the goals of political development. Finally, we need to examine government and administration, including armies, because they are the basis for both political stability and development. The kind of government that emerges in a Third World state is the central issue in the competition in the Third World.

How Democracy Comes to Fruition

We could digress at length here from the main purpose of the analysis by first defining "democracy." The disputes and literature on this topic are old and long, and we would stray if we tried to trace them even briefly. For shorthand, therefore, I have in mind "liberal democracy" in the sense that Giovanni Sartori has defined it in his recent book, *The Theory of Democracy Revisited*. For practical purposes, let us simplify the definition by saying that it is a political system in which (a) there is a constitutional system for deciding who rules; (b) the legal system guarantees individual rights sufficiently to insure that political opposition is tolerated; and (c) who rules is decided by periodic popular elections in which a majority of the citizenry is enfranchised to vote.

Such a system is "liberal" in the sense that majorities cannot disenfranchise all minorities; it is "democratic" in that majorities decide who governs. In developing countries, its "liberal" character may be limited without wholly disqualifying it as a "democracy" because in its early stages some quiescent minorities may be left out (as in the United States for a long time), but it must be sufficiently liberal to protect active political opposition groups that accept the constitutional rules.

Democracy, according to Huntington, looked like a general law of development from about 1800 until 1920.[3] Between 1920 and 1945, the direction was reversed as democracies failed, especially in Europe, and dictatorships tended to replace them. From 1945 to the mid 1950s, the number of democracies surged. Since the late 1950s, there has been no dominant trend. Huntington concludes that we may be at a point where the number of democracies may not increase appreciably for the foreseeable future. Since he made this judgment, the number has increased slightly in Latin America, but these democracies are far from fully established, and the prospects for reversals are considerable.

Obviously there are as many roads to democracy as there are countries that have made the trip, but common patterns do tend to emerge; in the political development literature, essentially five are readily identifiable. Although there may be other routes that could be included in this set, it is quite broad in capturing the varying circumstances in which democracies have emerged and the quite different causal factors that can come into play.

Dankwart Rustow advances a linear sequence. National unity comes first followed by a long period in which more participants are drawn into politics, creating a series of struggles, often accompanied by violence. At some point, leaders make a conscious decision to resort to democratic rules for resolving issues. Full-blown democracy requires a lengthy period thereafter during which democratic practices are fully accepted and internalized as the legitimate basis for government. Rustow's empirical cases are taken from Northern Europe reaching back over three centuries or more.[4]

The second pattern, noted by Huntington, is cyclical—despotism alternating with democracy. Peru, Argentina, and Nigeria are some of his examples. In these cases, democracy never becomes institutionalized to a degree that ensures its stability. Huntington also describes a third pattern, a "dialectical" one which is neither linear nor cyclical. A middle class develops within an autocratic state, bringing an "urban breakthrough" that permits this new class to displace the old regime. It may be through revolution or simply the collapse of the dictatorship. The new regime, built on democratic principles, proves stable, and a reversal does not occur.[5] Britain, more recently Spain and Portugal, and possibly Venezuela fit this pattern.

All three patterns involve periods of violence and disorder, and they require long development periods. Rustow and Huntington do not suggest that democracy is something that can be easily introduced into a developing country in a short time. Although the "dialectical" pattern involves a fairly dramatic and rapid transition, the period for developing a middle class, leading to the "urban breakthrough," takes a long time and depends on successful economic development.

A fourth pattern, identified by Robert Dahl, is a function of land tenure in preurban societies.[6] The appearance of modern democracies, of course, predates modern urban society. Because urbanization and political development are so entangled in the late developing states, urbanization and democracy are closely related in their experience, a fact accounting for the third path, the "urban breakthrough." Yet the United States, Canada, New Zealand, and Norway became democracies long before significant levels of modern urban society appeared. Dahl explains premodern, preurban democracies as the product of "free farmer" societies. They stand in contrast to "peasant" societies where the distribution of landownership is highly inequitable, concentrated in the hands of a few, and where a large landless peasantry provides the primary source of agricultural labor, as has been the case in Eastern Europe, Latin America, and elsewhere. In Dahl's view, this pattern is not really replicable today because the degree of urgency for economic and political development is too great to permit it. Perhaps this is true, but the important point seems to be that the diffusion of wealth and power through a large number of owners made democratic political institutions more acceptable, practical, and even necessary, whereas concentrated ownership combined with a large landless agrarian populace discouraged democratic institutions.[7]

A fifth pattern depends less on internal factors but fundamentally on external forces. Some democracies have been created by military conquest. The spectacular examples are Germany, Japan, and Italy after World War II. To all appearances these nations have developed stable democratic institutions able to manage domestic competitive political participation. Whether one can generalize from them to Third World states is problematic. Germany, Japan, and Italy already had large urban middle classes. They had all struggled with democratic processes before giving way to totalitarian political movements. South Korea is an interesting additional case where democracy has been quite slow in developing but nonetheless shows encouraging prospects in the last few years. Grenada is also an interesting case, one that may be more relevant to the larger set of Third World states if democracy becomes institutionalized there. The latest example, of course, is Panama. An urban breakthrough has been prevented there by Noreiga's regime. The American occupation should allow it to take place.

Initial study of political development after World War II focused on the relationship between economic development and democracy. As Seymour Lipset expresses it, "Perhaps the most common generalization linking political systems to other aspects of society has been that democracy is related to the state of economic development. The more well-to-do a nation, the greater the chances that it will sustain democracy."[8] Testing this proposition against a set of thirty European states and twenty Latin American states, Lipset found that the higher levels of per capita wealth, industrialization, organization, and education were in the democratic and less authoritarian states. Some students have reasoned that economic development would inherently create a large middle class which in turn would generate the transition to democracy.

At the same time, one could point to cases of rapid economic growth which did not bring a democratic transition. Japan and Germany in the late nineteenth and early twentieth centuries and the Soviet Union are examples.

Robert Dahl, Bruce Russett, and others have also examined the relationship between democracy and economic development, noting the same correlation as Lipset did. Asking if there is a causal relationship, Dahl cautiously observes, "I do not believe it is possible at this time to advance an acceptable causal theory that will account for all the cases."[9] While that may still be true two decades later, the economic performance of Marxist-Leninist states, especially as it has emerged in the 1980s, is providing evidence that suggests the causal connection is not only strong but very much a function of the diffusion of power through private ownership.

Because it will influence these conclusions from the case studies, I shall be explicit in stating my own view on this point. Effective political participation, or "contestation" in Dahl's notion of "polyarchy," requires effective institutions for participation, as Huntington asserts. Neither contestation nor institutions for such activity can have the necessary resources or genuine political independence to compete without independent wealth. Feudal rights over land and peasants maintained a significant degree of political competition in much of feudal Europe. Commerce and industry in a market economy broke the feudal political order precisely because it brought a new distribution of wealth that permitted new forms of contestation. Truly socialist economies without a large private sector and the legal basis for private ownership deprive the majority of the population of the resources necessary for contestation. That not only blocks the development of democracy but eventually stifles economic development. The command administrative economic system developed in the Soviet Union cannot handle the information flows essential for continuing economic progress. Bureaucracies necessary for central planning simply become overloaded and make millions of inefficient economic allocation decisions. Market economies, by decentralizing the flow of information through private ownership and legal contracts, have thus far managed the problem much better.

As Mancur Olson has demonstrated, to the degree political and business groups organize and collude to interfere with the market, they introduce inefficient allocations which lead to slower and slower economic performance.[10] The larger the state sector and private monopoly sector in an economy, the poorer is likely to be the economic performance. Not only do Soviet-type economies demonstrate this, appearing to be the extreme case of Olson's idea of social rigidities impeding the market, but the same is true to a lesser degree of many praetorian regimes and agrarian societies ruled by large landowner oligarchies. There may be deviant cases, but I take this as a general principle relevant to most states.

Lipset also found a correlation between religion and democracy. Protestant cultures more often seemed to enjoy both economic growth and democratic political development. Catholic cultures showed a mixed relationship to democracy as well as to economic success. Lipset did not investigate other religious cultures—Islamic, Hindu, and Confucian, for example. Huntington, however, has generalized about culture, going farther than noting that there is a correlation and suggesting that where immediate social goals are merged closely with messianic religious ideals, the culture is less tolerant of the compromises that make democracy possible. Where the two kinds of goals are not so closely merged, where they are separated in time of expected realization, democracy has a better chance. Protestant, Buddhist, and Hindu cultures present less difficulty for democracy, whereas Islamic and Confucian cultures have proven resistant to democratic forms and instrumentalities, particularly compromise. Catholic cultures stand somewhere between these two extremes—allowing for democracy in some cases, obstructing it in others.[11]

The best summary of the preconditions for democracy has been articulated by Huntington: economic, social, external, and cultural.[12] They serve as an excellent basis for estimating the prospects for any Third World state following a democratic course of political development.

First, as the economic precondition, democracy depends on wealth, although not only on wealth, as once believed. While the nexus may not be fully understood, wealth does make a difference. Poverty makes democracy difficult, although not impossible.

Second, the social context must include a middle class and a market economy. There are no democracies without market economies. Precisely why this is true, as we have noted, political scientists are reluctant to say, but the English experience may be instructive. Even in feudal times, wealth, primarily land, was never wholly the king's property. The concept of private property and a constitutional tradition of allowing increased participation in politics to be a function of property kept power diffused, creating a strong bulwark against tyranny and despotism. Russia, where the tsar always held primary ownership of all the land, disallowed this diffusion of political power. Tyranny was required if the tsar was to retain his right over all land. The failure of the nobility to break the tsar's monopoly of power seems to account, at least in part, for the absence of a constitutional tradition that would have allowed the social and economic articulation essential for a commercial middle class in the nineteenth century.

One of Lenin's major differences with his fellow Marxists concerned the revolutionary character of Russia's landless peasantry. He saw it as a critical force for overthrowing the old regime, but to inspire them to act, he had to promise the peasants ownership of land. The young Bolshevik regime felt terribly threatened by the new landed peasantry, and, of course, Stalin concluded that maintenance of hegemonic party power required taking away the peasants' land through collectivization. Again we see the connection between the potential for democracy and the diffusion of power through private property. To leave the peasants with land meant that sooner or later the Bolshevik party would have to share political power with competing groups.

Another apparent link between market economies and democracy seems to be in the role of economic growth as a contributor to democracy. Sustained growth has been realized only in market economies. Before the 1960s, this was not so clearly the case. The Soviet Union had recorded remarkable growth rates with a centrally planned economy. Part of the Soviet appeal to the Third World was the promise of rapid economic growth through central planning. The last couple of decades, however, have raised serious doubts about the capacity of command economies to sustain growth. Eastern Europe, China, North Korea, Vietnam, and Cuba all stand as monuments to the failure of command economies. As this reality becomes more widely recognized, it will be a major liability for Moscow in competition with the West in the Third World.

Third, external factors may offer a precondition for democracy. Military conquest by a democratic state can impose democracy. It should be noted, however, that conquest alone is not enough. A long postconquest period may be required to build the other preconditions. Korea is a case in point. Grenada could revert to a dictatorship if the other preconditions are too slow in coming. Before the 1990 elections, the freest elections ever held in Nicaragua were in 1926 under U.S. military occupation. The occupation shortly ended, and democracy never took root.

The kind of colonial experience a country undergoes seems to make a considerable difference for democratic development. At one extreme, British colonial rule as an external factor appears more conducive to postcolonial democracy than, say, Spanish colonial rule at the other extreme. Immigration, usually accompanying colonial rule, is one more external factor. Louis Hartz develops the thesis comparatively, showing that the class values brought by immigrants affect fundamentally the kind of politics that develops in the new states.[13]

Fourth, the cultural context makes a difference. Islamic and Confucian cultures, as we have noted, prove highly resistant to democracy. In the next few decades, democracy may not be a viable option in such cultures. Pakistan will be an interesting case to watch in this regard. It has tried to make the transition several times but has failed in the past. Turkey has had a similar experience over a longer history as an autonomous and secular state.

The Goals of Political Development

Perhaps the most important advance in political development theory has been the recognition that all the goals of development are not mutually compatible. Initially, Cyril Black, Daniel Lerner, and Karl Deutsch viewed modernization as a single manifold phenomenon, a view encouraged by the economic development theorists: growth, democracy, political stability, and so forth go hand in hand. By the 1970s, many empirical studies were proving that all of these goals could not be pursued successfully at the same time. The "compatibility" view began to give way to the "conflict" view.

Huntington identifies five goals for political development: (1) economic growth, (2) social equity, (3) democracy, (4) political stability, and (5) political autonomy.[14] Empirical studies show what is almost intuitively obvious—that economic growth conflicts with the other four. Moreover, democracy is often incompatible with political stability. Much progress in political development studies has derived from examining these conflicts.

The conflict of goals of development forces us to ask how they should be prioritized. If they cannot all be successfully sought at once, then they must be sought in some sequence. In the European experience, a few states stumbled into a successful sequence that has been reasonably well mapped by Rustow in his linear model of development. While that experience has some relevance for the Third World, in one regard it cannot apply. The time available to meet popular indigenous demands and the demands stimulated by external sources—for example, U.S.–Soviet competition in the Third World—has shortened. Literacy and modern communications create a global awareness on a mass scale that forces governments in Third World states to address most of these goals simultaneously or to use repressive methods of rule to keep some of them off the agenda. As we noted, Robert Dahl has emphasized the significance of this compressed time schedule for political development.

The most difficult dilemmas for American policy arise from trying to support political stability and democracy simultaneously. Ideologically U.S. policymakers cannot postpone democracy. Yet they realize the imperative of political stability. They want to see economic growth, but they know that takes time. They can tolerate a waiting period for social equity, and they know that inequities are likely to remain a permanent feature of all societies. American officials involved in assistance programs tend to realize that stability is the prerequisite for all the other things they seek. The media and the public, however, are inclined to want democracy above all else.

The challenge from Moscow has been greatest for the development goal U.S. policymakers seem least effective in pursuing, political stability. As Huntington puts it, "The real challenge which the communists pose to modernizing countries is not that they are good at overthrowing governments (which is easy), but that they are so good at making governments (which is a far more difficult task)."[15] None of the goals of development can be realized unless government and public order can be maintained.

Political Institutions and Stability

Huntington's great contribution to political development theory has been to sharpen the focus on institutions and government, to put the "political" back into development theory after the initial series of studies tended to emphasize everything else but the state and institutions. For him, "The most important distinction among countries concerns not their form of government but their degree of government."[16] Recent events in Eastern Europe and the Soviet Union may seem to call this proposition into question. If change on such a dramatic scale had been precipitated by group and mass action from below alone, there would indeed be a question about the degree of institutionalization in these states. But, in fact, the attack on institutions and the mobilization of mass demand for change were initiated from above, by Gorbachev and his supporters. Romania may be an exception; the events in all surrounding countries certainly played a role in inspiring imitative action. Without Gorbachev's policies, it seems unlikely that Ceauşescu's regime would have collapsed as it did. The modernization phenomenon in the Third World stimulates social and political forces for which the old institutions of governments are seldom adequate. As these requirements for governing exceed the institutions, the institutions "decay." With decay comes a decline in "order" unless new institutions are built to meet the new requirements. If order is to be maintained during modernization or reestablished after the collapse of the old order, institution building must succeed, first of all, in creating state institutions that can manage the process of change.

This seemingly obvious and cogent observation was rather late in being recognized in the field of political development theory because economists were among the first to work seriously on Third World development and because the political scientists, particularly Black and Deutsch, focused on economic activity, social and technological change, communications, and many other symptoms of the process. They exercised a detachment more proper for sociology and anthropology, noticing the large behavior patterns at the expense of examining the stresses on government and institutions of rule. Huntington has not been alone in calling for a change in viewpoint and focus. Joseph LaPalombara, for example, called for a change at about the same time, emphasizing governing and institutions as the critical objects for the study of political development.[17]

The elegance of Huntington's analysis is difficult to capture in a brief summary, but its logic is as simple as it is brilliant. It rests on three equations. First, more people are mobilized in the modernization process, which puts new demands on the institutions. The newly mobilized masses expect to maintain their former standards of living at least and to live better if possible. These expectations, of course, require successful economic growth if they are to be met. If economic growth is negligible, then frustration is the inevitable result; thus the equation,

$$\frac{\text{social mobilization}}{\text{economic developn,ent}} = \text{social frustration}$$

In other words, if economic development keeps pace with social mobilization, then frustration is low, but if it does not, then frustration is high.

Second, social frustration creates demand for mobility opportunities. Thus,

$$\frac{\text{social frustration}}{\text{mobility opportunities}} = \text{political participation}$$

Third, political participation is constrained by political institutions and their capacity to embrace broader participation and to make effective policy meaningfully. Thus the third equation,

$$\frac{\text{political participation}}{\text{political institutionalization}} = \text{political instability}$$

This indicates that weak institutions unable to handle the new demand for participation will produce political instability.

When these three ideas are used to analyze particular political systems, it becomes clear why old governments and political institutions resort to repression under the stresses of modernization. Because they cannot handle the demand for greater political participation, they try to slow down or stop social mobilization through the use of force by police and the military. As a very rough distinction, Huntington divides all polities into two categories, *civic* and *praetorian*. Where institutionalization is adequate to handle social mobilization, the system is *civic*. Where institutionalization is inadequate and the government must enforce order by police and military rule, the system is *praetorian*. Civic systems are not all democratic. The old Soviet system falls under the civic category because it possesses institutions to tie up and control social mobilization, to "govern" without direct military rule.

The remainder of Huntington's analysis deals with the plethora of issues surrounding the development of institutions that can deal effectively with social mobilization and frustration. Why does the military so often intervene in politics in the Third World? What are the dynamics of revolution? How can an authoritarian ruler reform the system? How does one deal with a large landless peasantry? How can land reform be achieved? How do political parties emerge?

Perhaps the most relevant for our analysis here is Huntington's point about praetorian systems and the proclivity for the military to intervene in politics. As political decay sets in and as social frustration and political participation increase, overloading institutions, the army is the last resort for maintaining order. Some military leaders may be politically ambitious, but, in most cases, they have cogent objective reasons to intervene. The civil government's institutions are collapsing under the demand for political participation.

Not infrequently, military rulers return power to civilian leaders after a time, and, when they do, the prospects of retaining a "civic" system depend on the existence of political parties that are sufficiently disciplined and organized to provide an effective governing cadre. If the system is to be democratic, it must have more than one party and established rules for electoral competition.

The Marxist-Leninist Development Model

In the development literature, relatively little attention is devoted to a textured examination of the Marxist-Leninist model of political development.[18] This task has been left to the Soviet and China area specialists, and they, as a rule, tend either to be less steeped in political development theory or to consider it conceptually inappropriate for Marxist-Leninist systems.[19]

Where Marxist-Leninist regimes have come to power, they generally draw on the Soviet experience. Local conditions have prevented a complete emulation of some aspects of policy and institutions, but all generally follow a pattern of institution building that derives from Soviet experience.[20]

The best examples are in Eastern Europe. There the Red Army backed and insured the installation of communist parties, which immediately began a process that led to these results:

1. Marxist-Leninist ideology is accepted as the official basis for the regime's legitimacy and programs for social, economic, and political transformation.

2. A single ruling communist party is modeled on the Soviet example. A mass party, it tends to include 5 to 10 percent of the population. As an elite party, its members penetrate and control all institutions of society. "Democratic centralism" within the party requires strict discipline similar to a military officer corps. In principle, party members are full-time professional revolutionaries ready to make any sacrifice for the party. Periodic purges of the party ensure its revitalization and discipline. Control of the party is ensured by carefully managed central assignment of party cadres to all important party and state posts.

3. In the early stages of consolidating power and building institutions, terror is used as an instrument to force change, to eliminate political opposition, and to impose new social and economic patterns on the society. In later stages, the use of terror subsides to lower levels and subtler means adequate to maintain a general fear of behaving independently and rejecting collective social and economic activity.

4. A party monopoly of the media is imposed and sustained, disallowing public dissent and turning the media into an instrument of social mobilization and education for party goals.

5. A state command economy is imposed, disallowing all but a few small pockets of private enterprise, usually private farm plots. In the industrial sector, allocations and production are directed by a central planning apparatus and a system of subsector management is carried out by ministries and sometimes territorial jurisdictions. In the agrarian sector, collectivized agriculture is instituted to ensure state control over production and distribution.

6. The military and police are transformed into party-controlled institutions, and unlike other institutions, have a very high level of party membership, approaching 100 percent in the officer corps.

This system of Party rule depends heavily on building a vast network of state and voluntary institutions in which the population is mobilized and directed. The state administration is led by the Party, and it is largely occupied with managing the economy. Trade unions, collective farms, youth groups, and voluntary societies proliferate to engage the wider masses, to occupy their time and energy, to direct them, and to ensure that they are not permitted to engage in antiregime activities. Within all of these organizations, individuals are entangled in collec-

tives, small subgroups that exploit peer pressures for social confor-
mity. The individual is disallowed an identity for action outside these
small collectives. The police develop networks of informers throughout all institutions and small collectives which keep close watch over
deviant behavior, trying to anticipate the tendency and block its manifestation in actions. The absence of a private sector of any kind leaves
the individual with no choice but to join a collective for employment,
education, and leisure. The aim of education is transformed, beginning
at the elementary school level, to instill proper ideological training for
perceiving the world and society and for observing proper normative
behavior.[21]

The history of the Soviet revolution from above in East Europe is the
record of the building of these institutions and instruments of control.
In North Korea, Vietnam, Cambodia, and Laos similar patterns of institutionalization occurred. While the speed and sequence has varied, the
final product has been the same in Cuba, Nicaragua, Ethiopia, South
Yemen, Angola, and for a time in Grenada. Albania, Yugoslavia, and
China followed very similar patterns but without direct Soviet tutelage.

Another set of states, which has developed strong client relations
with Moscow, has not followed the pattern of domestic institutional
development. Syria, Iraq, Libya, Egypt, and Somalia, and a few others
fall into this set. Indigenous regimes in those states developed their
own authoritarian patterns, emulating Soviet patterns only to a limited degree. Very important, they never let Soviet cadres penetrate their
institutions to a degree that made a Communist party takeover possible.
In particular, they kept their officer corps and their police and intelligence services wholly free of Soviet controlling penetrations. Even
more important, they refused Soviet offers to provide personal security
for the leadership. In Ethiopia and South Yemen, control of the leaders'
security became the critical Soviet lever for imposing additional penetration and eventually the full set of Soviet institutions.

The first major constraint against this pattern of Soviet institution
building is a shortage of properly trained party and police cadres. Local
personnel were normally taken to the Soviet Union for party training,
but this requires time. Until a sufficient number are trained to take the
key leadership roles in the system, surrogates must be found. In the
Middle East and Africa, East Europeans as well as Soviet citizens were
used before the fall of 1989 and the political upheaval there. Cubans,

of course, assisted in Ethiopia and South Yemen. In Nicaragua, Cubans have provided the mainstay of trained cadres. In Grenada, North Koreans, East Europeans, and Cubans played a role.

Two kinds of local institutions have proven difficult for Marxist-Leninist regimes to subdue. Churches and religious organizations in some cases have never been wholly brought under control. The Catholic church in Poland is a spectacular example. Second, the peasants have proven difficult to control. While the system of collectivized agriculture has been successfully installed in some states, others have gone only part way in imposing it, leaving large parts of the agrarian society to farm in traditional patterns.

These regimes also have difficulty in subduing ethnic minorities, especially where they have developed some sense of modern nationalism. Even where communist regimes are successfully built but are in the hands of a local national group, Soviet-type control runs up against "national communism," which does not always follow Moscow's line. China, Yugoslavia, and Albania were the first clear examples. Today, Vietnam, North Korea, and Cuba are showing signs of national communism, but Moscow has been able, at least until recently, to maintain a reasonably strong influence over them because of threats to these regimes from the United States and other states.

If we measure these regimes against political development goals, they stack up well in achieving political stability and social equity (at very low income levels, to be sure). But they have poor records in democracy and political autonomy. In most, the early years have brought rapid economic growth, but this initial spurt does not become a self-sustaining dynamic analogous to that of successful market economies. Instead, the economic bureaucracy and the absence of competitive market pricing become brakes on growth because they encourage inefficient investment and disallow effective criteria for resource allocations.

In the case of China, Yugoslavia, Albania, and to some extent North Korea, Marxist-Leninist regimes have done well in political autonomy. As Huntington says, they are good at building political institutions to overcome political decay. In economic development, initial successes have been followed by deepening economic problems. In no case has a Marxist-Leninist regime overcome the systemic obstacles that its political institutions pose to long-term growth. When a regime has tried to reform through genuine rather than apparent decentralization of economic authority—as in Yugoslavia and China—it has enjoyed some temporary success followed by both economic and political problems. Economic decentralization weakens political institutions, which causes political leaders to draw back from fundamental economic reform, to linger with halfway measures rather than let a competitive market work. In spite of the fanfare about Yugoslav, Hungarian, and Chinese success with economic reform in the 1970s and early 1980s, promising initial results have not been sustained.

The distinguishing features of the mature Marxist-Leninist regimes seem to be a weakening of their early strength in institutionalization and a permanent economic stagnation that thrives on the parochial interests of the political and economic bureaucracies. Until recently, none of these regimes has proven unstable to the point of collapse or transformation to a different type of political system. Such change has occurred in most of the Warsaw Pact states of Eastern Europe, and we seem to be on the threshold of seeing some kind of transformation in the Soviet Union.

How the change has begun is important to note. It has not come from below in the first instance. It has been initiated by the leadership in the Soviet Union. There is no reason that the Soviet system could not have continued on its path of stagnation and bureaucratic decay for a decade or so longer. Had its leaders chosen that path, they could have kept the lid on change in Eastern Europe, even in Poland where initiatives from below have developed dramatically, although that probably would have required Soviet military intervention. The process of collapse of the East European Marxist-Leninist systems was effectively catalyzed by the general secretary of the Communist party of the Soviet Union, Mikhail Gorbachev, when he called General Jaruzelski in August 1989, encouraging him to compromise with the opposition's demand for participation in the government. The Hungarian Party leadership had already become the leaders of systemic change; they were merely waiting for the opportunity. Thus Hungary quickly followed the Polish example, taking it further. Again, Gorbachev seems to have counseled retreat in face of popular pressures in East Germany. By the end of 1989, all of the regimes in Eastern Europe had come under unmanageable pressure for transformation. In 1990, they have begun the process of trying to reinstitutionalize their participatory systems. In many regards they have been thrown into a political development process analogous to that in many Third World states. To be sure, their political cultures and large industrial working classes make them exceptional, but many of their developmental tasks are analogous.

The easy conclusion to draw from these events is that the kind of U.S.–Soviet competition in the Third World with which this study is concerned is near its end. That would be too simple, and it will probably prove wrong. The nature of that competition is certainly changing, but it may be too early to say that the Marxist-Leninist approach to political and economic development in the Third World has lost all its appeal.

Philip Roeder has recently examined the Marxist-Leninist model of development and defined its early and late stages.[22] He argues that, in the early stage, institutionalization, as Huntington defines it, did not take place. Rather, Soviet institutions imposed "departicipation" on the population, denying them mechanisms for expressing demands and affecting policymaking. Instead, the people were coopted into these new institutions for "coproduction"—that is, for contributing their energy to the regime's development goals. The leadership was able to proceed with its own economic development aims without permitting popular political participation. Eventually, as the system proved incapable of adequate economic development, spontaneous withdrawal from institutions of coproduction began to occur, creating a new participation gap. Huntington's model of development, he contends, simply does not account for the Soviet experience.

For our purposes here, two points are important. First, it may not be that Huntington's model is invalid for the Marxist-Leninist model of development. It could be argued that it is a special case of praetorianism, that Huntington merely misclassified it when he put it in the category of civic regimes. Marxist-Leninist institutions provide the new oligarchy with the institutional means to repress political development while proceeding with economic development. Such systems are a uniquely stable form of praetorianism for several decades until the failure of their economies becomes too much for even the leadership to accept. Depending on how the leaders go about dealing with the growing economic and social crisis, they may destabilize the system. They do not have to destabilize it, and in some cases—Cuba, Vietnam, and China, for example—they have not.

The second point concerns the connection between democracy and economic development. The much maligned totalitarian model of

Soviet politics was originally intended to explain why such systems are different from other kinds of dictatorship. One of the major defining traits in that model is a centrally planned economy based on the virtual exclusion of private property and market economics. When Robert Dahl observed, in his book *Polyarchy* in 1971, that the causal relationship between economic development and democracy could not yet be explained with a general theory, one of the reasons he cited was the apparent success in economic development achieved in the Soviet Union. It seemed possible to have high levels of economic development without democracy and market economies.

Since Dahl made that observation, we have seen a number of authoritarian systems make a fairly peaceful transition to liberal democracy, what Dahl calls "polyarchy." Portugal and Spain are examples as well as a number of Latin American countries. Those systems always had private property in the agrarian and industrial sectors, and the competitive market played a large role in their economies. "Contestation" for participation in policy-making, the kind that Dahl sees as the mechanism for moving to polyarchy, was easier because resources for such contestation—that is, private ownership of property and capital—were more widely diffused among those new contestants for political power.

The Marxist-Leninist systems, those most nearly approximating the totalitarian model, did not permit that kind of diffusion of control over resources through private property. Today in Eastern Europe, where transitions are taking place (first in Poland where the diffusion of ownership was always greater) the most pressing issue is how to introduce a market economy. That seems as critical for the transformation as introducing democratic electoral processes. Failure to do so promises political instability. Whether Marxist-Leninist systems can do so successfully, of course, is still an open question. They could fail to achieve growth in time to cope with new political forces.

The initial dramatic political changes through free elections may give the appearance of a successful transition to democracy, but many of the policy decisions essential to transform the economies of these states could prove impossible for parliaments to make. Relapse into authoritarianism in some cases, therefore, cannot be wholly discounted. In the Soviet Union, notwithstanding the move toward a more competitive electoral process, the move toward private property and market economics is very small, virtually stymied in early 1991. Is genuine progress toward "polyarchy" possible in the Soviet case without a shift to a market economy? Or, to put it another way, can the economic stagnation that has created the behavior Roeder finds in the late stage of such a system be overcome without a market economy?[23] If it cannot, then we may be seeing evidence that would cause Dahl to rethink his view of the relationship between democracy and economic development.

The relevance of this for the Third World cases is central. The Marxist-Leninist model of development could still hold strong appeal because it offers two advantages. First, it deals effectively with instability and growing demand for participation. It allows the elite to hold the power without sharing it more widely. It provides institutional patterns to control the mobilized population and involve it in "coproduction" in the political economy. Second, it promises successful economic development, at least initially—for several decades if the Soviet case is the measure. For political leaders seizing power in Third World states, a couple of decades of economic growth is not a bad prospect. Later decades, when economic stagnation is bound to set in, can be left for future leaders to deal with. Meanwhile, the more urgent need— political stability within fragmented and civil war–torn societies—is likely to be much preferred to prospects of long-term economic growth. If Marxist-Leninist systems are merely a more durable form of praetorianism, they may be attractive alternatives to less stable, right-wing praetorian systems.

While the American-Soviet competition may well be ending in the form we have known it, it is too early to conclude confidently that the competition between two different ideas about political and economic development—ideas that lie at the root of American and Soviet differences in the Third World—will also end. The Marxist-Leninist model can easily find new proponents even if the Soviet Union casts it off. Its capacities for mobilizing power and maintaining stability in countries struggling with modernization are likely to retain their attractiveness here and there. At the same time, American support for democracy is not likely to disappear, although willingness to provide resources for the struggle may abate. Any way we view the future of Third World political development, it seems probable that the United States will find Marxist-Leninist competitors for the next five or ten years, if not far longer.

IV

The Indigenous Sources of

Internal Wars

Clearly the development process alone, without the interference of East-West competition, contains several sources for internal war. We could identify them abstractly by pairing the conflicting goals of development. A more useful way is to keep in mind the major aspects of political development theory as it has matured and to focus on the problem of political instability in sets of actual cases.

Much of the Third World has at one time been under colonial rule, and the early stages of modernization began during colonial rule. While each empire had its own particular institutional forms, they all were able to contain mobilization and repress frustration for a time. In some cases, the imperial states withdrew before the capacity of those institutions to maintain order was exceeded. In others, they were expelled by internal wars. Since the European empires have been disestablished, that form of warfare is not very relevant today. There are exceptions. Some of the republics within the Soviet Union, of course, see themselves as effectively Russian colonies. A few of them might well resort to national liberation struggles involving open warfare. The war in Afghanistan, as well, can be put in the national liberation category, but it is largely over, although Soviet hegemony is still extant in Kabul. When political autonomy is granted to the indigenous populations, they generally have a mix of traditional political institutions held over from precolonial time and administrative structures introduced by the colonial power. The capacity of these institutions to maintain stability varies from state to state, but most of them are weak, not adequate for the rise in social mobilization and demand for economic equity. The colonial influence leaves many of the characteristics of the former European ruler state. The patterns of institutionalization in former British, French, Portuguese, and Spanish colonies seem to hold many of the same development problems for these new states that were experienced by the European states in their move to democracy. The former British colonies have tended to be more successful, although some exceptions are conspicuous, for example, Burma and Pakistan. The former Spanish colonies are distinctive, even after a century and sometimes longer, for resisting democracy, for retaining aristocratic class structures and large landless peasantries. French former colonies retain a strong attraction for French centralized administration and French culture. The exceptions are where the French left very reluctantly, in Vietnam and Algeria.

Additional generalizations are possible, but in looking for the sources of internal war and conflict, we can see that the kind of colonial institutions, the way decolonization took place, and the degree to which colonial institutions have provided the political institutionalization required by modernization are all factors making political instability and internal war more or less likely. Spanish, Belgian, Portuguese, and French colonies in that order seem to have more difficulty in building adequate new institutions. The British have done the best, and some Francophone states have remained stable.

The cultural context, as several students of modernization emphasize, also determines the likelihood of war on the one hand or political stability on the other. Islamic states, no matter what the colonial experience, are prone to internal war and little success with modern political institutionalization. Praetorian regimes or radical repressive regimes are common in these states. They maintain political stability by repression which denies mobilization and participation, or, in radical cases, they use mass organizations and top-down control of new institutions to contain and exploit the mobilization.

The ethnic and religious makeup of Third World states is a strong factor in the prospects for political stability. Homogeneity makes it more likely. Heterogeneity makes it less likely and much harder to achieve. In many of the cases of multiethnic and multireligious states, interstate borders are in dispute. Ethnic or religious groups are sometimes split by international borders. The Middle East, Africa, and South Asia are particularly troubled by such fragmented societies and by subgroups straddling state borders. By comparison, Southeast Asia and Latin America have fewer such cases, but they too have such problems. Clearly these are states where periodic outbreaks of internal and external war are likely.

Social and economic fragmentation also follow other lines. The most common one is a bifurcation between a small landowning elite and a large, landless, and poor peasantry. Where there is a strong authoritarian regime committed to modernization and not under landowner domination, the bifurcation has been occasionally overcome through land reform. Taiwan, South Korea, and Pakistan are examples. Several Latin American regimes and the Philippines are cases where the problem is acute and the regimes either are too weak to implement land reform or are opposed to it. Such states are excellent targets for insurgency movements based on the discontented peasantry.

In summary, these indigenous factors—the nature of the colonial institutionalization experience, the religious context, ethnic heterogeneity, border disputes, and a landless peasantry—make political stability difficult to achieve and internal (and occasionally external) war virtually certain.

The Third World State Versus Enemies and Patrons

Because internal wars are about control over the state, about who is to rule, the state inevitably becomes the key belligerent in the conflict. For the state to win, it must prove that it can rule and deny the opposition the power to engage in violent conflict against the state and society. Winning an internal war, therefore, is not only about military operations; it is also about building effective political institutions. If the opposition defeats the state, it must also replace the state, creating institutions adequate to rule. Whoever wins must be able to maintain order. That means building institutions and governing.

This self-evident observation is important to underscore. American efforts in counterinsurgency, particularly in Vietnam, took it into account, but they did not always show awareness that winning at counterinsurgency is not dependent on succeeding in all five development goals at once. On the contrary, many of the programs pushed by American advisors in Greece, the Philippines, and Vietnam were aimed at achieving progress in several development goals simultaneously.[1] Economic growth, social equity, and democracy are desirable development goals, but they are not necessarily essential for winning the internal war. Achieving political stability, by contrast, is synonomous with victory in internal war. Political stability may be achieved through institutionalization of the mobilized society, the repression of the mobilization, or a mix of both. Let us note, however, that "winning" in this sense is never final, only temporary. No political order has ever been permanent. Internal war, therefore, always hangs over the head of any stable system, even if the probability is quite low.

The Third World state and the incumbent political leadership face two challenges during internal war: first, dealing with the internal needs for political institutionalization and commanding the means to control social mobilization; second, dealing with foreign patrons like the United States.

In most official literature on counterinsurgency and in much of the unofficial writing on the topic, it is assumed that the United States, as the patron of the beseiged client state, is a positive factor—one that strengthens the client through assistance and helps it become strong enough to win the contest for rulership. Is the assumption sound? Not at all. Consider some of the more obvious problems U.S. patronage creates for its clients.

First, it brings a strong bias for democratic institutions, a system of government that depends on a diffusion of power within the society and an internalized set of rules about deciding political issues. The incumbents of a besieged regime are hardly interested in dispersing power; they are more inclined to monopolize it for the purpose of defeating the insurgent forces. The patron-client relationship, then, throws the client government into pursuit of conflicting goals: strong central authority and democracy.

Second, the United States favors social equity, and, while it can tolerate inequity temporarily in order to accumulate development capital, it is highly inclined to use American funds for purposes of greater social equity. The infusion of U.S. aid inherently diffuses power. It puts resources into the hands of a wider set of the elite, officials whose loyalty to the present regime is sometimes mixed, sometimes nonexistent, and seldom high.

Third, the client's dependency on the United States can easily undercut its claim to national feeling and autonomy. It may look more and more like a "hired lackey of American imperialism." The more visible the American presence, the easier it is to make the label stick. Over time, the label may take on reality because the United States insists that its fiscal aid be contingent on conditions the client regime does not prefer but is compelled to accept.

Fourth, the client regime is caught between two competing sets of demands—domestic and foreign—and, to deal with the conflict, it often resorts to duplicity toward both domestic groups and the foreign patron. Inevitably the duplicity is uncovered, creating distrust on both fronts, domestic and foreign. Shafer has described this phenomenon in some detail in three cases—Greece, the Philippines, and Vietnam.[2] The Greek Army and Philippines President Magsaysay sidestepped much of the American advisors' guidance and built less corrupt and more responsive military capabilities. Because these governments defeated the insurgencies, the United States achieved one of its aims but not the others—democracy and economic prosperity. In the case of Vietnam, the client regime did not succeed in steering between the two sets of demands.

Fifth, the client can become dependent on American aid to such a degree that it cannot survive without it. In Vietnam this became increasingly the case by the mid-1960s. The government of South Vietnam lost more and more of its tax base to the Viet Cong as the war went on, dropping to an estimated 10 percent in 1970.[3] U.S. aid tended to compensate for the loss, thus removing some of the government's incentive for regaining the tax base from the Viet Cong.[4]

The second problem—diffusion of power through U.S. aid—and the fifth—allowing the United States to become the de facto tax base for the client regime—are particularly pernicious. In Vietnam not only did they have a profoundly negative impact on the government, but also abundant U.S. aid contributed to the insurgents' resource base. It is likely to be a very exceptional case where more than a marginal U.S. assistance program does not effectively prevent the client regime from succeeding in an internal war. If the local regime cannot compete effectively with the insurgents, denying them the capacity to tax the populace, to extract resources, it cannot win. It may not be an exaggeration to say that the crux of an internal war is taxation, or resource extraction. Organski and Kugler argue that over ten years during the Vietnam War, the total of U.S. and South Vietnamese resources committed to the war equalled the total committed by North Vietnam and the USSR in only one year.[5] In other words, the North Vietnamese and the Viet Cong taxed the USSR more successfully than the South Vietnamese government taxed the United States! What Organski and Kugler omit is an estimate of how much of the U.S. contribution actually fell into Viet Cong hands. That would make the resource balance favor the North Vietnamese even more.

The capacity to extract resources, or tax, is also a good index of a government's ability to rule. Foreign aid given to the government or to the private sector, or a mix of both, tends to dilute the taxing capacity of the recipient government. Thus we are driven to the conclusion that the centerpiece of U.S. support to client regimes for dealing with an internal war, economic assistance, profoundly undermines the policy aim for which it is intended. Where the political institutionalization is already well developed, as in the cases of Israel and Egypt, the impact is not necessarily the same, but even there U.S. assistance encourages deficits and avoidance of dealing with pressing domestic fiscal problems.

Private capital assistance is another matter. It too can be adverse in its effect, as in the case of massive loans of petrodollars that created the large foreign debts in South America during the 1970s, but the record of foreign capital for its impact on recipient states is normally different. According to Peter B. Evans, it has more often strengthened the local state.[6] Several patterns can be found. The state may become an intermediary between the local commercial classes and foreign capital; it may become a substitute for the commercial class by building state-owned enterprises; or it may become a countervailing bureaucracy vis-à-vis the transnational business bureaucracies, controlling and regulating them. In all cases, the autonomous role of the state grows.[7] This stronger role for the state may not ensure either growth or social equity, but it does throw doubt on the dependency theory proposition that the autonomy of the Third World state is undercut by its acceptance of foreign capital for economic development. It also stands in sharp contrast to the impact on client governments of economic assistance from a patron state.

Kiren Aziz Chaudhry raises interesting questions about the influence of these three patterns of transnational capital on the autonomy of the recipient, but she confirms the view that a state's capacity to tax is a good index of its ability to rule.[8] In a study of Saudi Arabia and the Yemen Arab Republic, she compares two types of foreign capital flow over periods of economic "boom" (1973–83) and economic "bust" (1983–87). Saudi Arabia received its foreign capital primarily through state-controlled oil sales. Yemen received capital largely through labor remittances earned abroad. In the Saudi case, capital came directly to the state bureaucracy, whereas in Yemen it went to private citizens, families of the workers abroad.

In both cases, the state allowed the institutions for extracting resources indigenously from the populace to atrophy during the boom period. In other words, state and local institutions declined in administrative competence because they did not have to collect taxes. External sources of finance tended to substitute for taxation. In Yemen, local cooperatives sprang up based on contributions for funding local needs. The business community became more independent of the state bureaucracy, and the state developed greater autonomy vis-à-vis the business community. In Saudi Arabia, because the state controlled the dispensing of monies, local business circles remained dependent on the state apparatus, virtually in its pay.

When the "bust" came in 1983, both states had to reimpose internal resource extraction, that is, taxation. In the Yemeni case, because the state had broken its ties with the business community, it could resist lobbying against greater taxes. Moreover, it took advantage of the new local institutions, using them as extractive structures. The Saudi business community, by contrast, much entangled with the state, was able to lobby effectively against austerity and reallocation policies. The state had no new local institutions, as existed in Yemen, to play off against the business community. Chaudhry says, "Labor remittances, by contrast, accrued directly to millions of Yemeni migrants through an informal, decentralized banking system that fed the buoyant private sector with virtually unlimited amounts of foreign exchange. Unlike oil revenues, labor remittances concentrated economic opportunity in the private sector." [9]

In many ways, Saudi oil revenues were like direct government aid grants. The Yemeni labor remittances allowed capital to bypass state control. In both cases, the impact on the state's administrative capacities was deleterious, but in the Yemeni case, adaptation to the conditions of austerity was easier. Most important, in both cases economic austerity was the factor stimulating the state to adapt and rebuild its capacity to rule locally. The conclusion is highly instructive. The way foreign capital flows into a developing state makes a large difference for institution building and political participation.

The critical variable, however, remains the political capacity of the recipient government. Lewis Snider, analyzing the foreign debt service performance of fifty-eight developing countries for the years 1970–84, shows that "political capacity can be decisive in correctly predicting the probability of a government's suspending its external debt service payments."[10] Snider's definition of political capacity is twofold: (1) the ability to penetrate society to exercise effective authority over as many citizens or subjects as possible within a state's jurisdiction, and (2) the ability to extract resources from society in support of national objectives.[11] His analysis rests on three variables: (1) political capacity to extract fiscal resources, (2) capital flight, and (3) creditors' assessment of the government's capacity to manage the economy. The first variable is the best predictor, according to this model, of states which suspended debt service payments.

In explaining the delinquent debtor state, Snider reasons that "a weak ability to raise and allocate revenue to cover the public spending gap without fear of adverse political repercussions was one reason why it resorted to foreign borrowing." Furthermore, "The more it used the foreign borrowing to finance the public sector deficit, the more the distributional effect duplicated the use of other forms of government spending. It built up constituencies who see public spending as an entitlement. This is particularly so when the public borrowing was done by parastatal firms."[12] The implication, of course, is that foreign borrowing by nonstatist firms competing in a more or less free market does not have this debilitating impact on the government.

A state's apparent capability to tax, however, can be misleading. As Snider points out, Third World states which raise most of their revenues by taxing trade, especially the exports from extractive industries, may do so without necessarily penetrating society and exercising authority over all citizens. Political capacity, therefore, is best indicated by the capacity to levy direct taxes because that requires greater administrative capability and penetration of society by government.[13]

Thus, Snider's analysis of a large number of countries shows that Chaudhry's two case studies are hardly exceptional. The capacity to rule is directly related to the capacity to extract resources from all citizens. Direct economic aid to governments, especially in countries with statist economic firms and constituencies, is certainly not going to stimulate greater political capacity. On the contrary, it is almost certain to reduce it.

Because winning an internal war depends on building a strong state administration, this contrast in the effects of private capital and direct government economic assistance takes on special significance for U.S. policy. It does not mean that aid is always pernicious. It means that the modalities for its transfer make large differences. It also suggests that U.S. strategy in assisting client states engaged in internal wars must take account of nongovernmental transnational institutions, an area that is generally neglected in U.S. policy toward such states. It also means that the role the local government plays in dealing with transnational capital makes a difference. Direct economic assistance may well obstruct the emergence of a strong free market and growth.

The American predicament is that it tries to practice colonialism by ventriloquy. Given its official position on colonialism and its respect for international law and the principle of self-determination, it cannot take direct control and install an effective system of public administration as the British frequently did. Instead, it builds a network of advisors, paralleling the client state's institutions, and tries to persuade the local incumbents to speak and act according to American advice. Even if the advice is sound—and the chances of this are small because the advisors bring their own ethnocentric views of how to govern (although there are exceptions when advisors know the local language and politics quite well)—and even if it is followed, the indigenous administrators and military officers tend to be seen as puppets, not legitimate independent officials. They are vulnerable to propaganda attacks by the insurgents.

Finally, building democracy while fighting a civil war is a virtually impossible task for some Third World states. Yet American policy cannot support for long a regime which scorns democracy for very long. Public opinion and media insistence on democracy soon find resonance in the Congress, and the Congress puts limits on the executive branch's programs for assistance, making them contingent on democratization.

The only way out of these dilemmas, colonialism by ventriloquy and the requirement to build democracy, is direct U.S. invasion and U.S. military government. Without a basis for declaring war, this is not a politically viable alternative, and such a basis in Third World states is rare indeed, Grenada and Panama being about as close to examples as we are likely to find in the near future. To be sure, there are many additional reasons why direct U.S. rule would be highly ill-advised as a general policy, but as an analytical excursion, the logic is instructive.

The power of the logic has prompted calls from U.S. congressmen and media pundits for deeper U.S. involvement in Kuwait and Iraq after the Gulf War.

A close client relationship with an imperiled Third World state, therefore, can prevent the development of a stable indigenous regime, one with sufficient institutionalization to win the internal war. That was the case in South Vietnam. El Salvador could have the same experience. It does not have to, but it could if the insurgents shift their strategy from major emphasis on internal war to emphasis on building an alternative political administration. In this event, the war would continue, but the primary front would shift to competition in institution building and resource extraction. The case of the Philippines is also relevant. The New People's Army has pursued a strategy of institution building and taxation. Unlike the Farabundo Marti National Liberation Front (FMLN) in El Salvador, it seems to be far less dependent on outside aid.

V

Where U.S. Involvement in Internal Wars

Is Probable

From our analysis of the sources of internal war, it is clear that such wars are highly probable throughout the Third World. Neither is this news to anyone who follows international affairs, nor is it helpful to U.S. policymakers. Can our analysis be any more precise, any more helpful in identifying where such wars will be of political significance to the United States, where U.S. interests are sufficient to make our involvement likely? The answer is yes.

The ambiguities inherent in defining national interests, "vital interests," and various other kinds of interests are well enough known. Our purpose here is not to enter that debate but rather to take a pragmatic and operational approach to interest definition, the approach normally taken in policy circles (and much debated in academic circles). In the first instance, our interests in other parts of the world are what we say they are and what government officials, foreign leaders, and the American public believe they are. No American president starts out with a tabula rasa and defines afresh what will and will not be United States interests. He inherits a set that is written in treaties, implicit in policies, and effectively asserted by political groups. He may redefine national interests, but that takes time and policy resources for convincing the Congress, the public, and other actors in the definition process. As a rule, they remain fairly stable, but they can change sharply as they did in the Persian Gulf region in 1980 after the Soviet invasion of Afghanistan. President Carter committed the United States to repel foreign military invasions from the region with the Soviet military largely in mind. Some voices challenged this new definition of our interests there, but President Reagan confirmed his agreement on the issue in 1981, and it has effectively become a strategic interest for the United States to meet a foreign military invasion there with force. With the dramatic change in Soviet foreign policy since 1985, this definition of interests may change again, and there are signs that it has already begun in the Department of Defense's annual directive to the military services, Defense Planning Guidance for 1992–97. The American definition of its interests in South Vietnam altered only slowly, over a decade.

Our analysis requires not a global definition of interests but only a reasonably sound assessment of what our presidents, the Congress, and the public are likely to believe are our interests in those regions outside the traditional East-West geographic axis of postwar competition—that is, what is roughly called the Third World. It also requires a further narrowing to regions and states where we would likely see it in our interests to become significantly involved in helping a client state cope with an internal war. In other words, a sound assessment requires both a political and an analytical judgment about where the United States would probably seriously consider either a direct or indirect commitment to an internal war.

Any two analysts will probably give different answers to that judgment question, but there would be a large overlap in the answers of any ten analysts who are reasonably familiar with U.S. defense and foreign policy. In the early years of the Cold War, we were prepared to compete almost anywhere. As the decades passed, we began to limit the regions and states where we would risk such involvement. A rather sharp watershed came toward the end of the Vietnam War with the Nixon doctrine, which committed the United States to reduce its security commitments in some regions. Since that time we have effectively ruled out fairly large parts of the Third World for more than marginal military involvement, that is, some military technical assistance.

In Southeast Asia and the South Pacific we have drawn back to two states where we still have security treaties: the Philippines and Thailand. (With Australia and New Zealand, we are a party to ANZUS, but neither country is part of the Third World.) Of course, we are still supportive of the Association of Southeast Asian Nations (ASEAN) states in those regions, but beyond the Philippines and Thailand, it is doubtful that we would easily become engaged in an internal war on the side of the incumbent regime. While we might be more willing in the case of some of the small island states in the South Pacific, larger states such as Indonesia and Malaysia would require a considerable redefinition of U.S. commitments to entangle us in their internal wars..

The prospects for anticommunist insurgencies that might draw our support are not attractive. The most obvious case, Cambodia, is terribly confusing and complex, and therefore offers no attractive options for such U.S. support, although there has been some congressional enthusiasm for involvement in Cambodia. Moreover, Secretary Baker has taken limited steps that could involve the United States in trying to reach a settlement, but he lacks a public consensus for going much further.

With the rapidly changing nature of Soviet foreign policy, there is even less incentive for U.S. involvement except in the two states to which we are committed formally. A strong argument can be made that our interests are not sufficiently great to include even these states. Certainly the Philippines provides basing for a U.S. military presence which is desired by ASEAN and which provides a stabilizing factor in the region, but without an aggressive Soviet policy there, that presence is less critical. Moreover, we could still project military power into the region from other basing, although it would be more difficult. We could, in principle, find alternative basing for our military presence in the region, and some official steps have been taken in this regard with Singapore. For our analysis here we will assume our interests are still sufficient to require us to stand by our treaty commitments, but we will also acknowledge that the depth of U.S. commitment to these interests is not nearly as great as in other regions. If they become costly we might give them up early.

Next, let us consider Latin America. The region can usefully be divided into two parts, those states on the Caribbean littoral and in Central America, and the remainder, all the states in South America not on the Caribbean littoral. While we certainly would be interested in the second set of states, significant U.S. involvement in internal wars there can be ruled out. Some would argue that drug trafficking from Colombia or other states in that set gives us sufficient interest for involvement, but if we consider the true nature of drug production, we will realize that stamping it out in Colombia and Peru will simply allow other producers throughout the Third World to make up the difference. We may become involved in antidrug internal wars, but it seems doubtful that interest alone will sustain our commitment over any significant time. Our present enthusiasm for such military and police operations is likely to flag fairly quickly.

That leaves the first set of Latin American states. Internal wars in these states have a direct impact on the United States. They prompt migrations northward. El Salvador, for example, is not another Vietnam as some have suggested in encouraging our policymakers to abandon it. One striking difference is the eight thousand miles of ocean that separate Vietnam from the United States! Cuba is a military security problem for the United States. It is the only state hostile toward the United States other than the Soviet Union which has the military means, admittedly limited, to attack the United States. Cuban aircraft and submarines could actually cause military damage to the continental United States. Admittedly, such a contingency is remote except in the event of a war in Europe and Soviet success in dragging Cuba in on Moscow's side. That, to be sure, is a fading prospect. With the proliferation of ballistic missile technology, the potential for other states to acquire some limited capability to hit the United States is real, even if improbable. These are a few of the reasons that this part of the Third World cannot be ignored to the extent that Southeast Asia can. We are indeed likely to remain involved in one way or another in this region's internal wars.

What about Africa? In the sub-Saharan region we have been involved in supporting the National Union for the Total Independence of Angola (UNITA) forces, and we helped Zaire in a couple of crises in Shaba. While we may want to continue such involvement, we cannot really consider the region so important as to require it. We have the choice, without great risk, to avoid such actions. In the Francophone states to the north, the French have taken a major role. We have assisted the French, but we need not become directly engaged here. Egypt is probably the only state where we have sufficient interest to support the incumbent regime in an internal war, and that is because of its strategic importance in the Middle East, not in Africa. Ethiopia and Somalia, to the extent they affect stability on the Arabian peninsula, become a concern for U.S. interests, but that concern is less today as Ethiopia struggles with ethnic strife against its Marxist-Leninist government. Africa, therefore, need not demand our involvement in its internal wars, at least not without a major change in the strategic alignments in the world. We are likely to be able to handle our interests in Africa through diplomacy and other nonmilitary instrumentalities, as we have with South Africa and a number of other states on that continent.

The subcontinent in Asia is another region where U.S. involvement in internal wars seems neither probable nor advisable. We have, of course, played a large role in Afghanistan, and we have strong interests in a stable Pakistan; but again, this is much related to the Middle East and our concerns with Soviet intentions toward Southwest Asia and the Middle East. India, the dominant power in the subcontinent, has internal wars and involves itself in Sri Lanka's internal war, but we have no good reasons to be a party to these conflicts. Pakistan and India could engage in open conflict, perhaps involving the use of nuclear weapons, but this would be an external war, not of the class we are considering.

The remaining region, the Middle East and Southwest Asia, is a different matter. The strategic importance of oil—plus our ties to Israel, Pakistan, and Turkey—makes us likely to see our interests as affected sufficiently for us to become a party to some internal wars in this region. As long as oil plays the role it does in the Western industrial economies, our strategic interests here will endure. We simply cannot take a benign view of the impact of internal wars on those interests. We may not need to become a party to them, but again we might. The crisis created by Iraq's invasion of Kuwait raises many uncertainties in this regard. The U.S. response, deploying large conventional military forces to Saudi Arabia and expelling the Iraqi forces by force, is bound to have a number of unanticipated and undesirable effects on the domestic politics of the states on the Arabian peninsula, perhaps even more widely in the region. If these effects entail internal wars, in addition to the interstate war that has already taken place, U.S. involvement is entirely possible. At this writing, the Kurdish uprising and its defeat has already prompted some U.S. direct involvement on Iraqi territory, and U.S. military presence in Kuwait appears to be destined for a long stay.

With this assessment of where our more critical interests lie in the Third World, it is possible to reduce dramatically our military force requirements to be prepared to deal directly with internal wars. Could we reduce the areas further if we knew that the Soviet Union had actually dropped out of the competition? While that factor would change the likelihood of conflicts, the internal dynamics of these regions, including radical movements that seek to destabilize regimes we support, keep the prospects of internal wars affecting our interests reasonably high. The end of the Cold War may help, but it will not reduce the problem to naught.

We are left, then, with three regions where we are likely or willing to deal with internal wars. We could reduce them to two by opting out of the Philippines, but let us assume that we will not. The Caribbean and Central America, parts of Southeast Asia, and the Middle East and Southwest Asia are the regions we must examine more closely for the probability of internal wars.

Let us next reflect on political development theory and try to refine our ability to anticipate more precisely where internal wars are probable. We can take the sources of internal war as we have identified them—the nature of the colonial experience, the religious context, the ethnic heterogeneity, border disputes, and landless peasantries—and examine each country in these regions for these factors. While they are extremely important, looking at them alone would probably cause us to miss the critical factor, the political factor. Some states with a number of potential sources of internal war are quite stable. Turkey, Pakistan, and Iraq, for example, ought to be prospects for internal wars by these measures. Mexico might be included as well as others. Few analysts, however, would consider internal disorders in these states likely to exceed the capacity of the regimes to manage them, particularly if the Soviet Union does not pursue a policy of aggressive support for the dissident forces.

Another way to look at the problem is to consider what Huntington calls the "degree" of government. Where the degree of government, or "institutionalization," is high, stability tends to be greater. It follows, then, that we should look at the governments for their degree of institutionalization, their capacity to deal with the problem of social mobilization that economic and political development bring. Huntington's three equations, it will be recalled, direct our attention to the connection between social mobilization, economic development, demand for participation, and institutions that accommodate participation.

When institutional development falls behind the pressures of these other variables, instability is greater. And since preventing internal wars is really about maintaining stability, it follows that where institutionalization is low or unsuccessful, the probability of internal war increases. On the other side of that struggle, it is also true that where insurgent institutions are strong, the probability of internal war is greater. The war is about whose legitimacy, whose institutions, will prevail.

Can we develop a simple taxonomy of regimes according to their degree of government? If we can, then we can apply it to the states of the regions where the United States has critical interests and make better judgments about where internal wars are likely.

We can develop the taxonomy a number of ways, using the work of different scholars. We could, for example, take Robert Dahl's concept of "hegemonic" regimes—dictatorships with very little inclusiveness for participation and no competing political groups—and his concept of "polyarchies"—regimes that are both inclusive and have competing political groups, that is, pluralist or democratic regimes. Making this scheme operational is not easy, but presumably we could identify what he calls "hegemonic" regimes and further identify those within the set that have growing mobilization which is not being institutionalized successfully. Internal war is virtually inevitable in these cases if a counterelite begins to institutionalize the disaffected population. Polyarchic regimes, of course, would be less vulnerable to internal war. So would highly inclusive hegemonic regimes. And of course, hegemonic regimes with little inclusiveness of the populace would be stable as long as social mobilization was nil.

Another way to approach the classification task is to use Huntington's concept of "civic" and "praetorian" regimes. Both democratic and Marxist-Leninist regimes are "civic" by his definition in that they offer adequate institutions to control the mobilization. Between these two extremes, we could add left- and right-wing authoritarian types, regimes that have developed adequate institutions to retain stability under the pressures of modernization, institutions based on the ideology of legitimacy. Syria, Iraq, Libya, and Mexico, for example, would fall into the left authoritarian category. They are not Marxist-Leninist, but they profess leftist leaning ideologies; and they institutionalize participation in a top-down, authoritarian fashion, as Marxist-Leninist regimes do, but without the full set of Soviet-type institutions. Right-wing authoritarians take much the same approach but from a different ideological perspective. The major difference between the two is their attitude toward private property and economic controls. In both, the state may play a large role, but the right-wing authoritarians are more inclined to accept a larger degree of market economics.

The distinctive feature of the praetorian regime is that it either cannot or will not accept greater participation. It faces growing mobilization and economic frustration in its populace and responds by trying to repress the resulting demand for participation. In reality, it is opposed to political development. It is attempting to prevent political development and participatory institutionalization. Praetorian regimes, therefore, are excellent prospects for internal war. They need only a small insurgent leadership capable of challenging the rule of the incumbents by violent means.

There is yet another type of regime worth mentioning in this classification effort. Some scholars have called them "traditional" regimes. Old, long-established governments, monarchies, feudal structures, or tribal structures are still in place in some Third World regions. The impact of social mobilization has not yet overwhelmed them, and thus they remain stable. The small Persian Gulf sheikdoms and Saudi Arabia are examples. They have been able to survive for a number of reasons, especially through astute use of oil revenues to prevent social mobilization. In Dahl's scheme, they are hegemonic. In Huntington's scheme, they are simply traditional regimes that have avoided the sequence indicated by his three equations—social mobilization leading to instability.

Internal wars in the regions in question are most probable in those states with praetorian regimes. There social mobilization is high, economic development has not prevented social frustration and demand for participation, and institutionalization is wholly inadequate. Instability and internal war are likely. Traditional regimes are also candidates for internal wars, and for some of the same reasons.

U.S.–Soviet competition in the Third World, of course, has made the probability of such internal wars much greater, especially because Marxism-Leninism has provided both an ideological justification for such wars and the organizational know-how for building insurgent movements. The Reagan doctrine has prompted an American effort to develop a democratic alternative for such insurgencies, but it has largely amounted to supporting already extant insurgencies, and it has not really developed effective organizational concepts. The National Endowment for Democracy presumably has this task, but its efforts are still at an inchoate stage. Whether they will persist and emerge into a well-developed and coherent system is an open question.

In Central America and on the Caribbean littoral, we have had two Marxist-Leninist regimes—Cuba and Nicaragua. The United States, of course, has supported an insurgency in Nicaragua. As with most Marxist-Leninist regimes that have had time to build Soviet-type institutions, it has withstood the insurgency's challenge. It did not, however, wholly eliminate political opposition; and under the twin pressures of the Contra insurgency and foreign diplomatic pressure—apparently including its sponsor, the Soviet Union—it ran the risk of free elections and lost. The transition to a new system, firmly established, will take time; and it could fail, particularly as long as the Sandinistas control the military. Cuba is in a fairly advanced stage of the Marxist-Leninist development model. Instability there, therefore, should not be ruled out. Depending on the course it might take, U.S. involvement also remains a possibility. In the near term, however, the Cuban regime has the appearance of stability, and Nicaragua is in a state of transition.

A number of fairly well-institutionalized democracies are also to be found there: Costa Rica, Colombia, Venezuela, Jamaica, the Dominican Republic, and the several West Indies island states. Panama now seems likely to join the democracies.

Haiti has been a praetorian state which has fallen into internal war, and what will emerge is not yet clear. It could eventually become a stable right-wing authoritarian, or it might revert to praetorianism. Democracy is not to be ruled out, but the prospects do not look good.

Mexico is a left-wing authoritarian regime that proves quite stable in spite of many internal difficulties in maintaining stability. Regional disorders are not to be ruled out, and, were they to become serious, the United States might conceivably become involved; but on the whole, Mexico seems to be inherently stable notwithstanding many frustrated groups' desire for greater participation. Moreover, Mexico is showing signs recently of moving away from its leftist orientation in favor of expanded private enterprise.

How should we classify El Salvador, Honduras, and Guatemala? In the 1970s they were praetorian regimes, indisputably. Today they all have democratically elected governments. They may not have had the freest elections, and political intimidation and corruption have not been absent in their recent democratic processes. Nonetheless, competition has been permitted, and the election results honored.

As we examine two of these states in our case studies, it will become apparent that democracy is more apparent than real there. The concentration of economic resources and landownership in the hands of a few oligarchs and military leaders makes it virtually impossible for opposition political parties to gain the resources and grass roots organizations essential for effective participation. These states may be more properly classified as praetorian, notwithstanding their young democratic institutions. Honduras stands apart among the three because the number of landowners is much larger than in the other two, creating a much greater diffusion of wealth and more resources for political competition. But even Honduras is a borderline case unless the regime elected early in 1990 succeeds with its bold economic program. Internal war in all three is ongoing (at a much lower level in Honduras), and understandably so. Soviet-Cuban backed and trained insurgencies exist, as does a large, frustrated, and socially mobilized population.

What about Southeast Asia? The Philippines is remarkably like these three Central American states. Formally it is a democracy, but in substance it has much in common with the praetorian type. Under Marcos, it was essentially praetorian; and President Aquino has not basically altered that situation, particularly the degree of landowning concentration in the hands of a few oligarchs. Competitive political institutions are very fragile, with little or no grass roots institutionalization.

Thailand is truly a unique case that defies easy classification. It retains elements of a traditional regime in its monarchy. Frequent military intervention in politics has given it praetorian qualities. Yet landownership is reasonably diffuse, providing stability to the rural political order. Insurgencies have persisted over decades, supported by outside powers, particularly China. Democratic elections have been periodic. A market economy has been encouraged although not free of state and other interference. Thailand was never a colonial dependency, and its leaders' skill in diplomacy in dealing with its neighbors and regional powers has been remarkable. On the whole, Thailand looks to be quite stable, able to deal with its insurgencies as law and order problems, and unlikely to fall into a serious internal war.

In the Middle East, most of the moderate Arab states fall into either the traditional or the praetorian category. They are good prospects for internal wars, but the nature of the insurgencies is different from that of Central America and Southeast Asia. Here they are ethnically based. Moreover, the desert climate in much of the region does not lend itself to peasant-based insurgencies of the type seen in other parts of the world. While some have a strong leftist or Marxist character in their ideologies, they also are based largely on Islamic religious ideas.

Where are these insurgencies? The Kurds overlap Iran, Iraq, and Turkey, and they have been dealt heavy blows by all of these governments.

Moreover, their outside sources of support have weakened. The Dhofar insurgency in Oman was defeated and shows little sign of reviving. Syria has brutally repressed dissident groups within its boundaries. Iran has considerable potential for ethnic insurgencies, ranging from the Baluchis in the south to the Azeris in the north as well as a few small groups in the central part of the country. The present Iranian regime, which might best be called a left-wing authoritarian, seems quite capable of maintaining internal stability in spite of these dissident groups.

The Palestinians are spread throughout the region, fragmented among themselves, and not really forming an insurgency except in the recent developments in the occupied territories within Israel. They are, to be sure, a major source of instability in Jordan. In Lebanon, the PLO's struggle with Israel has thrown the entire country into a long civil war, which recently ended largely because of exhaustion by all sides and Syria's involvement.

Insurgencies and the kind of internal war we see in the other two regions, however, are not really the central problem for stability in the Middle East. Rather interstate wars predominate. Every subsection of the region either is in the midst of a war, has recently emerged from one, or is about to fall into one. The primary problems in the region are the Iran-Iraq War; conflicts involving Pakistan-India, Somalia-Ethiopia, Syria-Iraq, and North and South Yemen (unless their recent political union succeeds); the Arab-Israel confrontation; Lebanon, where civil war was catalyzed by Syrian and Israeli intervention and Palestinian presence; and, most recently, the Iraqi invasion of Kuwait followed by the U.S.-led counteroffensive. These wars, of course, are not the focus of our study.

There is, however, another kind of internal war possible in several of the moderate Arab states. Radical Palestinian groups and Shiites backed by Iran could possibly create sufficient disorder in the capitals of the Persian Gulf sheikdoms or in Saudi Arabia, Jordan, or Egypt to cause the collapse of a regime. This type of internal war, the pattern we saw in Iran when the shah's regime collapsed, is dramatically different from the Central American cases. A slight variant of the same type of war occurred with the collapse of the monarchy in Ethiopia and the Soviet-backed Mengistu regime sometime later. In the event of such a development in Saudi Arabia, Oman, or the sheikdoms, the United States might well decide to become involved. This kind of internal war, therefore, is of critical interest to the United States because it potentially threatens the major oil-producing states. The U.S. victory in the Gulf War in the winter of 1991 makes such wars less likely in the short run, but it stimulates domestic political pressures that could prove unmanageable if U.S. forces depart soon.

Unlike the Central American and Philippine cases, U.S. goals in these internal wars in the Middle East could not reasonably be the establishment of democracy. The preconditions are not there. To impose democracy would be a long and expensive undertaking, something the American public is most unlikely to support. It might well, however, be willing to support short-term actions to restore order in the major oil-producing states. Again, the U.S. military victory over Iraq could render these judgments off the mark or irrelevant. It could lead to long-term commitments entailing implicit involvement in the domestic politics of militarily weak oil-producing states on the Persian Gulf, perhaps including Iraq.

To sum up, the Third World regions where the United States has sufficient interests to become involved in internal wars are fairly limited. Within those regions, the probability of such wars can be narrowed to the praetorian and traditional regimes, those with inadequate institutionalization or economic wealth to deal with rapid social mobilization. In Central America and the Caribbean littoral, that means essentially three or four states in the coming decade, but it also includes a Marxist-Leninist state, Cuba, because it is supporting internal wars in three of these states. In Southeast Asia it really means only the Philippines. And in the Middle East it means the moderate Arab states and Israel.

Some analysts might quarrel with this selection of states for primary concern for U.S. policy. Indeed, it may omit a few cases where events make our interests look different and our willingness to become involved greater. If we orient our concerns with internal war to the selected regions and the most likely candidates, however, we are likely to have adequate military resources for dealing with the few surprise cases. This is not to suggest that we entirely ignore all other regions and potential candidates for internal war. Strategic interests can change. It is, nonetheless, to argue that we greatly narrow our focus from its traditional global spread and concentrate on the more probable areas and states.

VI

The Record of East-West Competition
in the Third World

....

Now that we have identified the countries where future internal wars are likely to concern the United States most seriously, it is useful to look at the record of past competition. Has the Soviet approach to the competition scored well? Where it has succeeded, what has been the key to its success? Have indigenous communist parties led revolutions? What role has external support played? Are there other distinctive aspects of Soviet successes that deserve our attention for dealing with the future?

Moscow's greatest success has been in states that the Red Army invaded. East Europe is the example.[1] Not a single communist party in those states had good prospects for seizing power without the backing of the Soviet armed forces. Stalin went so far as to devise a modification in Marxism-Leninism to account for these so-called revolutions. Marx had explained that the economic "base" of a society changes with the changing conditions of production. Socialist revolutions would occur only when the "base" created a large propertyless working class whose interests were at odds with the bourgeois "superstructure" of political and social institutions. No such conditions existed in East Europe. The Soviet presence there, however, did change the "superstructure" into a socialist one and direct it to transform the "base." This reverse causal notion, turning Marx upside down, was Stalin's explanation of the way socialism was to be built in Eastern Europe.

Marxist-Leninist parties did succeed in taking power in other states during and shortly after World War II. Yugoslavia and Albania built insurgent armies from the peasantry, appealing to the anti-German sentiment brought by the wartime occupation. Indigenous parties also captured power in China and North Korea after the war. Thereafter, no victories for Marxist-Leninist parties occurred for several years. And in all of the communist-led peasant revolutions, Moscow soon found itself without the kind of control it desired.

Vietnam became the next major communist success, another case of a peasant-based army riding the local nationalist sentiment against Japanese and colonial occupation. Only half of the country fell in this case, leaving South Vietnam for a later war.

Soviet analysis of revolutionary prospects in the Third World focused on "national liberation movements" and the opportunities they offered for class alliance tactics, making common cause with the local national bourgeoisie.[2] Moscow also paid great attention to the role of the military in these movements, seeing them as a progressive force, one to be captured if possible.[3]

The record of Soviet exploitation of national liberation governments and military leaders, however, is mixed at best. In the Middle East, the Soviet leaders bet heavily on Nasser and Sadat but lost. They have sustained strong ties with Iraq and Syria, but those regimes have not become Marxist-Leninist in character, and their autonomy from Moscow is considerable. Somalia is a similar case where they eventually lost out. Ethiopia and South Yemen, however, are different stories. Here the Soviet Union came to the aid of beleaguered military rulers, penetrated their security and military institutions, and made them pawns of Soviet policy, thus effecting a revolution driven by the new superstructure of Soviet-like organizations. The same pattern occurred in Angola. In Mali, Ghana, the Sudan, and Nigeria, this same tactic was followed but without the same success. Algeria also deserves mention because it succeeded as an insurgency, but it has shown considerable independence from Moscow.

In South Vietnam, the war began with an insurgency based on peasant recruiting and anticolonial sentiment. Moscow's early role is not so clear, but in the end a military invasion by North Vietnam was required for taking power and imposing Marxist-Leninist institutions. Cambodia and Laos followed with a mix of local communist guerrillas and invading Vietnamese forces.

The Caribbean region has a wholly distinctive pattern. Here the United States was primarily responsible for the success of insurgent takeovers. U.S. special forces actually trained Castro's forces, and the

United States stood by as he took power. The Sandinista takeover in Nicaragua was supported by the United States in its last phase, and it is most doubtful that it could have succeeded without U.S. aid through Panama and refusal to save the National Guard after Somoza fell.

Moscow also pursued an electoral tactic for seizing power. It was close to a victory with the Allende government in Chile, but Pinochet's coup nipped it in the bud.

Moscow has tried to remain publicly aloof from a number of insurgent movements with a radical leftist orientation. The Sendero Luminoso, or Shining Path, in Peru and the New People's Army in the Philippines are examples. The terrorist and guerrilla movements in Argentina and Uruguay are additional examples. Cuban-backed M19 insurgents in Colombia and the insurgents in El Salvador, Guatemala, and Honduras are others, but Soviet support for Nicaragua until recently has made the connection to these Central American cases more difficult to hide.

Grenada, of course, had direct Soviet involvement; and, with the Cubans, Moscow was well on its way to a success until the U.S. invasion.

Moscow's tie to the PLO is well enough known, but the degree of control and support remains a question—not just for the public but probably also for Arafat because of the potential conflicts of interests if Arafat were to succeed in winning a Palestinian state. That it would initially be a Soviet client has been likely, but Moscow's new foreign policy makes that most doubtful today. How the relationship would work out in the longer run is anyone's guess. It would create dilemmas for Soviet strategy.

Some clear patterns emerge from this review. First, reliable Soviet clients arise only where the Soviet military occupies the country. Afghanistan, of course, is an exception, but the battle for influence in Kabul is far from over.

Second, where extensive internal wars have occurred, led by committed Marxist-Leninists who have eventually taken power, stable Marxist-Leninist regimes have been built. With the exception of Cuba and Vietnam, however, those states have not cooperated closely with Moscow. Cooperation in these two cases has been dictated by the enormous material support that Moscow provides and the hostile international environment in which they live. North Korea also falls into this pattern, but at times it has tilted toward the People's Republic of China

(PRC) at Moscow's expense. More recently, it has leaned almost wholly on the Soviet Union.

Third, in the cases of Ethiopia, South Yemen, and Angola, Soviet penetration of the regime without a revolution, but in conditions of civil war, has succeeded. In these cases, Moscow has been put on the side of the government fighting against indigenous insurgencies, a struggle being lost in Ethiopia and possibly in Angola.

In summary, three patterns of Soviet success can be identified. The first, invasion and occupation, has for the first time met failure in Afghanistan. Given Gorbachev's foreign policy, this pattern seems un-likely to appear in the next few years. Second, local insurgencies which are led by left radical cadres are either likely to be receiving indirect support or to receive it later as their success looks imminent. Again, Gorbachev's new policy promises, if not a total cessation, then a major reduction of such aid. Finally, Moscow has pursued the tactic of pene-trating Third World military and national liberation governments with the aim of a coup followed by revolution from above.

On the whole, Moscow has not done well. Since Vietnam, Laos, and Cambodia, no Soviet-backed insurgents have taken power. The Sandi-nistas in Nicaragua had Cuban and Soviet backing, but U.S. policy was the key to their success. Coups have been more successful, but they have come in conditions of serious domestic political fragmentation and internal war.

Another dimension of the Soviet record also deserves special empha-sis. The Leninist view of war as an interclass phenomenon has not pre-vailed in a practical sense. International class solidarity has failed even in some instances where communist parties have taken power. Nation-alism and national interests have transcended loyalty to the Soviet-led socialist camp. Yugoslavia was the first to break ranks, and Albania and China soon followed suit. Romania, while remaining a formal member of the Warsaw Pact, for all intents and purposes soon went its separate way. Hungary and Czechoslovakia would have gone their way but for the actions of the Soviet Army.

A particularly serious blow to the official Soviet ideology on relations between "brotherly socialist countries" was delivered by the war be-tween Vietnam and China in 1979. In theory, such wars are impossible; yet they occur. Border clashes between the Soviet Union and China may not have reached a full-blown state of war, but they too undercut the Leninist principle of international socialist relations.

Is there anything left to the Marxist-Leninist idea of transnational alignments in war? The Brezhnev doctrine, of course, was based on it, but it is officially dead. To revive it in its old form would be impossible. Yet given Soviet ties to Cuba, Vietnam, and South Yemen, it may be premature to assume that no new transnational alignment is possible, were a sharp political reaction to occur in Moscow. Admittedly, such a reaction becomes less probable as the Soviet Union slides into growing domestic turmoil in 1991.

In the Nigerian civil war, Moscow refused to assist the rebels because they intended to separate their region Biafra from Nigeria as an independent state. Given its public backing of all state borders in Africa, Moscow abandoned the insurgents and supported the bourgeois concept of the state.

Gorbachev's emphasis on the United Nations in maintaining the present international order also signals a backing off from the traditional Soviet revolutionary view of the nation state. Soviet cooperation in the Security Council in condemning Iraq's invasion of Kuwait suggests that we are witnessing more than a tactical shift in policy. It indicates the degree to which the original concept of international class struggle has had to be adapted to growing popularity of the sovereign state which has grown out of the European tradition of international law.

A similar failure in the Soviet approach is marked by the absence of worker-led revolutions. Of the three patterns of Soviet success in supporting Marxist-Leninist transformations in other states, none have resulted from working-class movements. These transformations have occurred as a result of peasants who have been mobilized as soldiers— initially as guerrilla soldiers and later as soldiers in regular military formations. In the penetration of national bourgeois regimes, the control of the military has proven critical. Only where the military was adequately penetrated by Soviet-trained cadres did success occur. In Chile, the military defeated the attempt at a coup by a Marxist-Leninist penetration of the civil regime.

Finally, however, one aspect of official Soviet theory does remain operative. The use of transnational fronts and organizations and the mobilization of sympathetic forces by propaganda and agitation has subsided but not wholly disappeared. On the contrary, even the Gorbachev policy seems reluctant to abandon wholly these techniques for participating in internal wars, for transforming them from essentially

civil wars into wars involving transnational coalitions of groups, organizations, media organs, and direct official Soviet institutions such as
military advisors, intelligence links, and commercial organizations.

How has the United States fared in the competition? In actual cases,
it won in Greece, the Philippines in the 1950s, in Korea, in most of Latin
America, in much of the Middle East, in most of Africa (although its
involvement there has been small by comparison with the Soviet and
Chinese presence), in Thailand, in Indonesia, and in a number of other
cases. It did not really contest Soviet actions in Angola, in Ethiopia, or
in South Yemen, and it did so only marginally in Cambodia and Laos.
The single contested loss has been in Vietnam. Nicaragua appeared to
be in that category, but the Sandinistas have lost their formal incumbency. Cuba should also be included, although the contest was never
very seriously pursued after the abortive Bay of Pigs affair.

The American record, when viewed as a whole, is remarkably good.
It looks even better when its ideological principles are used as a measure of success. Its efforts at persuading the European colonial powers
to divest themselves of colonies have been far more successful than
Soviet support to anti-imperialist national movements. Even where
such movements have not developed friendly ties with the U.S.—for
example, in states like Iraq, Syria, and Iran more recently—they have
resisted Soviet infringement upon their own sovereignty. While the
Soviet Union has talked a great deal about rolling back colonialism, the
United States has done a great deal to roll it back.

The American concept of the sovereign state has certainly spread as
the internationally accepted norm. Here the United States has clearly
scored a major victory, one that has overturned Soviet hegemony in
Eastern Europe and now threatens Moscow's domination of many non-
Russian peoples within the Soviet Union.

Although the United States has unswervingly supported the idea of
national autonomy and sovereignty, it has also supported the principle
of transnational economic institutions, both for finance capital and for
production. And it has been the leading supporter of international free
trade and the free flow of information across international boundaries.
The American counterpart to the Soviet front organizations and other
transnational political linkages is nongovernmental commercial institutions. Government institutions also play a large role—military and
economic assistance, intelligence cooperation, the renting of military
bases, and security alliances. In the overall scheme of the competition,

however, the private sector transnational linkages bulk much larger for the United States than is normally appreciated.

As a consequence of the commercial linkages, states seeking economic development have increasingly turned to the United States and its allies in Europe and East Asia. In the postcolonial struggle phase of Third World development, when growth seems as important as independence, the American model simply offers more than the Soviet model. It cannot ensure growth, but its record is better, and the means for economic development are to be found in the West, not in the Soviet Union.

Viewed from the historical perspective of four decades of competition, the American approach clearly holds a large edge. While sponsoring national sovereignty with great success, it has also helped to create fledgling democracies in some cases. In a lesser number of cases it has sponsored successful economic development. In three of the five development goals—autonomy, democracy, and growth—many Third World states owe a debt to the American approach to the East-West competition.

Case Assessments: Test of Concepts

With our theoretical framework for understanding U.S.–Soviet competition in the Third World, we ought to be able to analyze cases and discover the degree to which it squares with reality as well as to gain some insights about the likely future dynamics of particular internal wars. The choice of cases needs to include ones where the nature and level of U.S. involvement varies. The contrasts in local government performance should tend to prove or disprove our hypotheses about functional and dysfunctional U.S. policies. "Tend to prove" is important to underscore, because particular cases can differ so dramatically that a conclusive proof or refutation would require that we examine every case in the world, and, even in that event, we could not be sure that some future exceptional case would not arise. We should, however, be able to get a gross sense of the efficacy of our policies by looking at a few cases.

In the El Salvador case, we are deeply involved, and we have nearly a decade of experience with our policies there. In Guatemala, the internal war shares many commonalities with the war in El Salvador, but the U.S. involvement is significantly different. Very little direct U.S.

support has gone to Guatemala over the past decade. In the Philippine case, U.S. military involvement is still marginal, but the trend is toward greater commitments of aid. The nature of the war has similarities with wars in Central America, but there are basic differences in the insurgent tactics and strategy. In all cases, Soviet involvement is indirect and difficult to assess in all its details but nonetheless illustrative of emerging variations of Moscow's lower profile approach to some of the Third World competitions. It depends on transnational groups, surrogates, and innovative ways of finding and providing resources. At the same time, the organizational patterns of the insurgent political structures have a distinctive Marxist-Leninist character. In sum, these cases provide sufficient comparative basis for demonstrating that our general propositions about U.S.–Soviet competition on the one hand and political development on the other in the Third World have enough grounding in reality to be taken seriously.

As a comparative framework for each, a common analytical approach is essential. It will have four components. First, because the United States favors political development toward democracy, there must be an assessment of the country's prospects for achieving democracy. Are the preconditions there? Is the incompatibility between democracy and stability irreconcilable? By following the four preconditions for democracy—economic, social, external, and cultural—as an outline and by examining the data for the particular case, we ought to be able to obtain reasonable answers to the democracy question.

The second component is an examination of the adversary to the regime, the insurgency. It should include a look at the political ideology and goals of the insurgency, the insurgency strategy, and the resource base—internal and external—of the insurgents.

The third component is an examination of the incumbent regime's response to political development, its military capabilities and strategy, and its resource base—internal and external.

The fourth component is an assessment of whose position is stronger —who is winning based on the analysis developed in the first three components. It should also provide the occasion to draw conclusions about the relevance of our propositions for prompting different U.S. policies toward the embattled state.

The El Salvadoran Case

Although formally a democracy today, El Salvador has no history of democratic practice to speak of. Like most of the Central American states, its evolution after independence from colonial rule has been a stubborn resistance to new forces attempting to enter politics. Political and economic power have been monopolized by a small elite, a social and kinship oligarchy—the so-called fourteen families.[4] It has surrendered some of its power only under duress, and it has been remarkably successful in restricting political participation until the past couple of decades. Its size has expanded, numbering closer to forty extended families, and it has had to share power with the military since the earlier part of this century. Since World War II, new social forces have been demanding a participatory role, contributing to the present crisis.

The outlines and structure of Salvadoran politics can easily be traced back to the country's colonial origins. The Spanish failed to find gold there and reluctantly turned to agriculture, exploiting the cacao plantations already developed and operated by the Indians. Importing black slaves to increase the work force, the colonialists also imported new diseases which decimated the Indian population. Moreover, cacao production fell on hard times by the early 1600s, and indigo was taken as a replacement export crop. During the seventeenth century, racial mixing made an ever larger portion of the population mestizo, and the increasingly small number of whites remained the landowners. By the early nineteenth century, racial distinctions had virtually disappeared except among a few whites in the landowning elites. Coffee was entering the agricultural economy where it would remain the key crop for over a century. Spanish rule ended, leaving the former colonials to establish and defend their own sovereignty.[5]

Brutality in Salvadoran politics has very old roots. The Indian labor force was essentially allowed to perish from economic privation and disease in the early colonial decades. The replacement mestizos were not treated any better, and, when their discontent boiled into a major rebellion in 1832, the regime repressed it ruthlessly, putting the severed head of its leader, Aquino, on public display in San Salvador as a warning against future resort to resistance. The security police were the mainstay of repression in the nineteenth century, while the military was primarily concerned with external security—motivated by a fear of invasion from Guatemala or elsewhere.[6] In the late nineteenth and early twentieth century, the Rural Police became the National Police, and the National Guard, overlapping the police and the army, was created on the Spanish model.

Another large peasant rebellion occurred in 1932, one that gave El Salvadoran politics a new shape lasting even today. The repression was enormous, taking about thirty thousand lives. To put it down, the oligarchy had to depend not only on the police but critically on the army. The army had previously enjoyed neither high social nor economic status. Recruited primarily from the lower middle class, it stood socially far below the landowning oligarchs. Before 1932, it had not shared significantly in the political rule of the country. The uprising thrust it into a central political role. By putting down the rebellion and rescuing the oligarchy, the army could claim more than a little of the political power. Heretofore the oligarchy alone had dominated the country. Hereafter, it would share power. As Thomas P. Anderson puts it, "A curious bargain was struck between the military and the oligarchy, giving one the reins of power, the other economic control."[7]

Another factor in the 1932 uprising helped to bring a new shape to El Salvadoran politics. Among its key leaders was Augustin Farabundo Martí, the man who would follow the same role as Aquino played in 1832, providing charismatic leadership and losing his life to government executioners. Martí, however, brought an important difference. He was university educated and well acquainted with the ideas of socialism, especially its Marxist-Leninist variant. Martí was a founding member of the Social Party (PSC) in El Salvador in 1925.[8] The opposition in El Salvador henceforth would include Marxist-Leninists, giving it a radical thrust that would grow stronger over time.

For the next half century, El Salvador lived under a praetorian system struggling to prevent the social and political mobilization that was inexorably occurring. Montgomery has aptly described it as a series of political cycles following a standard pattern. Each new regime resorts to greater repression, causing a reaction from two quarters, the amorphous public at large and a social reform–minded faction of military officers. The progressive officers lead a coup and promulgate reforms but soon give way to a reemergence within the army of the most conservative faction and a highly repressive regime.[9]

The immediate postwar period witnessed one of these cycles during which fairly serious reforms were introduced. While they generated some hope, they did not last. In fact, with the rise of a small urban and industrial sector and with the appearance of a middle class of some significance, politics were not moderated but became more sharply polarized. The Catholic church itself was drawn more into the political struggle, moving away from its traditionally conservative position. Vatican II (1962–65) and the Medellín Bishops Conference (1968) provided the theological guidance that permitted the clear turn to the left in the Latin American church. Its clergy decided that they could not remain neutral politically and that they could not square Christian theology with support for the practices of the military dictatorships. Lacking a serious moderate alternative, many in the clergy began to throw their support to the radical left under the banner of "liberation theology," an amalgam of Marxism and Christianity. Events in El Salvador in 1970 marked the practical turn, and by that time "liberation theology" was finding support among the El Salvadoran clergy, permitting cooperation with the Marxist-Leninist cadres of the most radical political groups. The regime's reaction was assassination of priests, eventually to include the popular Archbishop Romero.

In the late 1970s and early 1980s, U.S. policy changed toward El Salvador, bringing unprecedented involvement, both with policy advice and with resources. Responding to the Sandinista strategy of pushing revolution throughout the region and committed to promoting democracy in Central America, the United States launched a two-pronged strategy—one in the form of military assistance to cope with the insurgency and the other aimed at inducing elected government based on broad popular participation.

In some regards U.S. policy has achieved much. The insurgency might well have toppled the regime without U.S. military and economic support. On the political front, El Salvador has held three reasonably honest elections—one for a constituent assembly in 1982, one for the presidency in 1984, and one for a second presidential election in 1989.[10] This unprecedented try at democracy could hardly have occurred without pressure from the United States. It is superficially impressive that Duarte's Christian Democratic party held power in all three branches of government for a term and that now an opposition party—Cristiani, backed by the Republican National Alliance (ARENA) with 54 percent of the vote—has been elected and has taken office peacefully.

A closer examination of the conditions that make the institutionalization of a democracy probable, however, takes away much of the basis for optimism. The sharp polarization, economically and politically, and the weak development of political parties, labor, and professional groups do not suggest smooth sailing for the inchoate democratic system. Neither the army nor the oligarchy has surrendered its firm grip on the system. Let us review the economic, social, external, and cultural conditions as they have come to exist—conditions that political development theory suggests are critical for democracy to take firm root in a political system.

Economic

As we know from the political development literature, democracy correlates positively with economic growth. Willingness to compromise politically and the capacity to meet rising demands from newly mobilized social strata of a late-developing country are going to be more abundant if the total economic product is expanding steadily. Since World War II, the oligarchy and the military in El Salvador have tried to expand the country's wealth by industrial development and technocratic approaches to some parts of the agrarian sector. The results have been mixed but not all that bad until the 1980s. In the past decade, most economic trends have been negative.[11]

As a general indication, the per capita income has declined 28 percent over the 1978–88 decade. It fell from $1266 in 1978 to $940 in 1988. This drop is reflected in the declining growth rate, which fell from 7.3 percent in 1978 to 0.5 percent in 1988, a 93 percent reduction to virtually no growth. Taking a somewhat longer look backwards, World Bank figures show an annual growth rate of GNP per capita between 1965 and 1988 to be a negative 0.5 percent.

Some of this poor performance might be attributable to the drop in international commodity prices since El Salvador is dependent to a significant degree on commodity exports, but some of the other sectoral trends are also poor. Industrial growth was 5.3 percent in 1965–80; from 1980 to 1988 it was 0.4 percent, slightly better than the 1.4 percent negative growth for agriculture in this period. These declines are reflected in a parallel drop in consumption—4.1 percent annually in 1965–80, a negative 0.1 percent in 1980–88.

Although government consumption dropped from 7 percent in 1965–80 to 3.3 percent during 1980–88, private consumption also fell from 4.1 percent to negative 0.1 percent during the same periods, respectively. These two trends have contributed to a serious decline in overall gross domestic investment, which fell from 6.6 percent in 1965–80 to 0.1 percent in the 1980–88 period. Consequently the national economy has become increasingly dependent on external capital. Foreign debt, for example, rose from $176 million in 1970 to $1.8 billion in 1988, which amounts to an annual debt service cost of 2.9 percent of GNP. These simultaneous trends of declining national investment and increasing foreign debt have significantly impeded national economic growth.

Government consumption, of course, has had to increase to meet military expenditures, accounting for almost 26 percent of the government budget in 1988. This has forced cutbacks in education, health, and housing. More and more, the regime has had to turn to foreign economic assistance, which has grown by 370 percent in 1980–88, now constituting about $83 per capita, or 7.7 percent of the GNP.

To say that the economic outlook is bleak is an understatement. Most disturbing is the drop from the encouraging performance in the 1960s and 1970s. The sense of "relative deprivation" is bound to be strong, not a good omen for democracy.[12] Overall, one is forced to conclude that the economic preconditions for democracy are inadequate; moreover, they are getting worse.

Social

El Salvador's work force of two million people is only 40 percent agricultural.[13] Sixty percent is in the urban and government sectors. It breaks down to 16 percent in manufacturing, 16 percent in commercial activities, 13 percent in the government, 9 percent in finance, and 3 percent in transportation. While El Salvador's population remains a society with a large agrarian sector, it has already experienced a large move toward the urban areas. This is a potentially encouraging development, but it carries a disturbing dynamic. The population growth has outstripped the economy, and today 55 percent of the population is under 19 years of age. When this is coupled with the poor economic outlook, the prospects for social discontent and disorder come sharply into focus. To create jobs for the youth entering the work force each year would be a challenge for any economy, but for El Salvador it is clearly beyond its means.

Also related to this surge in population pressure is a dramatic increase in the number of landless peasants. Between 1961 and 1975, they grew from 11 to 40 percent of the rural population.[14] Furthermore, education is inadequate to make the younger generations productive in the work force, literacy being only 35 percent. Not surprisingly, in 1987 the underemployment rate was estimated at 45 percent (with 10 percent unemployment). Thus the society faces a growing population of young people who have virtually no prospect of making a living and raising a family.

The social institutions to accommodate this rapid mobilization of population are relatively new and wholly inadequate to the task. The oldest are the labor unions, which can be traced to the second and third decades of this century, but until the 1980s they remained very weak and were led by radical political elements. The prospects for their becoming significant parts of the social and political infrastructure were not good until the 1980s, when American influence in favor of democracy began to be felt strongly in El Salvador. Even now, the unions are very much controlled by proinsurgent political cadres, inclining them not to centrist and reformist action so much as to mobilization of political sentiment and action against the regime.

The Catholic church has been the most successful organizer of the discontented population. The Salvadoran Christian Peasants Federation is an example. Initially established by the Church, it soon became a defender of peasant rights and later joined with the Popular Revolutionary Bloc in the mid-1970s.[15] The Church also sponsored so-called Christian Based Communities (CEB), study groups that have tended to become political in their actions.[16]

Political parties are relatively new in El Salvador, dating from the 1950s, except for the PCS, the Communist party, which goes back to the 1920s. The National Conciliation Party (PCN) has been the party of the military and the oligarchy. ARENA, the National Republican Alliance, emerged in 1981 and now houses most of the extreme right wing of the political spectrum. In the center are the Christian Democrats, although right of center is probably more accurate. Democratic Action (AD) is a small party of the center formed by the Federation of Lawyers. In addition to the PCS on the extreme left, there is also the National Revolutionary Movement (MNR); the National Democratic Union (UDN), which is a legal front for the Communists; and a splinter Christian Democratic group (MPSC), which refused to participate with the military government in 1980.[17]

The parties are weakly organized, highly personalistic, and without an institutional base countrywide. They rise and fall depending on the personalities and strengths of their leaders. This is less true, of course, for the parties of the extreme left, particularly the PCS. On the whole, however, political parties across the spectrum are not institutions offering the majority of the frustrated electorate a means of sustained and effective participation in the political system. They are mere groupings of elites for electoral purposes. There has been hope that the Christian Democrats would provide a vehicle for the moderate elements in the growing urban sector of the society to balance the military and landed families, but the 1989 elections revealed that this party has a long way to go before achieving that kind of power base. ARENA was able to present a less bloody face by creating some distance between its candidate, Cristiani, and Orden's death squads and to win the election.[18]

Overall, then, we see in El Salvador rapid social mobilization exacerbated by demographic pressures, the greatest among the Central American states, and a woeful lack of institutions to overcome, manage, and regulate the growing privations and frustrations. These pressures would be a challenge for a highly developed democratic system. For El Salvador, they look insurmountable unless dramatic relief from massive emigration removes much of the pressure.

External

The Spanish, of course, have been the biggest and most significant external influence on El Salvador. In the century and a half of its postcolonial existence, the political, social, and economic patterns have remained remarkably unchanged, adapting to changing international commodity markets and to internal political challenges. The two major changes have come in the twentieth century.

First, the fourteen families and their extended circles have had to share power with the military. Second, Marxism has come from abroad to provide a new or additional rationale for revolution. The pace of these two developments has picked up in the post–World War II period. From the 1920s until the late 1970s, Moscow was the primary source of foreign revolutionary influence, but since that time Cuba has stepped into the major position. The military has taken its foreign influence more and more from the United States, especially since World War II. Before that time, it was profascist, actually anti-U.S., but the events of

World War II reversed the view in El Salvador that an anti-U.S. attitude in the military could be maintained.

Foreign business cannot be said to have had the dominant role in El Salvador that it did in the economies of some of the other Central American republics. In the 1930s, anti-industrialization laws were passed, and, when they were repealed after World War II, government technocrats followed a policy of protectionism for domestic industry—so-called import substitution favoring domestic firms. The result was not a significant expansion of jobs and productivity in industry but an increase in the jobs for bureaucrats.[19]

The major external influence in El Salvador in modern times has been very recent. Turning to the United States for assistance against the insurgency in the 1980s, the regime had to accept U.S. terms in many respects. That included a willingness to introduce elected government, reform in the military, and a reduction of human rights violations. On the surface, U.S. influence has made a dramatic difference. Today a functioning electoral system has provided for a peaceful transition from one party in power, the Christian Democrats, to another, ARENA. U.S. military assistance has caused reform of the general staff and an assertion of its control over regional units.

In spite of these two kinds of changes, political and military, the old power structure remains essentially undisturbed. Land reform has not gone forward despite American urging, or it has been subverted, not effectively achieving a transfer of ownership; and the oligarchy retains its dominant economic position. The military has kept regional or local command systems, as well as a central command, creating in effect two chains of command with some serious dysfunctional consequences.

Since the Spanish conquest the Catholic church has been a deeply entrenched institution, but since World War II it has brought a lot of external influence for social and economic reform. Unfortunately, the regime has resisted it, driving the church more and more to the side of the insurgents.

In sum, the original Spanish influence was downright hostile to democratic political development, and it has retained its hegemony until very recently. The two main external sources of influence today are Cuban and declining indirect Soviet support for revolution and U.S. support for democracy. The old elites are fighting a two-front campaign against both sources.

Cultural

A relatively small number of Spanish whites imported Catholicism and imposed it on a large Indian population. Today the population is 89 percent mestizo, or mixed Spanish and Indian, 10 percent Indian, and only 1 percent white. While there are a few Protestants, the country is 97 percent Catholic.

Neither the Indian culture nor the Catholic culture is positively disposed to market economics. Following Vatican II and the Medellín Conference of Latin American Bishops in the late 1960s, the Church in El Salvador took a negative stance toward both Marxism and capitalism. Its more active social programs for helping the poverty-stricken masses were certainly needed, but at best they were neutral on the overall problem of political and economic development.

It would probably be wrong to view the Church as an obstacle to economic development, but its tradition in Latin America has certainly not been to champion free enterprise. On the contrary, its flirtation with liberation theology tends to work against the general directions of democratic political evolution and capital investment in economic development. And the Church can encourage sympathy for the insurgency where the insurgents know how to appeal to it skillfully. Given the awful living conditions for much of the population, Protestant religious activities and influence are probably no more conducive to economic enterprise. Too many adverse social factors draw the religious leadership toward other priorities.

In one critically important regard, the Catholic church's recent emphasis on social issues changes its traditional role in politics. Previously it tended to support conservative and authoritarian regimes. The shift of its support away from the political right, therefore, is a change of great potential significance—not just in El Salvador but throughout the region.

As Thomas Anderson has pointed out, the cultural patterns of El Salvador do not favor compromise.[20] The consequence for democratic development has been highly negative. On the other hand, this cultural pattern tends to favor the noncompromising character of Marxism-Leninism. The same is true for the Catholic cultural tradition, the oligarchy, and the army. The influence of the university has not been to mitigate this cultural pattern but rather to reinforce it. Across the board, then, the cultural influences encourage an unyielding, absolutist approach to politics, a struggle for all or nothing—an approach most inhospitable for democracy.

To sum up, only one factor of the four—external—is positive in its effect on the prospects for democracy. U.S. policy alone pushes the regime forward on the democratic path while every other factor seems to make its success temporary at best and dangerously likely to fail in the foreseeable future. In the pursuit of the goals of development, how is the regime doing? Its economic score is miserable; social equity is disastrous; autonomy is limited by U.S. influence; stability is being achieved at great pain and loss of life; and democracy is a roaring success in the formal sense.

The El Salvador case is not only fragile: it is artificial, afflicted with the most severe conflict of development goals, and able to do very little to make progress on the fundamental issue of growth but pursuing all of the goals in a democratic political forum highly dependent on foreign economic assistance. The trends do not suggest a reversal in the near future of any of the negative developments, and they indicate a growing intensity of some of the most basic problems.

The Insurgency

The insurgency in El Salvador today is a mix of disparate groups and factions merged under an umbrella organization for military operations (FMLN) and another organization for political action, the Democratic Revolutionary Front (FDR). (See chart 1.) This structure was built in the 1970s for the most part but still fragmented until 1980 when the superstructure was imposed on the various groups and factions. The leadership for bringing it together and coordinating its activities did not come from within El Salvador. It was imposed from without.[21] The organizational fragmentation, of course, reflected competing ideological and tactical views on how to conduct the conflict with the government of El Salvador. The merger, therefore, also involved imposing some common ground for ideology and strategy.

The resulting ideology and organization carries the marks of both Soviet and Cuban influence. From the time Castro took power in Cuba through the 1970s, rather sharp differences between Moscow and Havana prevailed on how to advance revolution in the rest of Latin America. While the Cuban approach, most articulately proclaimed by

Chart 1   Insurgent organizations in El Salvador.

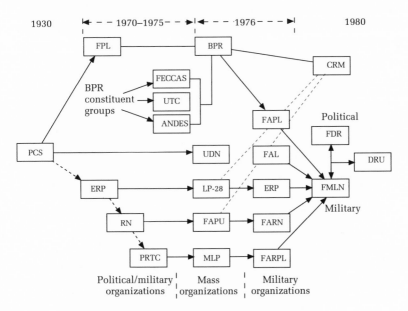

Political/military	Mass	Military
organizations	organizations	organizations

PCS	Salvadoran Communist Party
FPL	Popular Liberation Forces
ERP	People's Revolutionary Army
FECCAS	Christian Federation of Salvadoran Campesinos
UTC	Union of Rural Workers
ANDES	National Association of Salvadoran Educators
RN	National Resistance
PRTC	Central American Workers' Revolutionary Party
BPR	Popular Revolutionary Bloc
UDN	National Democratic Union
LP-28	Popular Leagues—28th of February
FAPU	United People's Action Front
MLP	Popular Liberation Movement
FAPL	Popular Armed Forces of Liberation
FAL	Armed Forces of Liberation
FARPL	Popular Revolutionary Armed Forces of Liberation
FARN	Armed Forces of National Resistance Committee of the masses
CRM	Revolutionary Coordinating
FMLN	Farabundo Marti National Liberation Front
FDR	Democratic Revolutionary Front
DRU	Unified Revolutionary Directorate

Source: "Strategic Country Assessment: El Salvador",
4 Feb 1988, SWORDS

Che Guevara, involved building peasant insurgent armies which would attack governments directly and seek to win a civil war, the Soviet approach placed the emphasis on the old Moscow-sponsored communist parties and added a new element, the development of "progressive" military elites in Latin American armies. Military coups in Panama, Ecuador, Bolivia, and Peru in the late 1960s and early 1970s brought to power military social reformers who nationalized foreign industrial holdings and welcomed Soviet diplomatic initiatives. In light of Che Guevara's abject failure in Bolivia and the absence of any promising insurgency movement, Moscow resisted the Cuban strategy, preferring the one that not only looked more promising but also invoked techniques with which Soviet operatives were more at home, more experienced.

Just as the Soviet Union had been surprised by Castro's victory in 1959 (in fact, it was more attributable to U.S. support than any other foreign influence), the Sandinista victory in Nicaragua was also a surprise (in fact, it was also primarily dependent upon a number of U.S. actions for its success). The Soviet Central Committee's International Department changed its tune rather quickly at this point and began to speak of great revolutionary opportunities in Central America. The Nicaraguan case, in the Cuban view, could be duplicated in several other Central American states if cadres and organizational support were forthcoming. The Soviet leadership came to share the Cuban optimism, and thus a coordinated effort was begun.

Concerning ideology, the Central American revolutionaries seem to have been fairly orthodox Marxist-Leninists of the Soviet type, although many of them were and still are not steeped in the intricacies of the ideology. The institutional structure of the Sandinista regime, however, follows very closely the pattern Moscow exported to Eastern Europe and Cuba—that is, one based on a single ideological political line, a disciplined Leninist-type party, a KGB-type police system, mass organizations, censorship, and a dominant role for state ownership of the means of production. The Sandinista political struggle with social and political opposition—particularly the Catholic church, the peasantry, and residual opposition political parties—is remarkably like the struggles in Eastern Europe from 1945 to 1953. The model of political institutionalization is in no way mysterious. It is a marginally adapted direct transfer of the Soviet model, and it has been heavily dependent on Cuban cadres for its initial construction. There simply have not been sufficient numbers of Nicaraguans adequately trained in the Soviet forms of governing to fill all the cadre roles.

The El Salvadoran insurgent factions were convinced by the success of the Sandinistas that they could achieve the same in a short time if they launched a major offensive. The Cubans and the Soviets, however, realized that they were not up to the task without major organizational consolidation and repression of factional quarrels among the several guerrilla groups. In the period of 1979–80, the Cubans managed to impose an organizational consolidation under the FMLN.

The complexity of this transition can best be understood by a look at the graphic display in chart 1. By the late 1970s, each of the five El Salvadoran guerrilla groups had a military structure and public political action front. The Cubans forced them to unite under the FMLN for control of the military arm and under the FDR for the political arm. (A unifying directorate, the Unified Revolutionary Directorate [DRU], sits on top of the entire structure.) The full story of this organizational fusion is difficult to piece together from unclassified sources, but it seems that the Cubans threatened to withhold resources to force the unification. The headquarters was located in Managua where Nicaraguan and Cuban strong-arm tactics could be easily available. That such tactics were required is suggested by the change in leading personnel in some of the El Salvadoran member groups.

The FMLN's strategy has taken much from the Cubans and the Sandinistas. Very soon after the new organizational structure was in place in 1981, the DRU announced its "final offensive," apparently modeled on the Sandinista final offensive in Nicaragua. It failed, of course, and the FMLN had to settle down for a much longer struggle.

The Nicaraguan insurgency was, in Cuban eyes, a vindication of some aspects of Guevara's "foco" type of revolution, an armed peasantry with some urban political front support, carrying the military fight directly against the government.[22] It was a shortcut as compared to the Maoist approach, which anticipates a long struggle during which the guerrillas not only base themselves in the rural areas but engage in massive propaganda, education, and organization of the peasantry— essentially becoming a government in the countryside which displaces the incumbent regime. The FMLN did not abandon the foco approach even after its failure at a "final offensive" in 1981. As time has passed, it has taken on more complexity and sophistication, but essentially it retains its emphasis on trying to defeat the government forces in a protracted struggle while hurting the economy through attacks on transportation, power, and other infrastructure critical to El Salvador's economic performance.

In the last few years, the FMLN has engaged in a number of nonfoco tactics, particularly in its dialogue with the government, initiated by President Duarte. It has also tried international appeals with peripatetic leaders abandoning their guerrilla apparel for suits and ties when they arrive in foreign capitals to meet the press and important people. By and large, however, it has stuck to its military strategy, confronting the army, suffering serious losses and setbacks, retreating into the mountain bases, restoring its supplies, recruiting new guerrilla soldiers, and once again stepping up its two-prong campaign—one against the army, the other against the economy. As Ernest Evans points out, a major modification of the foco strategy has been the insurgency's effort not to become isolated from sources of support. In practice this has meant working harder with mass organizations for popular support, especially in urban areas, and also maintaining an international support network.[23]

The FMLN's *resources* come from a variety of places. The public record does not provide an exhaustive record of the FMLN sources of materiel support, but the general patterns are clear. The key external source is the Soviet-Cuban connection which, until the Sandinistas lost the election, was managed primarily in Nicaragua. It involves not only direct supplies of weapons and materiel but also command and control. The DRU was located in Managua. Communications and other sophisticated technical support passed through Managua, which had become the nerve center for the insurgents not only in El Salvador but also in Guatemala and Honduras. Supplies traveled to Nicaragua for transit to El Salvador through indirect and complex routing. They came from North Korea, Vietnam, Eastern Europe, and a number of other sources—sometimes by way of Cuba, sometimes through Panama, sometimes directly by ship from the Soviet Union.

One might have anticipated that Nicaragua's key role in supporting insurgencies in Central America would have ceased when the Sandinistas had to turn over the presidency to Violeta Chamorro. This does not seem to have happened. The Sandinistas, of course, have retained control over the Nicaraguan military; and—while they may not be able to provide the same kind of haven as before for command and control functions of the insurgents in El Salvador, Guatemala, and Honduras—

supplies are getting through, especially to the FMLN in El Salvador. The Sandinista command of the Nicaraguan military probably allows it to continue a modicum of support beyond public scrutiny, perhaps even beyond the eyes of Chamorro's supporters in the government.

Much external support, however, originates in the West. Networks of international front organizations within the Western states raise funds and make purchases which are moved through one of several routes to the FMLN. The pattern became highly developed during U.S. involvement in Vietnam, and it received a sharp central focus in the Stockholm Conference campaign. In the Central American strategy, this kind of single focus has been avoided, and in its place a number of seemingly disconnected fronts and networks have emerged. The World Peace Council and World Federation of Trade Unions, veterans of the Vietnam struggle, are deeply involved. Organization front tactics have been pursued relentlessly in Western Europe and the United States where numerous groups have unknowingly contributed either direct financial aid or public relations support, often both. The extent to which Catholic and Protestant religious groups have been exploited successfully is unclear, but liberation theology has certainly drawn some clergymen into direct involvement in support of the insurgencies throughout Central America. The main point here, however, is to call attention to this transnational infrastructure that Moscow and Cuba have put together in support of the FMLN and other groups in the region. The byzantine labyrinth of cross-ties, networks, agents, routes, and communications can only be exposed and understood by highly competent intelligence services, and even then the picture is imperfect. Journalists sometimes do remarkably well at uncovering some of the linkages. Their evidence and the materials that Western governments have declassified, however, provide enough to let us infer confidently that these transnational resource mobilization efforts are extensive and of critical importance for the FMLN. And, of course, propaganda aimed at Western public opinion is as central to it as the material contributions.

Internal sources of material support are also important. The foco strategy, however, does not provide as extensive access to local support as does the Maoist strategy. Methodical taxation of the peasantry, organized extraction of weapons and ammunition from the governments, robbery of banks and businesses, extortion of bribes for passage and protection—these techniques of resource extraction do not seem to be as well developed in El Salvador as they are in other cases, particularly the Philippines. That is not to say that they are not important. Large numbers of weapons have passed from the El Salvadorans to the guerrillas. Food, labor, and medical supplies constitute some of the more important FMLN dependencies. Nonetheless, the FMLN has not attempted to govern locally in the comprehensive fashion characteristic of New People's Army (NPA) in the Philippines or the Viet Cong in Vietnam.

Overall, the insurgency is very much controlled and directed by Cuban and Soviet authorities. They have imposed their own organizational structure on it, and they have made it heavily dependent on foreign resources. The Cubans have had the upper hand in dictating the strategy, and they appear committed to vindicate once again their foco approach to taking power. The FMLN would become a much more serious threat to the El Salvadoran government if it shifted to the Maoist strategy, but a couple of factors work against such a change. First, the subjective preferences of the Cubans probably impede it. Second, it would shift the power within the insurgency away from the military wing to leaders in the political action wing. The militant guerrilla leaders undoubtedly would oppose such a diminution of their influence.

The insurgency has been a failure in its effort to defeat the El Salvadoran military in head-on clashes. While it has scored some victories, it has also suffered dramatic reversals, and during the mid-1980s it was reduced to about half its earlier size of ten thousand. With time, however, it will refill its depleted ranks from the exploding El Salvadoran population of youths. Its attack on the economy has been more successful. The degree of the success is evident in the downturn in all indices of El Salvadoran economic performance in the 1980s. Only foreign aid has kept the regime economically afloat.

The Government and Its Strategy

Insofar as it concerns the insurgency, the government has pursued a course it believed would yield stability.[24] This is, of course, one of the five general goals of development—growth, social equity, stability, autonomy, and democracy. During the 1960s and 1970s, it would be fair to say that the government was not pursuing all of these goals equally. Democracy and social equity were of less concern than stability and economic growth. Autonomy, of course, was probably a concern, but

the leadership was willing to facilitate foreign trade and business relations. It followed a pattern common to countries in the region, a pattern
that the dependency theorists would call a surrender of autonomy to
foreign capital.[25] While social equity may have suffered in the process,
the El Salvadoran government had hardly surrendered the country to
indirect foreign rule.

Stability was certainly pursued but not in the sense of a program for
institutionalizing the new levels of social mobilization into political
participatory patterns for democracy. Rather a praetorian pattern of repressing the demand for participation is more descriptive. As we noted
earlier, the old ruling families of the original latifundia elites in most
of Central America found it increasingly difficult to maintain order in
the early part of the twentieth century. The military emerged to handle
this task. It provided upward mobility for déclassé elements who found
status in the officer corps. The old elites had to pay them off for the
services they provided. The military in turn developed its own recruitment system through the military academy, which socialized officer
candidates by year classes. The class cliques emerging from the military
academy came to share the power with the old elites while denying parallel institutionalization and participation to other sectors of society—
commercial, white collar urban, urban blue collar, and so forth.

The repression of these other groups naturally produced frustration and eventually organized resistance. From these groups came the
leadership of the present insurgency groups. Some of these leaders had
privileged positions within the system, but, for personal and sometimes idealistic reasons, they abandoned the system to join movements
to overthrow it. The Communist party was able to find cadres from
these disenchanted elements, but its guidance from Moscow did not
encourage a resort to insurgency. Cuban influence prompted this development, particularly following the success of the Sandinistas in Nicaragua. Even so, the insurgent groups were not at first tightly controlled
by Havana; they were very much the creations of individual leaders
with minimal education in Marxism-Leninism. By the late 1970s, only
a few of the insurgent leaders could be said to have a strong grasp of
communist ideology and insurgency tactics.

The government was strongly anticommunist, and, in dealing with
what it considered to be Marxist elements, resorted to brutal repres-
sions and extrajudicial actions, including unleashing death squads.
Before the Sandinistas came to power and the Soviet-Cuban connec-

tion was activated to assist these insurgents, the regime could maintain its praetorian pattern of rule without serious threat to the stability of the system. Thereafter, the balance shifted against the government.

At this point, the United States began to become more heavily involved. Traditional forms of military assistance, though restricted by congressional limitations on engaging U.S. personnel in combat, were provided. The El Salvadoran military was supplied with new equipment and weapons, and training teams tried to teach the military units effective counterinsurgent tactics.[26] A very strong emphasis was placed on getting the general staff and its intelligence arm to operate in a professional manner. Progress was mixed, but by the mid-1980s, El Salvadoran military units were able to conduct search and destroy missions. Efforts to persuade the general staff to engage in small-scale patrolling into insurgent-controlled territories proved less successful. When it was tried, it met with success, but the El Salvadoran military retained its preference for larger unit actions, which were occasionally successful, especially when the guerrillas were willing to stand in major engagements. This sledgehammer approach has remained the main tactic. Sometimes the army attacks guerrilla units, but other times it simply executes large shows of force in regions where the guerrillas are not present or have departed. Supported with U.S. intelligence, the El Salvadoran military has directed much of its effort at interdicting guerrilla supplies. Success has been mixed at best.

A major handicap for the counterinsurgency campaign is found in the system of provincial military leader autonomy. Each regional military chieftain exercises considerable latitude in how he conducts military operations. At the same time, he bears a major responsibility for regional civil administration—that is, governing the country at the local level. Guerrilla units learn that retreating after an action to another region will generally free them from pursuit. Countrywide coordination of the military campaign is weak in this regard, failing to ensure that forces in all regions work together. Furthermore, the military commander is also occupied with public administration, including ensuring his own wealth and prosperity.

The U.S. advisory effort has pressed the El Salvadorans to create civic action programs to parallel its military operations, and in some cases local commanders have acted on the advice. The programs, however, have not delivered much in the way of improved living conditions for the peasantry, and security is provided only sporadically and temporarily. The U.S. programs have been traditional U.S. AID assistance, including pressure for land reform. The regime, however, has resisted carrying through on land reform. Moreover, the program aims to create cooperative peasant ownership of land, not individual private holdings. Thus, even if it were wholly implemented it would not produce a significant number of "free farmers," the kind who might be stalwart supporters of democratic government.

The government's tax policy has ostensibly been changed to achieve greater social equity through public spending. Taxes have been increased, but they have been spent for social programs that benefit primarily the urban areas, leaving the peasant with little to show for his greater tax burden, to the extent that taxes are actually collected.

The tax program also aims to stimulate economic development through improving the country's infrastructure. The results have been marginal, in part as a result of the FMLN's strategy of attacking the economy and trying to create an insurmountable economic crisis for the regime. As we have seen from the data on economic performance, the FMLN has been successful in causing an economic downturn, but large amounts of official U.S. aid, an annual average of $390 million since 1981, have allowed the government to hold its own.

Here we should recall Chaudhry's study of foreign capital flows and taxation in Saudi Arabia and Yemen. Receiving foreign aid at an annual rate of eighty-three dollars per capita, or 7.7 percent of the GNP, the Salvadoran government is not very dependent on local taxation for resources, and accordingly its tax-collecting administrative capacity is weak. Furthermore, local military chiefs are in a position to take a healthy share if they like. Chaudhry's findings about the weakening impact of foreign capital on state administrative capacities for extracting resources seem to be borne out in El Salvador as well.

The ill effects of U.S. aid in the Salvadoran case appear to be threefold. First, because it follows the pattern of Saudi experience, coming directly into the government bureaucracy, U.S. aid does not stimulate the private economic sector in the first instance. Second, the bureaucracy's allocation priorities, which favor the urban infrastructure, do not allow foreign aid to stimulate local economic activity which could yield local contributions for public purposes such as schools, medical facilities, farmers' cooperative stores, and the like. Third, U.S. aid relieves the state bureaucracy of pressure to maintain an effective local administration that could collect taxes while also preventing the economic development that might prompt new and effective local institutions.

The regime's autonomy has clearly declined. The United States has become a dominant factor in governing the country. It has forced elections, first for a constituent assembly and then for a president and a legislature. Political parties have become more important in recruiting elites and in dictating policies. President Duarte not only sought to institutionalize the electoral system but also attempted new tactics in dealing with the insurgents, namely directed talks and a halt to the extrajudicial actions against persons believed to sympathize with the insurgents.[27] With the new president and the new coalition of political parties, a change in these tactics can be expected. Efforts to coopt the insurgents are likely to be shunned in favor of a much tougher approach, but negotiations are likely to continue.

Institutions for political participation have enjoyed a greater role under the Duarte regime, but they remain weak, consisting mainly of the political parties and the labor unions. Bringing these institutions into the political system is not easy because the mass organizations of the insurgent factions also compete. Since they do not genuinely accept the legitimacy of the system, their role is disruptive to say the least.

The law enforcement system is extremely weak. Rural policemen are notoriously corrupt, behaving in a way that does not enhance the population's confidence in the regime's ability to provide police protection. The courts, of course, are generally biased toward the preferences of the political elites in the regime. El Salvador has a long way to go in creating an independent judicial system that can provide the kind of justice required for a stable democracy.

Applying Huntington's concept of the ratio of political participation to political institutionalization, it is high, but under U.S. tutelage it has become lower, even in the face of insurgent opposition. It remains too high, however, to insure political stability without a large degree of de facto praetorian behavior by the military and the police.

To sum up, in the 1980s the regime has been forced by the United States to pursue all of the development goals simultaneously. Success in achieving the forms of democracy have been notable, quite remarkable under the circumstances. The economic growth goal, however, has slipped beyond the regime's reach. Foreign capital has shied away—not surprisingly, given the military situation in the country—and U.S. economic assistance is received directly by the government rather than allocated to the populace on a market basis. Its economic effect, therefore, is marginal, and its impact on local institutional development and the state's local administrative capacity is negative. It mainly takes up the gap between government tax revenues and public spending for government and the military. The social equity goal not only lies beyond the regime's means but also beyond its attention. Things have become worse for the less-privileged strata of society, and population pressures, reflected in the large cohorts below the age of nineteen, promise to exacerbate the situation in the years ahead. Political stability, however, has been maintained. The military has managed to meet the insurgent military challenge, and in the mid-1980s it reduced the guerrillas to less than half their 1980 strength. Slowly, however, the guerrillas have replenished their ranks, although they remain below earlier levels. Finally, political autonomy in a formal sense has been maintained, but the regime's dependency on the direct government-to-government transfers from the United States makes the reality quite different.

The regime's strategy seems to be to continue the pattern of military actions of the past few years while trying to achieve economic growth that will become self-sustaining. The prospects of success are not bright for a number of reasons. First, the insurgent strategy works against it. Second, transnational private capital is not greatly available. Third, the earlier economic strategy of diversifying both agriculture and industry to avoid being subject to the vicissitudes of international prices of a single commodity or product has yet to pay off. Social equity holds very low priority. Land reform, the most pressing step the regime needs to take, is not likely to be pursued except to the degree that the United States demands it and pays for it. Moreover, the land reform scheme, cooperative ownership, is not advancing individual ownership on which a small farmer democracy might eventually be built. As Huntington has pointed out, parliaments are notoriously poor at land reform. El Salvador's democratic system is unlikely to prove an exception. The goal of stability can be achieved as it has in the past, through military and police actions, but the prospects of greater political institutionalization seem much more problematic. Meeting the stability goal, therefore, will continue to compete with maintaining the inchoate democracy. Finally, autonomy has declined, but the new president may well reassert his independence vis-à-vis U.S. tutelage at the expense of a number of things—particularly land reform, social justice, and due process in the legal system. With the political change in Nicaragua in the spring of 1990 and the possibility of the FMLN's losing Sandinista support, President Cristiani could become much less beholden to the United States for military assistance. By the spring of 1991, however, the FMLN showed no serious loss of external support.

Net Assessment and Prospects

In 1989 the overall picture was one of a military and political stand-off between the FMLN and the incumbent regime. While the war has been formally an internal one, both sides remained basically dependent on transnational sources of support—material and political. A highly complex conflict has emerged with extensive infrastructures that extend far beyond El Salvador's borders. In reality, it has been and remains an external war as well.

One side has been operating within the outlines of the Soviet approach, albeit with great particularization for the local conditions. The other side has been living to some degree with the American approach, albeit uncomfortably and often reluctantly. The FMLN and its foreign supporter have been only marginally constrained by international law, whereas the government and its foreign sponsor have been seriously constrained by it. The FMLN has depended heavily on the Soviet Union, Cuba, and Nicaragua for supply, command, and control of operations. The Salvadoran government has been a fretful party to "colonialism by ventriloquy." The FMLN's foreign supporters have pursued the struggle not only in Central America but also through the media and front organizations in the United States and Europe. While considerable materiel support has flowed indirectly from the Soviet Union and some of its allies, financial support has been mobilized within Western countries. Direct U.S. support to El Salvador to some extent finds its way into insurgent hands. The greater the American largess, the greater this source of support to the insurgency.

Both sides are in a struggle over the resources within El Salvador. The regime's tax efforts are matched by insurgent levies on the peasantry for food and other material help. The insurgents have made major efforts to deny the regime economic means by directing their military operations at the economy. The regime has engaged in a marginally successful effort to interdict insurgent supplies.

Thus far, the insurgents have not challenged methodically in the Maoist tradition the regime's direct governance over the population. They have yet to build local government structures that push out the regime's administration in a total way. The guerrillas do hold some remote parts of the country, but they have not built institutions that effectively govern rural regions. They have, however, remained competitive in mass organizations at the national level.

The regime has built new political institutions at the national level, but they do not reach out very effectively to the broader populace; and many mass organizations, such as the trade unions, are still treated with suspicion by the parties on the right. Notwithstanding the remarkable shift to a functioning electoral system, the regime is far from building the institutions for political participation it requires for genuine stability. Deep suspicions remain between the legal political parties about the constitutional and legal norms of the new system; each wonders how far to trust its opponent in allowing policy-making and dispute settling to be accomplished by such norms.

How might the U.S. strategy be made more effective? If we apply some of the propositions developed from our review of political development theory and experience, we would raise serious questions about the large U.S. fiscal assistance to El Salvador. It undercuts the regime's autonomy. It has become a rival, or substitute, for domestic resource extraction. And it is not having a positive effect on the economy. Moreover, it is also providing some support indirectly to the insurgents.

The U.S. military assistance effort has allowed the El Salvadoran army to survive and sometimes win against the guerrillas, and the professional expertise of the general staff has certainly increased, although it still leaves a great deal to be desired. On the whole, however, U.S. assistance has not brought a decisive outcome, and the prospects for that are not good. At best it will prevent the insurgents from winning without allowing the government to win. It is a formula for an indefinite war until one or both sides are exhausted.

What about the larger U.S. goal of imposing democracy on El Salvador? The preconditions are wholly inadequate for a stable democracy to develop in the next few years. It would require many years and billions of dollars of aid to sustain the present U.S. tutelage role in cultivating democracy. Moreover, one of the key programs for transforming the economic base to make democratic politics strong, land reform, has been an abject failure in two regards. First, the concept of peasant cooperative ownership has more in common with East European and Soviet collective farming than with private small holder farming and market economics. Second, the old owners have swindled the program and taken back some of the land under false cooperative fronts.

Little or nothing has been achieved to break the statist hold on the urban economy. Subsidies, import substitution policies, and bureaucratic controls remain strong barriers to a genuine market economy. In many regards, the Salvadoran economy looks more like an East European economy with state ownership and collective farms than it does a market economy based on private ownership. The oligarchs, military and civil, are the functional equivalent of the Party, economic, and collective farm bureaucracies in Eastern Europe. And the landless peasants are in a position similar to that of collective farm workers.

In light of these economic realities, it is not surprising that new institutions are not emerging to participate effectively in the political process. Individuals wishing to support such organizations lack the resources to make them effective. What is worse, capital inflows in the form of U.S. fiscal assistance do not reach these individuals to any appreciable degree.

The Sandinista failure to win the elections in the spring of 1990, of course, has changed the balance in the war in El Salvador. Precisely to what degree, it is too early at this writing to tell, but if indeed Nicaragua ceases to serve as a base of support and a conduit for supplies and aid to the FMLN, then the Salvadoran insurgents will be facing a new situation. Their willingness to negotiate with the Cristiani regime undoubtedly is related to the new strategic situation. A number of different developments are possible.

First, the FMLN may well adapt its logistics to new routes and means. That v. ll require time, and in the meanwhile it will not be able to sustain a high level of military activity. If Cuba remains supportive, and if the network of international organizations can sustain significant financial support, then building a new logistics structure is entirely possible.

Second, Nicaragua, even under President Chamorro, seems to continue a modicum of support to the FMLN. As long as the Sandinista cadres control the army and the police, they can continue surreptitious support. While it may be below former levels, it could prove vitally important for the FMLN. Moreover, the domestic political struggle in

Nicaragua is hardly over, and, while it does not seem likely, a Sandinista return to power cannot be wholly excluded.

Third, facing a greatly reduced flow of external support, the FMLN could change its strategy to a Maoist approach. It could retrench, live largely off resources from within El Salvador, and begin a long period of building an administrative and political system, slowly taking villages and organizations away from the government.

Fourth, President Chamorro may eventually succeed in cutting off all Nicaraguan support. Cuba, under Soviet pressure, might well back off from its commitments to the FMLN. The impact could be so great that a readjustment of the logistics system proves beyond the FMLN's ability. While the insurgency might not collapse entirely, it could become only a small band of guerrillas in the remote parts of the country, incapable of being more than an occasional menace to law and order. In other words, the government would effectively have won the internal war.

The change in Nicaragua and these various possible developments highlight two critical points. First, they show the importance of the transnational sources of support for the FMLN. For analytical purposes, suppose the United States had invaded Nicaragua after invading Grenada. Not only would the present situation have arrived much earlier with much less bloodshed in Nicaragua, but the prospects for the FMLN would have been very poor indeed. Many lives could have been saved in El Salvador as well. Such an action by the United States, however, would have required that American policymakers interpret international law differently, taking the preponderance of the emphasis off "peace" and putting more on "justice" by raising the "self-defense" issue and characterizing Nicaragua actions with the FMLN as a casus belli. This is not to recommend such a course of action. It is offered only as an analytical excursion to sharpen our focus on two things: the fecklessness of the U.S.–backed counterinsurgency strategy and an alternative, purely military, strategy that could have defeated the insurgents fairly quickly.

Second, the new realities in Nicaragua raise serious doubts about achieving the U.S. goal of a stable democracy in El Salvador. If the FMLN ceases to be a major problem, what leverage will the United States retain on Salvadoran domestic politics? In other words, the U.S. and Salvadoran regime could win the war without winning the fight for democracy. Whether the United States had invaded Nicaragua in the early 1980s or waited, as it has, for the change through free elections in 1990, U.S. policymakers might still be faced with a military victory against the insurgents on the one hand and political defeat by the regime in El Salvador on the other.

The Guatemalan Case

Like most Central American states, Guatemala's political structure in the nineteenth and early twentieth centuries was based on an oligarchy of latifundia owners.[28] As the primary crop base shifted, the landowning oligarchy changed, but the basic system remained, usually headed by a peronalistic dictator, or "caudillo." As long as the strongman needed little more than police and administrative services from the military, the balance of political power remained stable, except in transition periods from one dictator to the next.[29] As modern military equipment and weapons began to make a modest appearance, which they did during World War II, the military began to develop an institutional coherence that made it able to challenge the old power structure.[30] Jorge Ubico, the last of the traditional caudillos, was overthrown in 1944, marking a major break in the system.

The military was instrumental in Ubico's downfall.[31] Angry over his corruption and eager to promote change but not of one mind about how to do it, the military put a three-man junta in charge. It soon fell into quarrels; one of the three was assassinated, and Arbenz, an officer who thought of himself as a "soldier of the people," was elected president in 1950. Losing his political base in the army, Arbenz turned to civilian groups—particularly social reform elements—for support and continued the revolutionary change. Land reform proceeded, and leftist labor leaders and members of an inchoate urban intelligentsia pushed for broad social change. The army stood apart, withholding support, and when Castillo Armas, backed by the United States, launched an invasion from Honduras, Arbenz was easily overthrown.[32] Armas, reasserting control over the army, began reversing much of the social reform, also returning land to the small group of large landowners.

To use Huntington's term, the system became "praetorian." The military stopped the trend toward broader political participation and the institution building that had begun. For the next three decades, the political system essentially retained this praetorian form. The senior military held the balance of political power, and changes in leadership tended to come with rigged elections and coups by younger officers who found their superiors increasingly corrupted by high office. The army's lead in becoming a more modern institution gave it the dominant position in the political system, one it refused to relinquish even as greater social mobilization occurred with concomitant frustration and demand for greater political participation.

This was Guatemala's political condition in the 1970s and early 1980s. In 1985, however, the regime held elections, and a president and a congress were elected. A mix of factors prompted the shift to an elected government, but at least three stand out. First, the military was ambivalent about its own ability to manage the economy and the insurgency. Second, the insurgency had become much more serious because of the Soviet-Cuban sponsorship through Nicaragua. The new Soviet-Cuban policy was trying to repeat the Sandinista success not only in El Salvador but also in several other countries—namely Honduras, Colombia, and Guatemala. Third, the U.S. policy of providing no aid to right-wing dictatorships meant that Guatemala had been denied this source of support for a number of years. Like El Salvador, however, the preconditions favoring a successful transition to democracy were weak at best, as a review of them vividly demonstrates.

Economic

By two key indicators, GDP and population ($10.2 billion and nine million people), Guatemala has the largest economy in Central America. While the industrial, manufacturing, and service sectors have experienced modest growth since World War II, agriculture remains the major sector of the economy. Fairly rapid economic growth in the 1960s and 1970s allowed further industrialization and significant modernization of the public sector infrastructure. That, of course, increased the size and skill levels of the small urban labor sector.

Like the rest of Central America, Guatemala fell into a serious economic recession in the 1980s. By 1987, however, there were signs that Guatemala was again beginning to grow, primarily the result of major policy reforms which have caused modest increases in private sector investment and production.[33]

Let us look at the Guatemalan economy in more detail. Individual income was nine hundred dollars in 1988, forty dollars below the Salvadoran level. Over the period of 1965–88, Guatemala achieved an annual average of 1 percent growth in GNP. The 1980s, however, have seen a downturn, particularly in the industrial sector. During the period of 1965–80, it grew at a 7.3 percent annual average; during 1980–86, it fell to a negative 3 percent. All other sectors also turned in negative performances in the 1980s. Private consumption fell in the same two periods from an annual increase of 5.2 percent to a negative 1.2 percent. The population, therefore, has strong reason to see economic performance as far from encouraging. Although these consumption rates overlook an increase in average earnings per employee (1 percent during 1980–85, up from a negative 3.2 percent in the 1970s), there has been a downturn since 1985.

Some of this recent poor performance is attributable to international trade and commodities prices as well as internal management. The foreign debt has risen from $120 million in 1970 to $2.6 billion in 1988, and the debt service has grown from 1.6 percent of the GNP in 1970 to 4.4 percent in 1988, a change that explains some of the negative economic performance. Unlike the Salvadoran insurgency, however, the Guatemalan insurgency is not as damaging to the domestic economy.

Government consumption has remained rather stable, increasing from about 7 percent in 1965 to 12 percent of the gross domestic product in 1988. While the data on the Guatemalan budget is not as complete as for El Salvador, it is worth noting that Guatemalan military expenditures have not bulked as large. In fact, they were 11 percent of the gross domestic product in 1972 and only 1 percent in 1990. These figures, however, give the wrong impression unless we remember that the rapid growth of the economy in the period of 1965–80 makes the latter percentage much larger in real terms. A sense of the real growth in military expenditures can be gotten from noting that the military budget was $9.3 million in 1963, $61 million in 1979, $142.5 million in 1983, and $115 million in 1990. Growth in manpower shows the same expansion—9,000 in 1963, 14,000 in 1979, 29,000 in 1983, and 43,000 in 1990. By contrast, El Salvador spends about 30 percent of its budget for military purposes, a function of U.S. assistance and the kind of war that is being fought. Guatemala's government spending also differs from that of El Salvador and the Philippines in spending less for infrastructure such as transportation and communications, but it is somewhat higher in allocations to medical services.[34]

The Guatemalan government receives considerably less foreign economic assistance than El Salvador, but it has grown from $64 million in 1982 to $235 million in 1988.[35] Per capita the government receives $27

from foreign grants, about twice that of the Philippines but considerably below El Salvador's $83 per capita. With the decline in U.S. assis-
tance, Guatemala has sought other sources with some success, but they
have not provided large amounts of government-to-government aid.

Guatemala's tax revenues, especially income tax revenues, have been
below the levels of other Central American and South American countries as a percentage of GNP.[36] In 1972, for example, personal taxes com-
prised 12.7 percent of the total, 36 percent came from taxes on goods
and services, and 26 percent came from taxes on international trade
transactions. The higher percentage for foreign trade and indirect taxes
and the low percentage of direct taxes, following Lewis Snider's hypothesis, reflect a weak capacity to extract resources, thus a weak civil
administration. Taxes have also been levied more heavily on the rural
population, less on the urban dwellers and landowning elites. Under
pressure from the United States and the International Monetary Fund
(IMF), however, Guatemala passed tax reform legislation in 1986 that
modified property, income, and value-added taxes, broadening the tax
base and reducing evasions. The results are modestly promising. (Compared to 1972 levels, personal taxes rose to 20 percent of government
resources by 1988; taxes on goods and services declined to 28 percent;
and taxes on international transactions increased to 37 percent.)

Overall the economy remains predominantly agrarian. Before World
War II, it was based mainly on coffee growing, but the government
forced diversification to sugar, cotton, cattle, and fruit. Some urbanization and industrial development has occurred in the postwar decades,
but it has been slow. Because the regime has received much less direct
government-to-government aid, Guatemala has had to live more on its
own means. It did, of course, receive an infusion of private capital, reflected in its large foreign debt of $2.6 billion. That explains in part the
high growth rate before 1980.

The present state of the Guatemalan economy can hardly be said
to be conducive to democracy. The past decade, however, may be an
overly negative basis for judging because the debt problem and the
international markets for commodities made the Guatemalan situation
unexceptional. In the previous decades, there was growth and a modicum of urban and industrial expansion. Third World debt relief could
ameliorate the Guatemalan economic situation considerably; restoring
commodity prices to profitable levels, however, may be something that
the world markets will not do. All in all, one is forced to conclude that

the economic preconditions for democracy do not exist; furthermore, without some dramatic changes in foreign debt and export opportunities, they are not likely to improve significantly in the 1990s.

Social

Guatemala is more rural than El Salvador. Its labor force in 1988 consisted of 57 percent agricultural workers, 14 percent in manufacturing, 13 in services, 7 in commerce, 4 in construction, 3 in transportation, 0.8 in utilities, and 0.4 in mining.[37] The trend, however, has been toward fairly rapid movement to the nonagricultural sectors. In the period of 1956–80, the agricultural sector lost 11 percent of its laborers to gains of 20 percent in industry and 42 percent in services. At the same time, about 50 percent of the labor force was either unemployed or grossly underemployed.

The social trends are what we would expect of a developing country. Social mobilization is occurring as the agrarian population moves to urban sector employment. At the same time, that movement is exceeding the economy's capacity to supply jobs—thus the large number of unemployed. To what extent are institutions developing to provide some degree of political participation?

Thirteen political parties exist, and eight parties or coalitions of small parties have representation in the 116-member congress.[38] Political alignments in the congress shifted in the 1990 elections from those of 1985, but both the National Centrist Union (UCN) and the Christian Democrats (DCG) continue to dominate. In the 1990 elections, the DCG lost 23 of its 57 seats while the UCN added 19 to its previous 22. There is a working system of political parties, but they could hardly be said to embrace fully the lower strata of the society pouring into the urban sector. Nor are the parties able to deliver much that these people want and need to develop a solid commitment to the political system. Furthermore, no major coalition exists to support the next president, be he Carpio or Surano.

Business organizations are fairly well developed, and they are the oldest private sector institutions with significant political influence. They proliferated rapidly in the 1940s to a point that they had to come together in umbrella organizations. The most influential is the Federated Chambers of Agriculture, Commerce, Industry, and Finance (CACIF), which brought under its roof a large number of small businesses as well as two large older associations—one for agriculture and one for commerce and industry. ANACAFE, the coffee growers' association, also enjoys considerable influence. The Guatemalan Agricultural Association (AGA) aggregates the other landed agricultural sectors.[39]

Organized labor got its start in the 1920s primarily under Communist leadership but was soon virtually destroyed. In the revolutionary decade immediately after World War II, labor unions were legalized and encouraged. By 1954, the General Confederation of Guatemalan Workers (CGTG) claimed control of 500 affiliated unions with 104,000 members. The National Confederation of Guatemalan Peasants (CNGG), a rural counterpart labor organization, claimed 1,700 affiliated groups with 250,000 members.[40] After the coup in 1954, both were denied their legal status, and within a year only 23 legally recognized unions remained with about 27,000 members. Organized labor remained at about this level into the 1970s. The regime tried to manage unions by introducing moderate leadership, and the AFL-CIO assisted in creating the Confederation of Federated Workers (CTF). By 1976, however, it was the object of government repression. More troublesome in the government's view was the National Confederation of Workers (CNT); it had originally been organized by Christian Democrats but later broke that tie for a more leftist orientation and a relation with the outlawed Communist party and Guatemalan Labor party. A new umbrella committee, the National Committee of Trade Union Unity (CNUS), was formed in 1976, and it became the main object of the regime's efforts to repress the labor movement. A clandestinely organized peasant labor movement, the Committee for Peasant Unity (CUC), appeared in 1979 and achieved increased wages for cotton and coffee pickers through a strike in 1980, but employers often ignored the agreement.

The story of the efforts at institutionalization of the labor force, rural and urban, is one of violent struggle. The regime's policy of trying to moderate and coopt the labor movement was short-lived, and the old policy of repression has left the field open to radical political leadership, primarily the Communists.

Professional organizations have never been strong, although an organization of journalists has played a role of trying to protect members against the government violence. Its success has been marginal, however, and the same is true for the Guatemalan Bar Association. The

Democratic Front against Repression was formed in 1979 by a Christian Democratic congressman. It quickly counted some 150 groups within its membership, but its success has been minimal.

Praetorianism has kept the Guatemalan political system sharply fragmented, disallowing participation by the growing numbers of groups and organizational efforts within the private sector. Political institutionalization is at best inchoate, fragile, and constrained by the social fragmentation inherent in the society at large. The military is the most solidly developed institution, and it has provided most of the political leadership in the past. Today, however, it is caught between its traditional role, largely political, of sustaining a praetorian system and its role in fighting the insurgency. The same tension in El Salvador has to some extent pushed the military in the direction of more attention to professional military affairs, and a similar tendency can be observed in Guatemala. Curiously, in Guatemala the role of U.S. military advisors has been very limited. Yet a trend toward professionalism is occurring. That development leaves a vacuum in the civil sector where civilian groups under praetorianism heretofore excluded can participate more fully in the political system. In other words, the internal war has had some role in pushing the regime toward greater political participation and greater political institutionalization. That probably accounts in part for the present effort to let a democratically elected government rule.

External

Guatemala's external influences are highly analogous to those in El Salvador until most recently. Spanish colonial rule left its pattern in Guatemala as it did throughout Latin America. After the Spanish left and by the late nineteenth century, U.S. business was the major external influence. Like other Central American regimes, Guatemala felt itself very much at the mercy of American policy, and its population did not identify with the political system as their own autonomous government. Moreover, dictatorial rule in the interests of a few wealthy landowners and military leaders did little to encourage a strong sense of support for the government. The U.S. role in overturning the leftist government in 1955, to be sure, reinforced the image of the United States as a de facto colonial power treating Guatemala as a dependency. U.S. military assistance naturally could be seen as evidence, but that ended in the late 1970s. The legacy of U.S. interference in Guatemalan politics, particularly the role of the United Fruit Company, will be extremely difficult to overcome with the political left, even its most moderate wing.

The past decade has apparently caused a somewhat different self-image in Guatemala. Because of the U.S. human rights policy and Guatemala's deplorable record, the country was largely cut off from its traditional ties to the U.S. Whether the Guatemalans liked to believe it or not, realities forced them to deal with genuine autonomy. Neither North American business interests nor U.S. government aid programs were abundantly at their disposal as they had been in the past.[41] Guatemala was largely on its own, and the political and business elites were at first quite ill at ease with this new condition.

The contrast with El Salvador is critical for our analysis, because here we have a country much like El Salvador—a country facing similar political, economic, and military challenges but one that has not enjoyed extensive U.S. assistance, very little by comparison with El Salvador. Their comparative performances offer a measure of the apparent impact of U.S. military and economic assistance. In the Salvadoran case, U.S. aid has been enormous; in Guatemala, it has been trivial. Yet in Guatemala, per capita income is higher than in El Salvador, and the war against the insurgency has been more successful. Perhaps more surprising, without U.S. pressure, Guatemala has introduced democratic forms of selecting its rulers; although it has done so somewhat later than El Salvador, it has nonetheless conducted elections and taken the military out of direct rule.

To be sure, levels of U.S. aid are only one variable in these contrasting cases, and a number of other variables—for example, demographic pressures in El Salvador, the relative quiescence of the Guatemalan Indian population, and the different proximity of the two countries to external bases for the insurgents—have contributed to the different performances. Because U.S. policymakers, however, tend to assume that economic assistance is a highly critical variable and because the difference in levels of aid is so large, the performance differences between the two states must appear strongly counterintuitive. If aid does play a large role, then it must be negative; or it must play a very small positive role, disproportionate to its cost.

Cultural

Like that of El Salvador, Guatemala's culture is a Spanish veneer over a predominantly Indian cultural heritage. The major difference is the stronger residual Indian cultural influence. The population is 56 percent Ladino, that is mestizo, or mixed white and Indian and also Westernized Indian. Indians themselves make up almost half of the population, 44 percent. While Spanish is the official language, more than 40 percent of the populace speaks one of the eighteen Indian dialects as a first language.[42]

Catholicism is the majority religion, although Protestants had reached the 20 percent level by 1982. Mayans make up a small minority. The strong Catholic influence makes Guatemala essentially a Catholic culture, but to see it as that alone would be to overlook a serious and basic fragmentation in the culture. The Indians are almost wholly excluded from the political and social system. The tensions between the two halves of society create a major problem for political development. While some success in political institutionalization has occurred and while a democratically elected government rules, it actually represents at most half of the population, the Indians standing effectively outside it. They retain deeply rooted cultural values and attitudes which even Spanish influence has not diminished significantly. They do not vote, and they have no representation within the congress. When we consider that half of the population within the system, the Ladino, are also only partially represented and that peasants and unemployed are either poorly represented or not represented at all, then the extent of social and political institutionalization looks much smaller. In a political sense, the Indians are largely quiescent, not moving to the cities as part of the social mobilization with the Ladino. Were they to become socially mobilized, then the pressure on the political system would be enormous.

The Catholic church over the decades has had its ups and downs with the regime. In the latter part of the nineteenth century, the clergy split between liberal and conservative factions, and when the liberals won out the Church lost its tax exempt status. On the whole, in the twentieth century, the Church has been conservative, and it openly expressed concern over Arbenz's programs of reform in the early 1950s. After the fall of Arbenz, the church was rewarded by the regime with a restoration of its pre-1871 privileges. More recently, however, the church has found its clergy affected by liberation theology and the inclination to look favorably on much of the revolutionary activity.[43] Given the politically conservative stance of the evangelical Protestants and the Catholic flirtation with the political left, the army has been inclined to mistrust the Catholic clergy, and a number of clergy and lay church workers have been assassinated by the death squads.

The cultural base in Guatemala is far from conducive to democratization, and to a large degree it fosters radicalism, left and right. This is true in ethnic as well as religious matters. Compromise and political coalition building across religious and ethnic lines have virtually no tradition in Guatemala, and the political experience of the past century has only reinforced this absence.

To sum up, the preconditions for democracy in Guatemala are not favorable for the most part. The present regime is highly exclusive. It includes much less than half of the population as participants, and the institutions to handle this half are weak. Its economic performance is moving in the wrong direction. Its cultural base is not promising for democracy, particularly the fragmentation between the Ladino and the Indians. The most positive factor is the change in external relations. Forced to accept its own autonomy from the United States, it has responded by attempting to install a democratic regime. Perhaps it can survive, but, for it to do so, economic and social conditions will have to change—perhaps not dramatically, but they will have to improve, providing a sense of hope and confidence in the political system. All this must happen, of course, under the conditions of an internal war, a serious challenge to the regime.

The Insurgency

The sharp polarization in Guatemalan politics and the early appearance of Communists—the 1920s—essentially handed the political left to the Communists. Insurgency, however, did not come until the early 1960s, and, when it did, dissident army officers—some trained by the United States—led it. Soon, however, in 1962 when the Rebel Armed Forces (FAR) formed in the mountains, Communists took charge. Until then, Moscow's policy of working within the labor movement, the intelligentsia, and among "progressive" military officers was followed. In Cuba, however, Castro had set a new example of how to take power by going to the mountains, and Cuban foco strategy was adopted in

Guatemala. The government met this offensive with an offer of negotiations which caused a split in the FAR leadership in 1966. When
President Méndez Montenegro's amnesty was rejected by the FAR, he
launched the army on a ruthless counterinsurgency campaign which
soon claimed nearly eight thousand victims. By 1968, the insurgency
was virtually destroyed. While it continued with kidnappings to create
the impression that it was still vital, it was forced to begin a strategic
reassessment.

A second insurgency group, the Guerrilla Army of the Poor (EGP),
was formed in 1972. It took its line from Vietnam's experience, and
today it is the largest guerrilla group. The Organization of People in
Arms (ORPA) was launched in 1979 from elements which had split
earlier from the Guatemalan Labor Party and the FAR. It looks for its
political base among the Indian population, and it has put little emphasis on traditional mass organizational work. The Guatemalan Labor
party itself, the PGT, had a splinter group, the National Leadership
Nucleus, break with its normal mode of mass work and launch a tiny
guerrilla effort which engages in assassinations but has no major insurgent formations.[44]

Just as the Sandinista victory had brought a new approach marked
by a consolidation of the leadership under the FMLN, a similar consolidation was attempted in Guatemala. In 1982, an umbrella organization, the URNG, was imposed on all four of these insurgent groups.
(See chart 2.) Clearly this pattern was not a spontaneous development
among the Guatemalan insurgents, who had enough differences over
strategy and leadership to make such a union difficult at best. Rather
it is part of the Soviet-Cuban strategy applied in Nicaragua and El Salvador in creating the Sandinista Front of National Liberation (FLSN)
and the FMLN. Success in guiding it from Managua, however, has not
been great. The separate groups have continued throughout the 1980s
to pursue more or less independent strategies with very little cooperation. The leverage that comes with control of resources, especially
transnational support—money, communications, public relations, and
training—rests with the Cubans and Soviets.

The insurgents' strategies reflect the complex challenge that Guatemala's social and economic structure present for internal war. From
the 1940s until the 1970s, the left's struggle against the regime was cen-
tered primarily on mass organizations, particularly in the labor movement. No centrist of moderate political leadership could exist for long

Chart 2　Insurgent organizations in Guatemala.

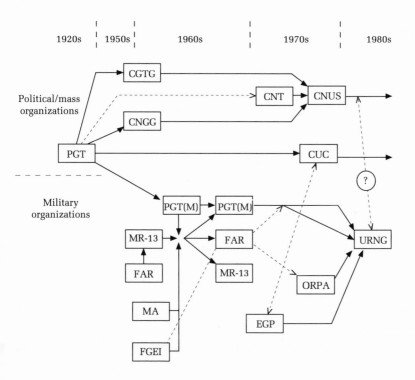

PGT	Guatemalan Labor Party (communist)
CGTG	General Confederation of Guatemalan Workers
CNGG	National Confederation of Guatemalan Peasants
CNT	National Confederation of Workers
CNUS	Committee for Trade Union Unity (umbrella organization)
CUC	Committee of Peasant Unity
MR-13	November 13 Revolutionary Movement
FAR	Rebel Armed Forces
PGT(M)	Guatemalan Labor Party (militant wing)
MA	Movimento 12 de Avril
FGEI	Frente Guerrillero Edgar Ibarra
EGP	Guerrilla Army of the Poor
ORPA	Organization of the People in Arms
URNG	Guatemalan National Revolutionary Unity

Source: Compiled from multiple sources.

in the face of the regime's fitful, brutal tactics of repression. Christian Democrats, Social Democrats, professional leaders, religious leaders, students, and even some reform-minded army officers were driven to radical opposition. The insurgent groups all contain a mix of these elements. They did not enter the insurgency as well-trained Marxist-Leninists; rather they brought a variety of ideological views to one common cause, armed opposition to the regime.

In designing a strategy, the insurgent groups face several major problems. First, they must take this influx of dissidents with their different ideological backgrounds and mold them into good Leninists, Maoists, or some other Marxist faction. This has not always been easy, and in the case of ORPA, which splintered from the FAR, it has not occurred, or it has occurred only recently. ORPA appeared to have non-Marxist leadership before the creation of the URNG umbrella structure.

Second, even as Marxists, these groups are far from united on how to conduct the war. The FAR leaders believe in armed combat, but they also have old ties to mass action in the labor movement. They appear to remain pupils of Che Guevara's foco strategy. The Sandinista victory in Nicaragua probably reinforces their conviction that direct armed struggle is the first priority. Yet the success of the FAR has not been great. In fact, it was badly mauled by the army in the early 1980s and required several years to regain its old footing.

ORPA essentially rejects political action for military action, seeks to fill its ranks from the Indian population, and tries to fight in both the mountains and in urban areas. Because it sees the Indians as the genuine revolutionary potential and because eradicating racism is a major objective, it has had to seek some ideological grounding in the Mayan culture and traditions. Whether this can be easily amalgamated with Marxism is a serious question, and as ORPA brings Mayan and Indian values to its political program, the clash with modernity is likely to sharpen. Yet it can point to the size of the Indian populace and its inherent hostility to the regime and Ladino part of society as a genuine basis for optimism about revolutionary potential. After all, Lenin came to power in Russia in a "class alliance" with the peasantry because he recognized that the working class had no chance on its own. ORPA, however, seems to be giving the Indian class the leading role over others, and that must create serious problems for the URNG leadership in developing a common strategy.

The EGP takes an entirely different approach. Looking at the Maoist strategy used in Vietnam, its leaders are bent not just on building guerrilla forces but, more important, on creating a political infrastructure that allows them to govern large parts of the dissident population, on taking away the regime's authority and implanting an alternative de facto local government. This strategy, of course, is a long-term one which will require years, even decades. It has already proven moderately successful, however, in asserting its influence fairly widely in the country and is the largest of the insurgent groups. It believes not only in building infrastructure in the remote rural regions but also in creating a mass organizational base in the urban areas. Nor does it limit itself to particular regions but seeks to build cadres countrywide. The EPG was instrumental in the secretive formation and operation of the rural union, the CUC, which succeeded in creating rural labor strikes against plantation owners in 1979 and in 1980.

The small PGT splinter guerrilla group is the least significant of the four insurgent groups. Having broken with the Moscow-line communist party, it still has links to the labor unions. To what extent it has a strategy is unclear.

In addition to these two problems—the diversity of the ideological views that must coexist in the URNG until they can be eradicated and the considerable differences among the three insurgent strategies—a third problem confronts the insurgency. Most of the senior cadres have been in their positions for more than a decade and a half, some even longer. That means they have experience and insurgency skills, but it also means they may not have the kind of energy required to transform the struggle into a more promising organizational and strategy posture. And it means that they have fifteen or twenty years of personal quarrels and differences among themselves. As they have been unable to find a common strategy, political and military, over the past couple of decades, one must wonder if they can do so today.

Unlike the FMLN in El Salvador, the URNG has not been able, or perhaps has not tried, to attack the economy. That its base is in the mountains, of course, takes it away from the major economic activities and makes such a strategy more difficult. Geography in Guatemala does not favor such a strategy to the degree it does in El Salvador.

The insurgency's resource base is much smaller than the one enjoyed by the FMLN in El Salvador. The URNG continues to rely on attacks against military patrols and outposts to obtain most of its weapons and supplies. Having no sanctuary from the Guatemalan army, either within Guatemala or neighboring countries—although some use of Mexican territory is made—the insurgents have been forced to survive through mobility. Consequently, they have found it more difficult to establish a presence in remote rural villages where they can requisition food and shelter. While they had some success in Indian areas, the government's tactic of coopting, or forcing, the Indians to join the counterinsurgency has further limited the URNG's rural resource base.

In the urban areas, the insurgents were quite successful in the 1960s in extracting large sums of money through extortions and kidnappings.[45] In the 1980s, particularly in the later part of the decade, the government has been able to reduce this kind of resource extraction dramatically. At the same time, it has limited the rural base of support. The insurgents have, accordingly, become more dependent on external sources of support. Training of cadres continues in Cuba, and propaganda support is provided by Radio Havana. Cuban field advisors, however, have reportedly been rejected to preserve the national appeal of the insurgency.[46]

Soviet military support had been forthcoming until 1967 when pro-Soviet Communist party delegates voiced their opposition to the guerrilla strategies at the Organization of Latin American Solidarity Conference. After the Sandinista victory in Nicaragua, however, Moscow revised its view of the prospects for insurgency in Central America. But dispersal of Soviet aid is through Cuban channels.

Nicaragua has become a key supporter of the URNG. Supplies have been delivered through a Honduran pipeline. Perhaps more important, Nicaragua provides operational assistance and advice through a little known FMLN-URNG link.[47]

The URNG has reportedly made some gains in the late 1980s, but it is far from challenging the regime in the way that the FMLN is threatening the Salvadoran regime. Still fragmented, without able leadership, it fights on mainly with external support. The government is unlikely to destroy it completely, however, and in the worst of circumstances small guerrilla cadres would probably survive in the mountains.

The Government and Its Strategy

Internal war was a manageable problem for the government in the 1960s. U.S. Special Forces support with counterinsurgency training and equipment—especially night vision devices and remote sensing equipment, aerial bombardment with napalm, small unit search and destroy missions, active psychological warfare tactics, civic action programs, and extensive use of photo and human intelligence—gave the government a large edge against the poorly equipped and trained guerrillas.

Throughout the late 1960s and into the 1970s, the army pursued a strategy of occupation and pacification that resembled the U.S. "strategic hamlet" approach in Vietnam at the time. A military base was established to secure the oil-producing infrastructure along the Guatemalan-Mexican border, and more than fifty model villages—each with a school, church, drinking water, roads, market, and meeting hall—were constructed to isolate the insurgents from the population.

The late 1970s and the 1980s have witnessed the expansion of the conflict to significant proportions. The government and the army have been influenced in counterinsurgency tactics by a number of sources—mainly U.S., but also French and Israeli. Until the 1980s, the government mixed army operations against guerrilla formations with brutal attacks by vigilante groups who indiscriminately assassinated urban leftists, numbering thousands in their victims. The excesses with these tactics reached a painfully high level under President Lucas García (1978–82), and, as his term approached its end, even the army did not support him against a coup.

Brigadier General Ríos Montt, a member of the usurping junta, soon emerged supreme, a born-again Christian whose proclamations of justice and amnesty gave the appearance that he might begin a period of healing. In fact, he launched a severe campaign of repression, including a stepped war against the guerrillas, Operation Victory 82, which was supposed to end the twenty-year civil war within one year. Notorious for its disregard of human rights, the campaign claimed thousands of victims, many of them entirely innocent. Ríos Montt tried to deideologize the war by proclaiming an offensive against the left and the right and promising to clean up the corruption of the Lucas Garcia era. In fact, little was done to those he promised to purge, and most of the culprits escaped unscathed.

A new strategy did begin to take shape under Ríos Montt. Enjoying some sympathy among the younger officers, he inspired them to carry the war to the countryside in a fashion Lucas García had not. The Guatemalan army scoffed at the El Salvador tactics of large search and destroy operations followed by withdrawal from the area, allowing the guerrillas free run again. The Guatemalan army began a program of local civil defense organizations, providing some arms to villagers and signing them up to keeping the guerrillas away. This "beans and bullets" strategy promised some economic assistance as well, but army bullets were more plentifully provided than beans. Carrying the war into the highlands among the Indians, the army set up hamlets, invited the Indians and peasants to live in them, and declared areas outside them "free fire zones." Operations within the free fire zones were ruthless. Indian groups who had not initially entered the protected areas changed their mind in many cases, providing a modicum of success against the guerrillas. By keeping military units in the area, the government has been able to limit and to some degree cut back the insurgents' strength.

Ríos Montt's political support for this strategy, however, soon waned. His reliance on a select group of army advisors and Protestant fundamentalists alienated large parts of the business community, the Catholic church, and the conservative military hierarchy. In 1983, General Oscar Mejia Victores successfully overthrew Ríos Montt. The next year, the government returned to its model village program in rural Indian communities. General Mejia made good on his promise to hold elections, and in December 1985 Mario Vinicio Cerezo Arévalo, a Christian Democrat, won the runoff election. His decision to hold direct talks with the URNG in Spain in 1987 displeased conservative groups, civilian and military alike, but Cerezo survived an effort to overthrow him. The verdict on this latest attempt at democracy is still very much in question, but, in the winter of 1990–91, Cerezo served out his term and a new civilian president was elected, Jorge Serrano.

The government's problems have been exacerbated by the trends in the economy. In the boom years of the 1960s and 1970s, economic privations were not as severe, and that made it more difficult for the insurgents. The economic hardships of the late 1980s have taken away this cushion from the government and favored the insurgents. While direct economic assistance might ameliorate the problem for a time, it can be no substitute for private sector expansion. Much of the direct assistance would inevitably be skimmed off through corruption, and the large foreign debt would deter private capital from coming back to Guatemala on a significant scale. Clearly foreign debt relief would be a bigger boon for the regime than direct assistance.

If we consider the five development goals—economic growth, social equity, autonomy, stability, and democracy—we see at once that there is a de facto prioritization by which some of them receive little or no attention and others are pursued actively if not always effectively.

Guatemala enjoyed a respectable economic growth in the 1960s and 1970s, over 7 percent annually. Traditionally the government has kept a very tight budget, spending no more than it collects through taxes. In the post–World War II decades, however, it has drifted away from that practice, and it has also changed its policy toward acquiring foreign debt. The international market drop in commodity prices in the 1980s whiplashed the regime just as it did the rest of Latin America. At the same time, Guatemala has not been a recipient of large foreign economic assistance as El Salvador has. Remarkably, however, its per capita income is about the same as El Salvador's. Equity in income distribution, to be sure, is another matter. Turning its economy around is critical for the regime, but its control over the variables is limited. Foreign debt relief clearly would be the most helpful economic assistance measure for Guatemala. Without relief, the goal of restoring economic growth is probably not within the regime's reach.

Social equity seems to be lowest in priority among the development goals. Junior military officers talk about it when they become upset with corrupt behavior among senior officers, but, after coups in the name of ending corruption, little more is heard and nothing is done to improve social equity. The revolutionary decade, 1944–54, to be sure, remains a living memory of a time when this goal had high priority, particularly in the land reform program, which was reversed after 1954. The land reform option is the single greatest step toward the equity goal the regime could take today. It might well lower agricultural productivity by breaking up the large commodity export–producing plantations, but the political and social gains would clearly be worth it, and it would set back the insurgents quite seriously. Because parliamentary democracies are poor at land reform, the main hope for such a program lies in a highly determined reformist military clique.

The autonomy goal is a point of distinct success. The U.S. policy of cutting off aid because of human rights violations, to be sure, contributed significantly. The regime was left with no choice but to take greater responsibility for its own fate, although government and business circles have been uncomfortable with such enforced independence. It has taken some of the wind out of the insurgents' propaganda sails. They have tried to make an issue of the presence of U.S. Special

Forces personnel, but the low U.S. profile still undercuts their charges. The issue will not disappear, however, because the U.S. role in the overthrow of Arbenz in 1954 remains a vivid memory.

Stability, of course, has been the highest goal in the regime's priorities. The cost has been high because of the tactic for achieving it. Ruthless praetorian repression has made political development virtually impossible. Rather than institution building to expand participation, political exclusion has been the practice. The challenge of political development is enormous, particularly in light of the bifurcation between the large Indian population and the Ladino, the majority of the remainder. The regime, however, has made little effort even at broader inclusion of the Ladino sector. This, of course, makes President Serrano's efforts to maintain a democracy not very promising. Without a sustained benevolent attitude within the army, he has the smallest prospects for success.

This brings us to the democracy goal and the somewhat surprising decision by the ruling circles to make a serious try at democracy. The government confronts not only the absence of adequate political and social institutions but also the Ladino-Indian fissure. Of these two fronts, clearly building institutions is the most critical in the short run. Until the urban sector—labor, professional groups, and business circles—develops adequate modern institutions and spreads its base to the Ladino part of the rural society, there will be no counterbalance to the army. One consequence of the insurgency has been to give the army enough to do so that it is more willing to let such political development be attempted.

A significant factor in the army's support for a democratic government has been its desire to reestablish strong ties with the United States and regain lost military and economic assistance. Were the United States to accept this opening and provide such support, it would not be the best for Guatemala. Lack of U.S. support has forced it to deal more effectively with the insurgency. If the democracy is to be lasting, the key factor will be an enlightened military leadership. Dankwart Rustow's point about the role of leadership, the necessity for the competing elites to decide that they want to institutionalize a rule-based political system with genuine electoral competition, is critical in Guatemala's case. It cannot happen in the present regime without strong support from the military.

Net Assessment

The internal war in Guatemala is a standoff. It is a race in political institutionalization, a race in asserting effective government over the population. The insurgents, if they come to an agreed strategy, a Maoist approach, will challenge the government much more seriously. At the same time, as they try to pursue that strategy in the Indian sector of the country, they may find it extremely difficult to mix Mayan culture with Marxism-Leninism, or even with Maoism. And they will find themselves astride the fissure that separates the Ladino and Indian sectors of society.

The government's willingness to try democracy is a positive sign, but it is only that. Even a serious and sustained effort to build a democratic system will run up against the social fragmentation between Ladino and Indian, between the wealthy landowning elite and the poverty-stricken masses, and even within the army. A second coup attempt, for example, against Cerezo Arévalo in May of 1989 has been attributed to a faction in the army which is upset over the government's negotiations with the insurgents.[48] If the inchoate urban classes could be enfranchised and given reasonable protection under the law, the government might build a democracy on the Ladino sector of society and through benevolent policies toward the Indians keep them politically quiescent.

Notwithstanding these positive developments, military success in the field and an elected government, the regime has only marginally faced up to its political development challenges. The formally democratic system conceals a praetorian reality. Economic and political power is still very much concentrated in the hands of a few military and civilian elites. Corruption and statism in the economy limit and distort market forces. Yet the urban and commercial sector is growing slowly, creating more pressure for political participation. Rather than sponsor new institutionalization, the military elites resist it, still resorting to nonjudicial measures against opponents. That leaves institutions such as the church, labor unions, and professional groups no alternative but to move to the political left.

In the countryside, the absence of land reform and programs to create a population of independent small farmers leaves a considerable landless peasantry for insurgent recruitment. If the regime merely made a strong effort to include the Ladino sector of the populace more effectively in the political system, it could probably leave the Indian sector excluded and quiescent, at least for the present. The insurgents have had limited success in mobilizing the Indians in any case.

In making the comparison with El Salvador, one is inclined to say that the absence of large U.S. military and economic assistance has been for the best. Given the political and economic realities, as well as the U.S. record of influence in Guatemala, it is difficult to believe that a U.S. country team with large assistance programs could have induced much more reform than has occurred. Nor is it likely that the counterinsurgency would have been more effective, and it might well have been less effective with more U.S. assistance. Admittedly, the military situation in Guatemala differs from the one in El Salvador. Over the past decade, the geographic proximity of Nicaragua to El Salvador has made it easier for the FMLN to acquire transnational materiel support. The URNG in Guatemala is more isolated, more difficult to assist from abroad, although routes through southern Mexico have been developed. Notwithstanding these differences, one is still inclined to conclude from a comparison of the two cases that U.S. expenditures in El Salvador have been counterproductive.

The URNG, to be sure, has not been the most effective competitor in this internal war. Still somewhat fragmented in its leadership, it has never really devised an effective overall strategy. As in the case of the FMLN, the political change in Nicaragua raises questions about the URNG's capacity to continue the war. The significant amount of technical support that has come from Managua could be routed to the URNG directly from Cuba or through southern Mexico. URNG leaders do not have the international standing of their FMLN counterparts, and they probably do not enjoy as much financial support from international front organizations. Their case is less well popularized in the United States. As long as Cuba remains a stalwart ally, however, they will be a significant problem for the Guatemalan government.

What if the weakening of Soviet support for Central American insurgencies continues to decline and Cuba is pressed to reduce its own contributions? The URNG's alternatives are fairly limited. First, it could try to adopt a more Maoistlike strategy and settle in for an indefinite and long war, deriving most of its resources from within Guatemala. This alternative would require the consolidation of a new leadership that could force a common strategy on all the subgroups in the insurgency. Second, it could de-emphasize the military component of its struggle and make its main effort penetration of the frustrated urban groups. Third, it could essentially lose the war, degenerating into a few bands of guerrillas living in remote parts of the country but with the means to conduct significant operations.

Once again, we see the possibility of a painful dilemma for the United States. The government could win the war without yielding much to democratic political development. The military's dominant political role would likely remain unchanged, and the economic oligarchs would be content with the formal appearance of democracy without the economic and participatory substance. Because American investment and involvement in the war is much smaller than in El Salvador, the embarrassment would be much less, but it would be a setback for political development in the region. Moreover, this de facto praetorianism would not likely last forever, and its collapse would unavoidably be bloody.

A conceivable way out of the predicament for Guatemala and El Salvador alike would be the emergence of a reform-minded military elite, not unlike the one in 1944–54. Such elites have arisen in developing countries in other parts of the world, but something about the recruitment and socialization process in Central American militaries seems to prevent their emergence there. Perhaps the inchoate trend to greater professionalism that the war has prompted in the Guatemalan military could eventually alter the traditional pattern of the military's political behavior.

The Philippines Case

Although it lies nearly halfway around the world from Central America, the Philippines shares much in common with El Salvador and Guatemala. The Philippines was long a Spanish colony, and the patterns of Spanish rule were deeply implanted. A small oligarchy of latifundia owners depended on low-cost landless peasant labor. The Catholic church shared abundantly in both ownership of land and in the political system, being formally tied to the Spanish government. Moreover, it was the main educational institution, teaching Spanish and religion in parochial schools. All of these features of Philippine political, economic, and social history, of course, are also characteristic of the two Central American cases. Moreover, all three lie in a tropical climate and share commonalities in agriculture.

The differences to be found in the Philippine case are not inconsequential, however. The indigenous demography is wholly different, not only in the ethnicity of the Southeast Asia peoples as compared to that of the Central American Indians, but also in the linguistic and ethnic diversity within the Philippines, which is much greater than in Central America. What is more, the Philippines have a Muslim minority, something not present in the Central American states.

There is also a major difference in the Philippine relationship with the U.S. The Philippines moved directly from Spanish colonial rule in 1898 through a very short-lived period of the independent Malolos Republic to American control. For almost a half century, the Philippines were subjected to American tutelage in democratic forms of government, beginning in 1907 when the lower house of the parliament was elected by the indigenous population.[49] A short time later the upper house was also elected in the same manner. Church and state were legally separated, and a system of public elementary schools was introduced which taught in the English language. The Philippine Military Academy was modelled on West Point, and the American concept of military subordination to political authorities was made an article of indoctrination which to some extent persists even today.

By contrast, Guatemala and El Salvador experienced a direct shift to independence and more than a century of rule by oligarchies and dictators followed by the rise of the army in politics and modern praetorianism in the form of government. They retained closer cultural ties to Spain; their citizens did not learn English; and they had mixed relations, mostly bad in the popular mind, with the United States. This is not to say that the Filipinos had only positive attitudes toward the United States. On the contrary, the memory of the brief Malolos Republic and independence has remained vivid in the minds of Filipinos, and both latent and manifest anti-American feelings have persisted.

The American influence on the Philippines, however, did not by any means displace the Spanish social, economic, and cultural patterns. They remain today in modified form as enduring obstacles to political and economic development. The Spanish landowners were displaced by Filipinos, and the old social inequities have in no sense eroded. The role of the Catholic church remains strong. And political parties remain as narrowly based as in Central America. In many respects, the American influence has only imposed a veneer on the more deeply rooted Spanish patterns which have reasserted themselves in the post–World War II years of independence. The tendency toward oligarchy, dictatorship, corruption, and exploitation of a large landless peasantry is remarkably like what we have observed in Central America. The practice of leaning on the army as the major base of political power, drifting into praetorian rule under Marcos, certainly has its parallel in El Salvador and Guatemala.

Finally, all three countries are trying to institute democracy, and all three have begun this effort anew in the 1980s. At the same time, all three are deeply engaged in internal wars in which the insurgents are Marxist-Leninists who directly or indirectly enjoy political and other forms of support from the Soviet Union.

As we review the economic, social, external, and cultural preconditions for democracy in the Philippines, we will observe many more similarities but also some basic differences.

Economic

Growth was impressive until the 1980s, but in the last decade it has slowed dramatically.[50] In 1988, the per capita income in the Philippines was $630, about two-thirds what it was for El Salvador or Guatemala. The growth of the GNP has been 1.6 percent per capita since 1965, remaining slightly ahead of population increases. The economy as a whole enjoyed significant growth in the period of 1965–80, the gross domestic product averaging 5.9 percent. The 1980s have brought a downturn in economic performance as the annual average of the gross domestic product has dropped to 0.1 percent. Private consumption, however, has increased, but the rate has dropped from a 5.0 percent before 1980 to a mere 0.8 percent annual increase since that time.

Agriculture has performed somewhat better, maintaining a positive 1.8 percent annual growth rate in the 1980s, but still a dramatic drop from the 4.6 percent annual average in 1965–80. Services also had a positive growth rate in the 1980s, but at 0.7 percent, it is far below the 5.2 percent enjoyed in 1965–80. Industry and manufacturing both turned in negative rates in the 1980s. Industry dropped significantly from 8.0 percent growth in 1965–80 to a negative 1.8 percent. Manufacturing fell from 7.5 percent in 1965–80 to negative 0.3 percent in 1980–88.

The downturn in the Philippine economy, of course, can partly be explained as a result of the collapse of international commodity prices and a large foreign debt, which grew from $1.5 billion in 1970 to $29.4 billion in 1988. Debt service has, accordingly, risen from 1.4 percent of GNP to 7.0 percent during the same period. An exacerbating factor has been the surprisingly large capital flight from the Philippines, estimated as no less than $10 billion and as high as $14 billion. Added to capital flight, which probably continues today, is flight of human capital. Middle-class professional people in large numbers find their way to the United States, normally with "green cards," permission to work. Too often they never return, finding ways to emigrate permanently. A return of both human and financial capital could dramatically change the Philippine economy, not to mention the political system.

Shifts among the economic sectors have been significant since 1965. While agriculture has remained about one-fourth of the gross domestic product, industry has increased to 34 percent and manufacturing to 25 percent. Services have declined by 9 percent in the same period. The overall size of the gross domestic product has actually increased by more than six times in this period.

General government consumption grew at about 8.0 percent annually over the period of 1965–80, slightly more than in the cases of El Salvador and Guatemala (7.0 percent and 6.2 percent respectively). Since 1980, however, it has been reduced to a 0.8 percent annual change. The decline in government expenditures can be explained partly as a function of the large growth in GNP before 1980, but they have also declined in real terms. Since 1972 they have dropped almost 70 percent for administrative expenditures. The savings have been transferred to defense, health, education, and other public sector spending. While health, education, housing, and welfare have enjoyed some growth, in real terms, defense has received the lion's share. The defense budget, however, is still only about one percent of the GNP, the lowest in Southeast Asia.[51]

Direct foreign aid for development assistance has gone up dramatically, from $300 million in 1980 to $854 million in 1988. The latter figure is 2.2 percent of the GNP for that year and equal to $14.30 per capita, almost half the Guatemalan rate but far below the El Salvador figure of $83.

Taxes have increased sharply since 1972, 97 percent for incomes, 50 percent for goods and services, and only 3 percent for international transactions. At the same time, total tax revenues as a percent of the GNP have increased modestly from 12.4 percent to 14.3 percent. Clearly, tax evasion has been rampant, although part of the discrepancy can be explained by changes in accounting procedures for separating state and local taxes.

The economic picture in the Philippines shares much in common with the two Central American cases. All three countries experienced fairly strong economic growth in the 1960s and 1970s, but it was largely offset by population growth. The 1980s brought a sharp decline in economic performance accompanied by surges in foreign debt. Government expenditures have been fairly modest, but they have experienced significant shifts to the defense sector as their internal wars have intensified. While all three have enjoyed large amounts of foreign aid to take up some of the slack in tax revenues and to sustain government expenditures, El Salvador stands out for receiving about four times as much aid as each of the others per capita. While they have all enjoyed some growth in industry, manufacturing, and commercial activities, they remain predominantly agrarian economies.

Social

Philippine society remains predominantly agrarian with about 50 percent of the populace engaged in agriculture. A steady move from the agrarian sector continues, however, amounting to about 10 percent of the population since the 1960s. The urban population was 39 percent of the total in 1985, showing a 7 percent rise since 1965. Industry and commerce employ 20 percent of the labor force; 13.5 percent are engaged in services and 10 percent in government; the remainder, less than 10 percent, are spread over several other smaller employment sectors. The official unemployment rate in 1987 was 11 percent, but that does not reflect the large number of underemployed workers providing a very marginal contribution to the economy.

The labor force has grown steadily over the past two decades, 7.7 percent annually between 1965 and 1985, and it is projected to continue to grow about 2.4 percent through the end of the century. Population pressure, therefore, presents a continuing challenge for the economy. Fairly spectacular growth rates are imperative if the ordinary individual is to have some sense of gradual economic betterment and a relatively less deprived existence.

Private sector organizations in Philippine society are too numerous to count. They cover all aspects of life—political, social, and economic. In the labor movement, for example, there are over two thousand registered unions. They have a total membership of just under 5 million, or 21 percent of the work force. There are, however, umbrella labor organizations that aggregate the numerous local unions. The National Congress of Farmers Organizations is the largest, numbering 2.7 million members. The Trade Union of the Philippines and Allied Services with 153,000 members showed its autonomy by resisting Marcos's effort to control labor through the Trade Union Congress of the Philippines, claiming 1.5 million members. The much larger Kilusang Mayo Uno with 350,000 members also kept its independence, but it is heavily influenced by the Communist party of the Philippines.

Business circles are well organized, and potentially they could exert a fairly strong influence on the political system. It would be wrong, however, to see them as similar to modern business organizations in advanced industrial countries because kinship ties cross-link them to government and political circles in a way that makes their formal appearance somewhat misleading. They are not static in this respect, however, and as the influence of the old families declines with a changing economy, they could help stabilize the democracy.

The same has been true of political parties. Patron-client relations from Manila downward to the local levels created a vertically integrated political system. Political parties, therefore, have had no horizontal aggregating role across groups and provinces. Nor have they traditionally had formal membership and local organizations. They have not become modern institutions for accommodating expanding demand for political participation. Rather they have remained loose election umbrellas for a political process played out among a narrow circle of wealthy elites, cliques connected more effectively by family and kinship ties than by party loyalties. Before and during Marcos's rule, the party system was essentially an institutional veneer over the traditional oligarchy of privileged families. Parties did not provide political participation and integration on a broad basis for affecting policy. They merely covered the narrow policy-making circle at the top and shielded it from popular pressures.

Marcos's Kilusang Bagong Lipunan (KBL) party during and after martial law, which existed from 1972 through 1983, in a real sense began to undermine the old party system, although Richard Kessler argues that it was already showing signs of change when Marcos initially declared martial law.[52] It followed the old pattern in that it knitted together the national, provincial, and local levels in a patron-client linkage, but Marcos did not share with the other oligarchies. His clientele slowly devoured more and more of the entire system of spoils and corruption.

In the post-Marcos period, there is a chance for a modern party structure to replace the old one if the new urban middle class asserts itself through organizations that integrate horizontally. The KBL has been wrecked, leaving the field open. It is, therefore, a race between new organizations and modern parties against the old clientele-patron system rising from the ashes of the KBL.[53] The military, of course, and the Communists will be members of the contest, and if they stand each other off in the internal war, they may leave the other newer social forces to build a different and more inclusive party system.

This is, however, a very optimistic scenario which assumes that the Marcos regime truly did destroy the traditional forces of oligarchy. An equally compelling argument could be made that land tenure is still so heavily concentrated in the hands of a few wealthy owners that the old power structure is far from broken. A genuine opportunity for change would require an extensive and completed land reform program. Without it, the insurgents retain a high potential for mobilizing a land-hungry peasantry in their ranks, a process that has already enjoyed more than a little success. Land reform, therefore, would not only undercut the old ruling oligarchy, but it would also strike a heavy political blow against the insurgents. Yet another factor that undercuts the optimistic scenario is the flight of the professional middle class, many of whom emigrate to the United States. The very forces Kessler rightly sees as possibly altering the system are weakened by the emigration pattern.

From the viewpoint of social structure, the Philippines has many features of a textbook version of a late-developing country. The urban sector is growing as the agrarian sector declines, but the new social mobilization in the cities runs into the oligarchic, kinship-laced, land-owning power structure of feudalism. A clientelist public bureaucracy and local government has become the heart of the political system, a block to political participation both by the new urban elites and by the mass of low-income, land-hungry peasantry. Using Huntington's concept again, social mobilization has exceeded economic development, yielding social frustration. To some extent, social mobility bleeds off the frustration, but its growing levels create growing demands for political participation. The political and social institutions for controlling this participation are sufficiently numerous and adequate in a formal sense, but on closer scrutiny they have more often repressed than accommodated the participatory demand.

A significant difference in the Philippine case, however, is that a thoroughgoing praetorianism has not been the whole formula for resisting the demand for wider political participation. President Marcos leaned on the armed forces as a source of power, but the military has not become as dominant in politics as it has in El Salvador and Guatemala. Marcos, a personalistic dictator who manipulated the formal democratic system through his vast net of kinsmen and clients, was able to control the military by the same means. It did not control him; although in the showdown with Cory Aquino losing the military was critical, a reasonably well-organized urban sector of society stood as a counterweight to direct military rule. Comparison with the Central American cases suggests that political institutionalization has proceeded much further in the Philippines than in El Salvador and Guatemala, although it remains precariously weak because of the exclusion of such a large part of the peasantry.

One other point of comparison in the social structure is important to note. Regionalism and localism are strong in the Philippines in a way that one does not find in the Central American cases. One of the functional aspects of Marcos's clientelist system was that it coopted regional and local leaders, giving Manila a modicum of control throughout the many islands and distinct ethnic groups. Breaking up this kind of structure for authority and allocation of political spoils can bring a dangerous bifurcation between urban Manila and local political chiefs. Neither the political parties nor the private organizations have the kind of control over regional and local politics to check this bifurcation. The Catholic church and some of the umbrella labor unions may prove exceptions, but it remains a serious impending problem.

External

We have already drawn the main outlines of external influences on the Philippine political system. The Spanish influence remains in many regards, but it has been partially countered by American influence. If we are to explain the rather significant differences between Philippine and Central American social structures, a slightly stronger institutionalization of the new urban forces and a lesser role of the military in politics, we would have to include American influence as critical. The long relation of the Philippines Armed Forces with the U.S. military has imparted to the former a disposition to stay out of politics, especially among the junior officers who are socialized by an education in the Philippine Military Academy. Corruption in the senior ranks, however, and the fight against the insurgency have the opposite impact, pushing the military toward a greater political role. Reasonably honest elections were imposed during American rule early in this century, and, although some would argue that Philippine political leaders always tended to be highly authoritarian (in particular Quezon, whose political dominance in the 1920s did reveal such tendencies), compromise in politics was often the case. The Central American cases had no such experience, and they are very belatedly trying to learn the art of compromise in political arrangements.

Another important external influence on the Philippines is the appearance of the Islamic faith in Mindanao. The Moro ethnic group on this island became followers of Islam at the same time it came to Indonesia, and they have resisted integration into the Philippine political system ever since. The source of separatist wars and insurgency for many decades, this Islamic influence creates a serious fissure for the political system.

The Japanese invasion is another source of external influence, one that allowed the United States to overcome some of the anti-American feeling when General MacArthur reconquered the island. Other than leaving a strong anti-Japanese feeling among the population, however, this effect has not been lasting. The resistance to the Japanese, however, did allow the Communists to gain a stronger foothold, especially among the Huks. Since then, the Communists have remained an important factor in Philippine politics, struggling among themselves over deference to the Soviet Union or China. The pro-Moscow Philippine Communist party (PKP) long held the upper hand, but the pro-

Chinese Communist party of the Philippines (CPP) eventually took the upper hand, reducing the Soviet influence to insignificance. In the late 1980s, however, the odds seemed to be shifting back in Moscow's favor.

In sum, the Philippines has been subjected to five incompatible external influences: Spanish colonialism, American tutelage democracy, Islam, Japanese occupation, and Marxism-Leninism. Vestiges of all five are still highly active factors in both the social structure and politics.

Cultural

The Philippines has a predominantly Catholic culture. This feature of Spanish influence has proven highly stable through the vicissitudes of Philippine political development. And, of course, there is a large Muslim population in Mindanao. The Catholics compose 83 percent of the population, Protestants 9 percent, and Muslims 5 percent.[54] A small Buddhist population, 3 percent, is also present.

Ethnically, the population is largely Malay (over 95 percent), but the linguistic map of the Philippines is not so homogeneous. Many local dialects persist along with some Spanish, and a fairly large percentage of Filipinos are able to speak English. Overseas Chinese make up 1.5 percent of the population and play a strong role in the urban commercial sector.

Literacy was estimated at 88 percent in 1988, higher than for either of the Central American cases. This, of course, is in large part the legacy of the public school system established by American authorities early in this century. For a Third World country the literacy rate is high but still below the rates of some of the Asian rimland states.

The Catholic church in the Philippines has played a strong role, not only in cultural matters but also in politics. Traditionally quite conservative, it has nonetheless experienced a leftward tilt on many social issues. Like the Catholic church in Latin America, it has been influenced by Vatican II to concern itself more with social and economic justice. Within the ranks of its clergy, there are radical priests with ties to the political left, including the Communists and the insurgents. This pattern is remarkably similar to the ones observed in the clergy in El Salvador and Guatemala. Cardinal Sin, the prelate in Manila, could not be considered radical, but he clearly supports reform. He withdrew his support from the Marcos regime and encouraged Catholics to back Cory

Aquino. Ultimately this policy proved to be one of the critical factors in bringing down President Marcos.

The Catholic church in the Philippines case has thus far been a positive factor in the most recent efforts to create a stable democracy in the country. Most of the clergy can probably be counted on to continue that support as long as the regime proves more inclusive in its participatory patterns and social policies. But elements of the clergy can also be found on the other side of the internal war. Given a choice between abandoning democracy for what they perceive as a path toward redressing social and economic injustices and standing behind democracy as it proves feckless in achieving greater social equity, many clergymen are likely to abandon the regime for more radical political solutions. Because of its strong institutional and administrative capacities, the role of the Catholic church could prove quite critical. Only a powerful praetorian regime could likely stand successfully if the church threw its full weight against the government.

The Insurgency

Insurgency is nothing new in the Philippines. It was almost constant throughout Spanish rule, and when the United States assumed control of the islands in 1898, it immediately confronted the same problem. The Moros proved particularly difficult to subdue in the first two decades of this century. The Hukbalahuk group in Central Luzon was long a source of disorder and resistance against the large landlords.[55] Many other smaller resistances have been common throughout the islands. Each group had its own parochial aims and political ideology, if these insurgents' ideas about how they should be ruled can be called an ideology.

The major change in the present situation is the growing dominance of Marxism-Leninism as the insurgency's ideology. Some will object to the use of Marxism-Leninism to describe it, insisting that it is Maoist, or closer to the Khmer Rouge or some other variant—perhaps an indigenous Filipino mix of Marxism and local ideological innovations. This may be true to some degree, but communism came to the Philippines through the Comintern between the world wars, and the Soviet influence on the Communist party there was for a long time quite strong. In the 1950s, however, it did find itself split between those more attracted to the Chinese model of revolution—Mao's peasant-based insurgency, political education, and de facto government in the insurgent-controlled areas. Magsaysay was able to defeat the Huk rebellion and its Communist leadership in the 1950s, and he tried to coopt the less radical Communists by legalizing their participation.[56] A former Communist of Moscow orientation, Turok, actually became a minister for land reform in the 1960s. The pro-Chinese faction in the Communist movement soon had the upper hand, reducing the pro-Soviet faction to irrelevance. That has remained the case throughout the 1960s and 1970s.

As China turned inward, accepted an opening to the United States, and became less interested in directly sponsoring revolutions in the region, the Philippine movement appeared to be isolated. That did not lead, however, to a decline in its activities. On the contrary, it turned more than ever to internal sources for support, and it became deeply committed to the Maoist strategy of a peasant revolution. This does not mean that it ignores the cities and work in mass organizations, particularly the labor unions, but it does mean that it builds its primary base in the countryside. Propagandizing, organizing, and actually governing larger and larger regions are more important early forms of struggle than direct military conflict with government forces.[57] Here the Philippine insurgency differs rather fundamentally from the insurgencies in Guatemala and El Salvador.

The military and main rural organizational arm of the Philippine Communist party (CPP) is the NPA. In some regards it is remarkably analogous to the FSLN in Nicaragua, the FMLN in El Salvador, and the URNG in Guatemala. It is an umbrella command and control structure for the many insurgency subgroups. (See chart 3.) The appearance of the NPA gives the insurgency in the Philippines a distinction from its past. It has been able to create organizational structures in sixty-five of the seventy-three provinces in the islands of the republic.

Western observers were surprisingly late in realizing this fundamental change. One could dismiss the insurgency as perhaps a serious nuisance—after all, insurgency has always been a problem in the Philippines—but it has never seriously threatened the regime, except perhaps in the 1950s. The regime had coped then; it would cope now as in the past. Nothing basically new seemed to strike foreign observers.

The change was in the aggregation—the building of a command and control network that could eventually coordinate insurgent groups throughout the whole of the country, perhaps even with the Moro in-

Chart 3   Insurgent organizations in the Philippines.

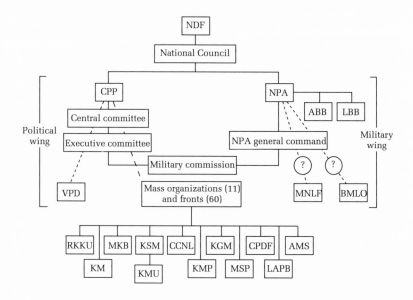

NDF National Democratic Front or National Democratic Underground Mass Organization (1973)

CPP Communist Party of the Philippines (1968) (Pro-Chinese and pro-Soviet factions)

VPD Volunteers for Popular Democracy

NPA New People's Army

ABB Alex Boncayao Brigade (urban guerrillas)

LBB Lorena Barros Brigade

MNLF Moro National Liberation Front (Muslim)

BMLO Bangsa Liberation Organization (Muslim)

RKKU Rebolusyonaryong Kongreso ng Kilusang Unyon (trade unions)

KM Kabataang Makabayan (youth)

MKB Makabayang Kilusan ng Bagong (women)

KSM Katipunan ng mga Samahang Manggagawa (workers)

KMU Kilusang Mayo Uno Mayo (militant labor)

CCNL Church Christians for National Liberation

KMP Pambansang Kaisahan ng mga Magbubukid (union of Philippine peasants)

KGM Katipunan ng mga Gurong Makabayan (teachers)

MSP Makabayang Samahang Pankalusugan (medical)

CPDF Cordillera People's Democratic Front

LAPB Liga ng Agham Para sa Bayan (science and technology)

AMS Artista at Manunulat ng Sambayanan (artists)

Sources: *South*, Nov 1988, pp.22-23; *Far Eastern Economic Review*, 17 Dec 1987, pp.34-42.

surgents (although striking common cause with them has not proven easy for the NPA). In the past, the regime could oppose separate groups with great concentration of military force and without worry about other parts of the country. In the 1980s, however, this changed. As Marcos shifted more and more of his army to Mindanao to cope with the Moros, he found the NPA turning up the heat in other places—not just in Luzon but on several other islands as well. He also found it able to exert influence within the labor unions.

The NPA also revealed another change that many observers, including intelligence analysts, have been reluctant to see. While the public appearance of having no ties to Moscow has been scrupulously maintained by the NPA, they were in fact reestablished in clandestine channels. And they have been expanded through international front organizations. Here we see the common footprint in organization and transnational networking that is well established in Central America with the FSLN, FMLN, and the URNG.

This pattern does not involve direct material support in the way it was given to the North Vietnamese and the Viet Cong—or to Angola, Ethiopia, South Yemen, and Afghanistan before December 1979. Instead it depends on a complex set of transnational organizational ties, political action programs, fund-raising, and clandestine intelligence work. (See chart 4.)

But before we continue to examine insurgency resources, it is well to look at the NPA strategy in more detail. Following the Maoist model of guerrilla warfare, the NPA, under the political leadership of the CPP, has followed a three-pronged strategy.[58] First, it has devoted great energy to building up party organizations in the rural towns and barrios. Second, it has formed small guerrilla units for the NPA, extending them into as many provinces as possible. Third, it has tried to increase its influence in the urban sector of society with the National Democratic Front and through organizational work in the labor unions.

While military work has not been neglected, the emphasis has been on political work—building a party infrastructure with cadre influence in mass organizations and particularly in rural areas. By 1985, the CPP had political organizations in about 20 percent of the 41,000 barangays in the Philippines, which allowed it to claim control of about 25 percent of the entire population. The effect of this organizational success has been the weakening, even disintegration, of local government at the barangay and town levels. To accelerate its work in the larger

Chart 4   External support provided to the Philippine
insurgency (CPP/NPA).

	Financial	Armaments	Military training	Shipping/ logistics	Diplomacy/ propaganda*	Diplomatic initiatives* sought
Soviet Union	X	X		X	X	
North Korea		X	X		X	
Vietnam		X		X	X	
Malaysia			X		X	
Singapore	X			X		
Japan	X				X	
Hong Kong	X					
Australia					X	
New Zealand					X	
Belgium					X	
France					X	
Netherlands					X	
China					◄———	X
East Germany					◄———	X
Yugoslavia					◄———	X
Hungary					◄———	X
Bulgaria					?	X
Cuba					?	X
Libya	?					
Albania						X
Spain						X
Italy						X
Greece						X
Latin American Liaison Office			X			
Southern African Liaison Office						X

*Denotes contact/link with Communist Party affiliate(s).
Sources: *Naval War College Review*, Autumn 1987, pp.96–99; *Far Eastern Economic Review*, 28 Jul 1988, pp.12–14; *Far Eastern Economic Review*, 17 Dec 1987, pp.35-42; *South*, Nov 1988, pp. 20–23.

urban areas, the CPP formed a new front organization, Bayan, which was designed to mobilize and attract noncommunists. By the end of the year, it claimed to influence over three million people, predominantly noncommunists. The CPP cadres were able to propel Bayan into more militant action through a general strike.[59]

On the military front, the NPA has grown throughout the 1980s, but it is difficult to determine precisely how much. Marcos's intelligence services probably biased their estimates downward, trying to convince both themselves and the American Embassy that the NPA was not as serious a threat as in fact it was becoming. In 1986, the official Philippine estimate was about 13,000 guerrillas, but at the same time American officials were placing the estimate at about 20,000.[60]

While it calls itself an army, the NPA is more accurately described as a network of small guerrilla bands—poorly armed in most cases, without modern communications, and unable to conduct more than small actions, primarily assassinations and ambushes. Occasionally it attacks small isolated military outposts and police stations, but it shows no inclination to fight large government military units. Its strategy is to eschew those kinds of operations at the present stage of the insurgency. Rather it directs its operations to destroy local government and to terrorize the population into support.

The CPP and the NPA have survived on very limited resources, and NPA units are often in desperate need of food and medical supplies. Reportedly, the CPP has turned down offers of direct foreign support, preferring to stick to its original strategy of living off the resources it can raise locally.[61]

It would be a mistake to conclude that the NPA is hopelessly weak because of this approach to resources. On the contrary, that is its strength. Lacking the foreign support of the kind that the URNG and the FMLN enjoy, it must extort and tax the population. More and more reports of the expansion of this taxation policy began to appear in 1985. The Maoist strategy is to build an insurgent government. There is probably no better measure of the degree of governing than the capacity to tax. What is given to the NPA cannot be given to the government tax collectors. Forcing local Party and NPA units to live off of what can be extracted locally strengthens their capacity to rule locally. The efficacy of this tactic is confirmed not only by intelligence reports but also by local priests who are told by their parishioners of the fear of the NPA and of their inability to resist its taxation efforts.

It cannot be expected that local resource extraction will remain the only form of support for the NPA. Its tactics have probably already changed considerably; there are indications that they have.[62] At some point, the NPA expects to be able to increase the size of its operations and stand against the regular army units. For it to do so will require considerable upgrading in weapons, ammunition, medical, and food supply, as well as improved communications. It is reasonable to surmise that this kind of upgrading is already taking place in some regions. In the meantime, it is very much in the CPP and NPA interest to maintain the impression that they are destitute and wholly without foreign aid. Such an impression not only reduces concerns of U.S. authorities but also reinforces the NPA's claim to being purely nationalist, the true claimant of the nationalist banner.

With the overthrow of Marcos and Aquino's assumption of the presidency through popular election, the CPP has had to reassess its strategy. This matter has been made somewhat more complicated by Aquino's amnesty policy and her release from jail of a number of Communist leaders. Moreover, her promise of land reform and greater social equity creates a problem for the CPP. There is some evidence that the reassessment has split the CPP leadership, that some are more inclined to come into legal forms of political competition and to de-emphasize the insurgency while others are convinced that the old strategy has merely to be adjusted to the new political realities of Aquino's rule.

From CPP and NPA behavior since Aquino's election, it is clear that the legalists have not prevailed. The NPA is protecting its rural base, even expanding it, and political work in urban areas has resumed. The minor change has been to avoid direct propaganda attacks on Aquino while attempting to isolate her government from the population and to exploit the political splits among her ministers. Another change is an effort to sharpen the nationalist issue by attacks on U.S. military personnel and facilities, highlighting the presence of the bases as evidence of residual colonial rule.[63] Many other such tactics, including direct negotiations with the government and changing party and front tactics can be expected. All the while, nothing is being surrendered on the NPA's front. The tax competition for control goes on, and the spread of the NPA's terrorizing influence has not ceased.

Too rosy a picture should not be taken away from this brief survey of the major outlines of the insurgency organization, strategy, and tactics. For Aquino's government, the battle is far from won or even reaching its most advanced phase. Neither the weapons nor the political forces are yet ready for it. At the same time, this insurgency has many more malignant characteristics for the Aquino government than do the Central American insurgencies. Manila's rule is being challenged on a number of levels, and the insurgents have created a base that cannot be quickly or easily eliminated. Successful military operations against the NPA still leave the local cadre infrastructure in place. The government must not only defeat the guerrillas. It must rebuild local government and sustain it against terrorist and political tactics.

The Government and Its Strategy

The Marcos regime pursued a set of policies that facilitated the insurgency. First, his patron-clientele system for dealing with local government left the CPP and NPA with only one serious opponent, the local Marcos client. Other potential political participants, unions, professional groups, and political parties were discouraged from trying to institutionalize the local population. The armed forces were extremely poorly supplied and their senior ranks corrupted, making the army much less of a challenge to the NPA. As long as the insurgents were fragmented, with separate groups opposing the local KBL appointee, Marcos's system could not really be threatened in a serious strategic sense. Once the NPA began to provide a network to command and control guerrilla units on a countrywide basis and, at the same time, the CPP built an equally wide network of party organizations, the balance began to shift to the insurgents' side. The local Marcos satrap was isolated and up against a coordinated campaign. Inherently unpopular in any case (although there apparently were exceptions), these officials were easy to expose as corrupt, easy to isolate from the local population politically. All the social and political inequities could be exploited without much competition. No noninsurgent institutions other than the Catholic church were in the competition on a countrywide basis. Moreover, the central government was wholly unresponsive in any case.

The economic downturn in the 1980s also exacerbated the inequities, making the regime a still more vulnerable target for the insurgents. From the villagers' viewpoint, there was no institutional alternative for expressing dissatisfaction, for participating in the political process.

Earlier economic growth had not been great, but, when it began to turn negative, the bind on the peasantry was acute.

The overthrow of Marcos removed the object of much hatred; it was also accompanied by organized political action on a massive scale, largely in the Manila area to be sure. This certainly demonstrated to non-Communists that effective political action is possible without the help of the CPP and the NPA. The big question remains, however, whether this was merely a temporary affair or whether it reflects a fundamental turn in Philippine politics and social policies.

We have already discussed the prospects of new social structures, particularly political parties, which might alter the system to create institutional competition—not only in Manila but also in the country-side. One analyst, Richard Kessler, had made a very cogent argument that the old system of clientele and kinship ties was breaking down when Marcos declared martial law in 1972. The KBL under Marcos began to squeeze the others out, dealing the old system further blows.[64] Will the reviving parties change their organizational approach and create countrywide formal institutions? Will they seek broad electoral support in competition not only with each other but also with the CPP?

One can raise serious doubts about their effectiveness unless extensive land reform is carried through rather quickly. What kind of constituencies can be built in the countryside? Certainly local government officials and bureaucrats would be an attractive target for party recruitment, and we anticipate that they will be pursued. But what about the peasantry? Their interests are in social programs and land reform. What party is likely to decide to carry their issues? Moreover, what prospects would it have in the legislature of delivering much that the peasants want? The record of peasant parties in achieving success in this regard is poor. Why will it be better in the Philippines?

Another problem for Kessler's scenario is the flight of the middle class through emigration. The potential leadership for restructuring Philippine party politics is not always willing to stay and carry on the struggle. The parallel problem for the economy is capital flight. The Philippine economic elites are not always willing to cast their lot completely with the system: they hedge their bets; their opposition, the insurgents, does not.

President Aquino, of course, can only do so much to press this kind of reconstructing. In her initial set of policy promises, she has indeed addressed the basic issues—land reform and making the army more effective in fighting the NPA. She has also tried to steal the banner of reform and social justice from the CPP and the NPA with amnesties and promises of reform. It is one thing to make promises, however, and it is quite another to deliver on them. One must grant her time. She certainly cannot deliver at once. Building an effective political base of her own is essential. While she has made it difficult for the opposition elites to reestablish their old patronage systems, she has also refused to build a new party of her own. That is perhaps wise, because it might leave her with a narrower base than she now has given her populist posture of standing above the fray and symbolizing hope for all groups.

A clear strategy on her part, nonetheless, has not yet emerged. Parts of one have. She must clean up the leadership of the military, provide it with better resources, and push it into more effective action against the NPA. She has taken some steps in this regard, but Marcos's dabbling with dissident military officers from Hawaii created obstacles for a time. Improving the military will also require money. Pouring resources into the military, however, will create new temptations for corruption and patronage.

Land reform, unless it is to be carried out by force, disenfranchising the present owners without payment, will require large sums of money. At the same time, depending on how it is carried out, it could reduce the agricultural sector's productivity for a time.

Social programs also require money, but, even if it is made available, the bureaucratic competence to administer such programs effectively is in short supply and threatened by the old tendencies toward corruption.

Almost all aspects of a comprehensive strategy for President Aquino require large amounts of money. Given the economic outlook for exports of commodities and given the protectionism for many industrial and manufacturing enterprises, economic growth is not likely to provide such fiscal resources in the near future. Restructuring the economy for greater future efficiency is more likely to reduce government resources.

Already tendencies are apparent in U.S. policy and in the aid policies of some other industrial states, particularly in Japan, to help the government with fairly large economic and military assistance. (The World Bank, for example, recently announced in Tokyo that donor countries and multinational institutions had pledged $3.5 billion in Official Development Assistance [ODA] to the Philippines in 1989.)[65] It is hard to gainsay the arguments for providing such support to President Aquino. If the political and administrative infrastructure existed and were being used effectively for the reform programs that are most needed and most likely to hurt the insurgents, these arguments would be more compelling, but given the actual situation they are not. Here we come back to the insurgents' taxation campaigns and the government's record of being unable to collect taxes effectively. Tax rates have increased dramatically, but overall revenues under Marcos actually fell. At the same time, the insurgents are taking more and more of the tax base away from the government.

The government's inevitable proclivity will be to become more dependent on foreign assistance, direct government-to-government assistance, while failing to recover much of the tax base from the insurgents. The government, if it follows these practices, will be turning foreign donors into its de facto tax base, allocating the monies to domestic programs and putting more resources into the countryside. Unless a much better set of local administrative and political institutions precedes this flow of resources, the insurgents will turn out to be the greater beneficiaries. As resources arrive in the countryside and even in the urban areas, the CPP and the NPA will go after them. Their policy of self-sufficiency in lieu of dependency on large foreign support will force them to do so.

This is precisely what happened on a grand scale in the case of the government of South Vietnam. Up against a Maoist-type insurgency which developed an extensive and ruthless system of tax extraction, it slowly yielded most of the rural and some of the urban tax base to the Viet Cong. At the same time, the U.S. government took up the government's internal budget gap, making more resources available. Worse yet, U.S. AID programs pumped money into village, district, and province administrations where it frequently found its way directly into Viet Cong coffers.

The conclusion one is encouraged to reach is that no direct assistance is better than a lot. Abundant aid makes it too easy for the government to shy away from the competitive taxation system the insurgency creates. If we reflect on the political development studies that show that transnational capital, that is, private investment, tends to strengthen the government, we may find another way to provide assistance that is more effective. If private sector institutions, transnational businesses and banks, move money into a Third World country responsibly, they put it in institutions that they find have the administrative capacity to spend it effectively to return a profit. Where such institutions fail, they go broke, and the lenders presumably take the losses. Recalling Chaudhry's study of capital inflows to Saudi Arabia and Yemen, we should be mindful that if they are channeled through the state bureaucracy, they do not have a positive effect either on economic performance or local administrative institutions. Private capital alone is only part of the answer. How it flows in and how it is used play an equally important role for political and economic development.

Private sector capital, therefore, if it is not filtered through the state bureaucracy, is less likely to find its way to the insurgents and less likely to be wasted by government bureaucracies. It builds its own administrative structures and tracks the consequences of capital transfers. It is not, however, wholly invulnerable. Foreign businesses and local firms have been known to pay the insurgents not to disturb their operations.

A positive outcome from foreign investment, to be sure, is not certain, and, unless the government can protect its institutions and local recipients from insurgent extortions, it cannot make good use of such an investment. If protection in the form of effective local government administration can be provided, however, the private sector can set in motion social and economic change that eventually erodes the old economic order. In the case of the Philippines, to achieve this, it would have to undercut the influence of the large landowners, cooperate with moderate labor union development, and provide enough jobs to bring economic relief to the landless peasantry. U.S. AID–sponsored development is not at all likely to achieve such results. Like U.S. counterinsurgency assistance, which we have called "colonialism by ventriloquy," aid sponsored by the U.S. government, or even in most cases by the World Bank, turns out to be "capitalism by ventriloquy."

The Philippine government has very limited resources, and it is strapped with a huge foreign debt. At the same time, it is losing control over more and more of its tax base. A government strategy to defeat the insurgents must face up to all of these constraints consciously and find a way to manage them. At the present time, debt relief would seem to be the most helpful thing that foreign governments could provide. The next most helpful thing would be for the government to deal aggressively with the tax competition with the insurgents, not necessarily collecting higher taxes but building effective local administrative structures. Only by denying its growing sources of internal fiscal and material means can it prove that it governs and not the CPP-NPA.

The army, of course, is key to making headway in this regard. The guerrillas are not yet showing capabilities to field large units for direct combat with large army units. The army, therefore, could regain the initiative. Here again, foreign assistance can hurt as well as help. Too much aid or the wrong kinds of military assistance will slow, not expedite, an effective military challenge to the NPA. The internal cohesion and determination of the army are far more important than largesse in military assistance. Until they are indisputably in evidence throughout the army, large amounts of military assistance will be ill-advised.

Comparison with El Salvador is instructive here. El Salvador is small compared to the Philippines, and the United States can much more easily shower the El Salvador military with abundant support. At the same time, the FMLN engages the army in large unit battles, facing the army's strong suite. The Philippine army is not facing the same operational challenges. They are much smaller in a technical military sense, but they are accompanied by the building of local organization and infrastructure that removes more and more of the population from government control. Disciplined organization in the army supported with abundant intelligence is the Philippine army's most crying need—not fleets of new helicopters, artillery, airplanes for ground attack, and the like. Those things can help in many cases, but they are much lower priority than discipline and organization coupled with tactics for keeping the insurgents away from villages and shopkeepers, peasants and clergy, local government officials and school teachers.

Unless the army can become effective in this regard in the near future, it eventually will face a better armed and more aggressive NPA. That stage of the insurgency has not yet arrived, but when it does it will be backed by a differently organized local population than the FMLN has in El Salvador. It will not be sufficient for the army to win a few engagements by mauling the guerrillas and driving them into the hills for a few weeks or months to heal their wounds. The population will be caught up in and institutionalized by insurgent political structures, removed from all real government control. It will supply the NPA with vast amounts of intelligence, and it will sustain the NPA logistics base, stealing from the government and the army. That is the character of a Maoist insurgency as compared to a foco insurgency.

Let us sum up this analysis of the regime's strategy by putting it in the context of the five political development goals—economic growth, social equity, democracy, political stability, and political autonomy. Either explicitly or implicitly, how has President Aquino prioritized them? Does her strategy involve a sequence of goals and a recognition of their inherently conflicting demands?

If one tries to infer answers to these questions from Aquino's public rhetoric, one would be forced to conclude that she is seeking all the goals simultaneously. She speaks out for economic growth as an urgent matter. At the same time, she proclaims a commitment to early progress in greater social equity, particularly concerning land reform. Democracy, of course, may stand slightly ahead of all other goals because a free election brought her to power. Political stability ranks high in her explicit concerns, although she has risked it occasionally by dealing gently with Communist leaders and military coup leaders. The negotiations over the future of the U.S. military bases have thrust political autonomy to the fore, and how hard she bargains has become a test of her commitment to Philippine independence.

Looking beyond her policy rhetoric to Aquino's actions, we do not see the same emphasis on all five goals. She has certainly struggled to maintain the present democratic system dominated by the old oligarchic circles, but she has achieved little in broadening its base throughout the country.

For all the talk about economic growth, she has not seriously considered the kind of austerity policies necessary to create a sound basis for growth. "Import substitutions," hidden subsidies to some businesses, and other obstacles to greater market effectiveness combined with an effective taxation policy remain beyond serious policy action. Instead, she acts as if the most important answer to economic growth is foreign aid.

Progress in social equity is nil. Land reform, which could create a strong sense of improved social equity in the rural areas—the places she most needs to win support—has little chance of implementation. Those who would lose land in a reform program have adequate power in the parliament to block it. Other kinds of wealth transfers for social equity, on a scale that would make much difference, are beyond the public budget. Nor is she trying to build a reliable countrywide system of civil administration that could distribute such transfers fairly.

Political stability remains fragile for many reasons, not least the weakness and unreliability of the army and regional civil administration. The weakness of political parties is also a factor. Aquino's policy actions to overcome these inadequacies have been meager to say the least.

Making the military base negotiations the test of political autonomy while calling for more foreign aid, as she is doing, is to confuse appearances with reality. Direct aid will undercut autonomy, whereas the income from the military bases, in part going directly to individual Filipino salaries, actually contributes to the government's autonomy in the same way private capital inflows to the private sector do. The Yemeni experience, as described in Kiren Aziz Chaudhry's study, is an instructive case in point.[66]

Both Aquino's policy rhetoric and her policy actions, when judged against these development goals, give the impression of a regime caught in a state of paralysis—drifting and apparently unaware of how to proceed. The inherent conflict in priorities seems lost on Aquino, while her determination to hold together the democratic system that brought her to power contributes little to building the kinds of institutions she needs to make progress toward most of the development goals. Hers appears to be a government without a strategy, attempting to muddle through without a clear view of the fundamental problems, not to mention a grasp of promising solutions. This is not to suggest that an effective strategy is easy to design and implement. Rather it is a candid assessment of Aquino's predicament.

Net Assessment

The tide was certainly with the NPA during the last years of the Marcos regime. The CPP was expanding political control at the government's expense. The NPA extended its network of guerrilla groups into almost all, sixty-five of seventy-three, provinces. While there were problems, resource shortages, and leadership quarrels, the insurgents were making sustained progress. With the overthrow of Marcos and Aquino's election with massive popular support, the guerrillas suffered a serious blow. She compounded it by offering a conciliatory hand of amnesty and a willingness to include the insurgents as legal political participants if they were willing to put aside their guns.

This juncture in Philippine politics brought the internal war to a temporary standoff. The government had a significant opening for attacking the insurgency, not only militarily but also politically. The insurgent leaders, however, seem to have rebounded after a period of confusion and indecision about how to proceed. They have readjusted their strategy slightly, taking into account her enormous personal popularity, and they have surrendered little or nothing of their political network and guerrilla infrastructure. By pushing the nationalism issue, particularly emphasizing it through attention to the U.S. military presence, they are taking a position that could eventually make Aquino subject to the charge that she is backing American colonialism in the Philippines. The insurgency seems to have worked out its strategy more quickly than Aquino has hers.

The external aspects of the internal war are also temporarily at a standoff. The government is seeking large amounts of foreign assistance and has reasonable prospects of receiving some, if not all, it has asked for. Whether the government is administratively capable of using that assistance effectively is a large and troubling question. The insurgency also seems more willing to seek and accept foreign assistance. Its administrative capacity to use the aid effectively is far more impressive than the government's.

The internal war in the Philippines is far from reaching a definitive conclusion, and the government certainly has the opportunity to turn the tide. Thus far, however, it has not really done so. It can struggle for many years, but time would not seem to be on its side until it has made some very major moves—particularly in land reform, economic growth, greater institutionalization of private organizations such as unions and political parties, and, most critically, strengthening the army. As time passes before these things are accomplished, the insurgents will take more and more control of the population, and their resources will increase; pushing them back will become much more difficult. At some point in the next three to five years, if the insurgency is not dealt some very heavy setbacks, the tide could move irreversibly to the insurgents' side.

The Middle East–Southwest Asian Challenge

Iraq's invasion of Kuwait, the U.S. deployment of large military forces to Saudi Arabia, and the stunning defeat of Iraqi forces by the U.S.–led military coalition are likely to mark a major turning point in the politics of the region. Dramatic change in Soviet policy toward the region, promising to end the East-West competition there, is an equally important new development. Before speculating on the meaning of this abrupt turn of events, let us review the state of the region and U.S.– Soviet competition up until the mid- and late 1980s. That backdrop is essential for analyzing the impact of the Gulf War and future prospects for internal wars.

For many states in the region, the main development problem is national identity and geographic sovereignty. The traditional societies in much of the region have had boundaries imposed on them that are somewhat artificial for purposes of welding a modern national state. Borders and territories, therefore, play a central role in political development and military affairs. If the region is broken down into subregions, it becomes clear that each subregion is plagued with seemingly intractable border struggles, irredentism, and ethnic strife.

The best known, of course, is that area including Israel and Arab confrontation states. It would not be an exaggeration to say that Lebanon makes no sense as a state. Conceived and drawn on the map by European diplomats, it has no single cohering majority that can assert legitimacy and maintain stability. Both Syria and Jordan are geographic artificialities, fragmented polities, still struggling with national unity and so lacking in the preconditions that a transition to democracy is at present out of the question. Egypt has a stronger basis for nationality identity and coherence than any other Arab state in this subregion, but it too has internal ethnic and religious fissures. With the Camp David Accords, it presumably has settled its territorial ambitions. Most other states, including Israel, have serious territorial problems. Diverse sources of immigration to Israel are changing its internal political structure so that it is beginning to take on signs of the social diversity characteristic of its neighbors, placing new, although manageable strains on its democratic government.

Some of the interethnic strife in this subregion in the 1980s has begun to look like more traditional insurgency warfare. In Lebanon this was particularly true, and, until the apparent end of the civil war in the fall of 1990, it remained true in the case of the uprisings in the occupied territories within Israel's boundaries. At the same time, these insurgent factions are quite different because they have de facto territorial bases, and they engage in occasional conventional military operations. Since its failed intervention in Lebanon in 1982–83, the United States has not been militarily involved. Moreover, this subregion and the Arab-Israeli conflict stand apart as a special case. It could be treated within the general set of U.S.–Soviet competitions in the Third World, but its distinctions are so great that our generalizations from this study do not readily apply.

Another subregion, the Arabian peninsula, is rife with border disputes and warring groups. The Saudis and Yemenis have long-standing quarrels. South Yemen and North Yemen have been periodically at war. South Yemen for a time backed the Dhofari rebellion in Oman. The small sheikdoms on the Persian Gulf are fragile entities which could easily suffer internal coups.

To the north, the subregion that includes Iraq, Iran, and Kuwait has been the scene of one of the largest and bloodiest territorial wars in the Third World since World War II. Although a final settlement has apparently been reached between Iran and Iraq, the situation will remain precarious. Iraq's invasion of Kuwait and its liberation by the U.S.–led military coalition forces have added another war to this conflict-ridden region. The Kurds, of course, have long fought Iranian, Persian, and Turkish rule, seeking their own autonomy. Both the United States and the Soviet Union have at different times backed Kurdish leaders. Because of their intractable character, the disputes in this subregion were probably no closer to a final settlement than the Arab-Israeli conflict was before the Gulf War's unsettling impact.

The Horn of Africa in many regards belongs to the larger regional grouping of the Middle East–Southwest Asian states. Its ties to the Arabian peninsula and Egypt rival, and in some ways exceed, those to Africa. Here, the Ethiopian-Somali dispute is both old and deep, promising continuing periodic wars between the two countries. Eritrea seeks its independence from Ethiopia, adding another fissure to the region. As with the other states in the larger region, borders, ethnic strife, and sovereignty are the basic problems.

Finally, Afghanistan, Pakistan, and Iran form another subregion beset by war, ethnic rivalries, and border disputes. Only religion unites Pakistan. Baluchistan sits in all three states in the subregion. India has its claims against Pakistan and vice versa.

A transnational political phenomenon also gives much of the region's politics a special character. Pan-Arabism complicates the region's politics and entangles it with most of North Africa. Based on Islam and an old belief that all Arabs are brothers, pan-Arabism confuses loyalties to the modern secular state with loyalties to a wider cultural, religious, and ethnic entity. In the 1950s, Nasser played heavily on the idea of transnational Arab loyalties in opposing British and French influence in the region. The United States' support for Israel allowed it to become an object of pan-Arab hostility. Egypt effectively wore the mantle of pan-Arab leadership for more than two decades until Sadat agreed to a peace settlement with Israel. Since then, other Arab leaders have tried to assume the mantle in order to manipulate support for their own policies. In the 1980s, Assad of Syria and Saddam Hussein of Iraq have vied for it.

In most crises, where state interests are seriously at odds with pan-Arab solidarity, pan-Arabism has been cast aside. Yet it has maintained a hold on the political attitudes of the man in the street, even when his government sets it aside. That fissure between much of the public and the leadership of Arab states allows some leaders to use the pan-Arab appeal against Arab leaders, especially when the Arab-Israeli confrontation is at issue but also when the United States asserts itself in the region. Thus it is a terribly complicating factor in regional politics among sovereign states.

Pan-Arabism also complicates the domestic political development of Arab states. Its transnational religious and ethnic basis stands as an obstacle to the development of modern secular states and governments. This kind of political development tends to offend traditional religious sensitivities as well as to provoke a duality in the individual's political loyalties.

Time and painful experiences resulting from the cynicism with which various leaders have tried to exploit pan-Arabism undoubtedly weaken it, but it will remain a serious factor in the region for years to come. In any internal wars in the Arab states, therefore, it will be a factor of considerable importance. At the same time, it can be overestimated. Too often, state leaders and group leaders have sacrificed it to what they believed were the interests of their own power.

U.S. Strategy

The U.S. strategy toward the region changed rather significantly twice during the Carter administration and then settled into a consistent pattern from 1980 to late 1990. Once again it appears to have been radically revised.

In the first year of the Carter administration, a series of new policies—resulting from the Indian Ocean arms talks, the conventional arms transfer talks, and the arms transfer policy and including a nuclear nonproliferation policy applied to Pakistan—intersected in the area east of the Suez to create a strong impression that the United States was downgrading its influence there. The arms control proposals to the Soviet Union rested on the assumption that the two superpowers should have essentially equal military power in the region. The arms transfer policy, putting a ceiling on how many arms the United States would sell globally, had its greatest impact on the buyers in this region, namely the moderate Arab states—Iran, Pakistan, and Ethiopia. Pressing Pakistan not to develop nuclear weapons and at the same time denying it transfers of modern conventional weapons merely strengthened its determination to acquire a nuclear capability.

By the summer of 1977, most of the regional leaders who had depended on Washington began to believe that the United States was following Britain in its earlier retreat from the region. They could not afford to cry out for the United States to remain; for their own safety they had to keep quiet and seek the best alternatives available in the changing power balance.[67]

By late 1978, the United States had lost its footing in Iran and Ethiopia. By the summer of 1979, President Carter had changed his mind about accepting military equivalence with the Soviet Union in the region. The Communist coups in Afghanistan and South Yemen and the Soviet foothold in Ethiopia stimulated considerable rethinking among President Carter's advisors. The Soviet invasion of Afghanistan prompted the so-called Carter doctrine, a commitment to expel a military intervention in the region and to reassert U.S. power there to maintain a balance of power for protecting Western oil supplies.

Throughout late 1979 and 1980, a series of steps were taken to reestablish a strong U.S. presence. Military access was obtained in Oman, Somalia, and Kenya. Military exercises with Egypt were initiated. The beginnings of the rapid deployment force and the command structure that would become Central Command (CENTCOM) appeared. Relations with Pakistan were improved and support for the Afghan insurgency began. The Iraq invasion of Iran brought concerns that Iran might attack the Saudi and emirate oil facilities. The U.S. AWACS (airborne warning and air control system) was deployed to Saudi Arabia to improve Saudi air defenses, and arms sales to Saudi Arabia were reconsidered.

The Reagan administration reconfirmed the Carter doctrine, carried through the organization of CENTCOM, and, after the abortive intervention in Lebanon, continued the Carter strategy of maintaining a balance of power in the region. As the Iraq-Iran War dragged on, President Reagan deployed naval forces for keeping the shipping lanes open in the Persian Gulf and disallowed Iran a decisive victory over Iraq, ensuring that neither side could upset the balance.

The expanded U.S. commitments included no assistance to governments against insurgencies and the concomitant concern with building democracy. Only in Pakistan was the United States in a position to encourage democracy, and even that was limited by the higher priority given to support of the Afghan rebels. The Camp David Accords brought a large economic aid commitment to Egypt, but it was not contingent on democratic reforms, rather on Egypt's relations with Israel.

The major problems for U.S. strategy in the region have been two. First, the Carter doctrine committed the United States to deal with external wars for the purpose of regional stability and a balance of power that ensures a free market for oil. That meant in practice that no country would be allowed to achieve hegemony over the oil-producing territories. This remained U.S. strategy up until November 1990. The deployment of U.S. forces for the defense of Saudi Arabia and the UN coalition in support of economic sanctions against Iraq reestablished the balance upset by Iraq's invasion of Kuwait. United States military power on the ground checked Iraqi military power, and that confrontation also changed the regional nuclear balance vis-à-vis Iraq in that Iraq, were it to acquire nuclear weapons, would be facing U.S. nuclear forces.

This is not the first time conventional military means have been employed for balancing purposes in the region. Other instances are military supply to Israel in the 1973 war, intervention in Lebanon in 1982, and the U.S. naval escort operation in the Persian Gulf in 1987–89. The Gulf War is only the latest of these. Clearly the U.S. military must have a wide range of capabilities to deal with these kinds of contingencies, but they exceed counterinsurgency and similar military means. Thus, these regional interstate wars fall outside our analysis of internal wars, but they form a backdrop for internal wars and are inextricably related to them.

The second problem for U.S. strategy is ensuring the stability of the moderate Arab states, the oil-producing states, and any other states deemed critical to U.S. interests. Solving it requires somewhat different military and nonmilitary options if the United States wants the choice of sustaining those regimes in power in times of crisis. Although these options may include major intervention forces, they have not yet required traditional counterinsurgency assistance. They have required the means to manage military sales and to provide technical assistance. They could also include an ability to deal with coups and sudden collapses of moderate but fragile governments in states critical to oil production and other aspects of U.S. regional interests. Major conventional forces, in most cases, could not deploy rapidly enough to cope effectively with these contingencies; therefore, a somewhat different capability may be needed.

The Iranian case is indicative of the structural and political hazard of instability in several moderate states in the region. The regimes are not based on popular sovereignty, and their societies are Muslim. At the same time, oil profits give some of these regimes very large incomes which they spend in vast projects involving U.S. and other Western private firms. The foreign presence brings cultural behavior and levels of consumption that clash with the Muslim culture, inspiring deep social resentment against Westerners. The regimes, of course, become closely identified with the foreign influences, creating a sharp social bifurcation between the wealthy ruling elites and the mass of the society. The oil wealth and the rapid economic change it buys threatens traditional society. The shah of Iran was seen as a puppet of this Western influence, a significant factor in his demise.

In Saudi Arabia, Kuwait, Oman, the sheikdoms on the Persian Gulf, and even in Jordan and Egypt, this social bifurcation can be observed. Although the United States enjoys some influence with these regimes, it is not in a position to sponsor democratic development in them as it is in the Central American and Philippine cases. That has left the United States little choice but to depend on the incumbent governments, notwithstanding the implications for political upheavals such support involves. The rulers of these states have perhaps wisely kept the United States at arm's length in many regards, an effort to prevent being seen purely as pawns of U.S. imperialism. Economic wealth, however, brings in Western cultural influence, from which the rulers find it increasingly difficult to distance themselves in the eyes of the clerics and their underclass followers. Envisioning military, economic, or political means for U.S. strategy to deal with this problem is difficult.

Yet failing to deal with it makes the probabilities of having to contain the resulting instability with military means much higher.

Certainly counterterrorist means are also a requirement for the U.S. menu of military capabilities. The case for them has broad support in the United States, and such capabilities must be maintained. The priority of this mission, however, can be higher than it should be. The terrorism problem in this region tends to distract our attention and constrain our strategy in a way that we should not let it do.

As General Gazit, former director of Israeli military intelligence, once observed in a seminar where the author was present, Israel gave so much attention to terrorism in the early 1970s that it was too distracted to recognize the signs of war in the Sinai along the Suez Canal. Terrorism is a form of warfare. It is a tragic nuisance, but it has not made a major strategic difference to any of the regional conflicts. Moreover, Americans become targets only to the extent that the United States loses its posture of having ties to both the Arab and Israeli camps. It is neither in the Israeli nor the U.S. interest for the United States to be at war with the radical Arabs and Iranian extremists. In the best event, U.S. interests will continue to be terrorists' targets, making counterterrorist means essential, but the point remains: they alone cannot suffice for U.S. strategy, and they should not be the main effort.

Occasionally, the view is advanced that the United States should stay out of all these regional quarrels and avoid the myriad problems involvement brings. We could do that, and, in the first year of the Carter administration, that strategy was adopted. But the implication of this course of action is, effectively, withdrawal from the region—not a wise strategy if we believe that we have vital interests there. There is no tidy solution for U.S. strategy in this war-plagued part of the world. Excessive focus on terrorism, rigidity in commitments, and radical changes in commitments all tend to undercut our major objectives—access to oil and the security of Israel and the moderate states that depend on the American connection. Moreover, our influence will remain limited by the extent of our power. We do not have the power to provide tutelage democracy for states throughout this very large area. Deep involvement in internal wars and regional conflicts, where they can be avoided, would seem most unwise. Prudence suggests playing at the margins, maintaining a balance of power in the region, taking high payoff initiatives only where the opportunity looks promising, and recognizing that political development leading to democracy in this part of the world will be decades, perhaps longer, in the making.

This was the outlook before the Gulf War. Both the situation and U.S. strategy have altered significantly in early 1991. Accordingly, the outlook has to be revised. Before doing so, let us consider Soviet strategy toward the region.

Soviet Strategy

Perestroika in Soviet foreign policy appears to have reversed Moscow's approach to this region fundamentally. Much that has transpired in 1990 and 1991 changes the entire complexion of great power influence there. To appreciate the present and future context, however, a review of the old competition is helpful.

Soviet strategy for the Middle East and Southwest Asia has taken some dramatic turns in the past decade or more. Until 1972, it bet heavily on Egypt, only to be expelled. In the 1973 war, it used its military force projection capabilities in a desperate effort to regain Egyptian confidence, but to no avail. Painting the U.S. and Israel as imperialist forces trying to reimpose colonial influence in the region, Moscow was able to maintain close ties with Syria and Iraq. The relationship has brought the Soviet Union greater influence in the region, and it earned much hard currency through arms sales.[68]

In these three cases—Egypt, Syria, and Iraq—the Soviet approach has been based on the assessment of the military leaders in these states as "progressive" political forces.[69] Lacking a significant working-class base and a large peasantry, these states have never offered a promising opening for Marxism-Leninism and Soviet influence. As pointed out in the general discussion of the Soviet approach to the Third World competition, Moscow reached the view that the revolutionary potential lay primarily within the armies in this region. The Kurds, of course, and the PLO are exceptions, but they are small in their potential when compared to the military elites of the Arab states. Moreover, clandestine techniques for penetrating the officer corps and for organizational leverage are Soviet strengths. The Soviet leaders were, therefore, following a classical Leninist analysis of the prospects and effective tactics. In these three countries, however, they have failed. The local military leaders proved capable of taking Soviet support without allowing

Soviet cadres to gain the leverage necessary for Marxist-Leninist coups. The same was true in Somalia with Siad Barre's regime.

In South Yemen and Ethiopia, however, things worked out differently. Here the Soviet strategists took an opening created by war, seated their cadres in key positions, and captured the regimes. The same thing occurred in Afghanistan with the Taraki coup in 1978.

Both in the Horn of Africa and in the Iraq-Iran conflict, the Soviet Union took a flexible approach, playing both sides to the degree possible. Given the choice between the strategically more important Ethiopia and the less important Somalia, when it finally had to choose, Moscow sided with Ethiopia, but only because it was forced to do so. In the Iraq-Iran War, again Moscow played both sides, but the opening in Iran was never wide. Immediately after the shah's fall, the KGB worked hard to build up its clandestine networks, and the Tudeh party came out of cold storage to reenter politics in Tehran. A little-noticed but important turn of events hurt the Soviet position in Iran very seriously. A KGB officer defected to the British, and he brought extensive knowledge of the Soviet clandestine structure. This information apparently made its way to the Khomeini regime, allowing it to neutralize these growing Soviet assets. Since that time, both suspicions between Tehran and Moscow and the lack of Soviet penetrations have worked against growing Soviet influence in Iran. In 1987–88, when the U.S. Navy provided escorts to Kuwaiti ships, Iran tried to drum up a new relationship with Moscow. The initiative went nowhere, probably because Moscow understood that it could not exploit the opening effectively with such a weak clandestine infrastructure. Khomeini would have the best of the deal. Moscow's interests in good relations with the United States at the time also may have played a role. And, to be sure, Iran's Islamic revolution was not something the Tudeh party or the KGB could easily use, especially given its adverse impact on the Muslim peoples in the Soviet Union.

The Soviet threat to the region, objectively, has been twofold. Moscow could have invaded with military forces, and there were signs in the early 1980s that such a contingency was at least considered in planning a strategy for Iran. Thereafter, this prospect has not been serious, and, given internal Soviet affairs, particularly incipient civil war in the Muslim regions of the USSR, it can be discounted for the foreseeable future.

Second, through diplomacy and military sales, Moscow could still pursue the old military coup tactic. Although it has not worked in Iraq, Syria, Somalia, and Egypt, Soviet initiatives for establishing diplomatic relations with Saudi Arabia and other moderate Arab states suggest that it has not been abandoned in the late 1980s. Moreover, the Soviet ties to the radical movements—the PLO and its various affiliates and related splinter groups as well as Libyan operatives—provide forces for creating disorders, intimidating Arab governments, and radicalizing the political situation in vulnerable states. The Iranian Revolutionary Guards in 1979 showed signs of having acquired Marxist-Leninist tactics in many of their activities, tactics they undoubtedly picked up from radical Arab groups who had learned them from the Soviets, or maybe even directly from Soviet agents. The problem with these forces, however, is that they are difficult to control. Given the choice of an approach like the one it enjoyed in Ethiopia or one in which it depends on these groups for creating a crisis and a political opening, the Soviet Union has traditionally preferred the former.

The main point to underscore here is that Soviet means for competition in the Middle East–Southwest Asia region have included a different set of instrumentalities than they have in the Central American region. The indigenous political and military realities are different, Soviet access is different, and peasant-based insurgencies do not figure significantly in most of the region.

For all of Moscow's efforts, the Soviet strategy has enjoyed only mixed success. It has allowed Moscow to be a major factor in the region, and it has earned the Soviet Union large amounts of hard currency in arms sales. At the same time, it has not yielded permanent gains, or to use Soviet terminology, a significant improvement in the "international correlation of forces" for the "socialist camp."

Net Assessment

A net assessment of U.S.–Soviet competition in the Middle East–Southwest Asia region before the Gulf War must give the United States a significant edge in the late 1980s. In the late 1970s, Moscow was making a comeback after losing in Egypt. The string of coups—Afghanistan, Ethiopia, and South Yemen—and the growing Soviet military and naval presence in the region showed a Soviet willingness to go quite far in destabilizing the region and in taking its chances on achieving a strong position in the ensuing chaos. Furthermore, the U.S. inclination to pull back from the region in 1977—evidenced by a new arms transfer policy (which limited military sales to the region's moderates), the Indian Ocean arms talks and the conventional arms transfer talks with Moscow (which promised a reduction of U.S. naval presence), and greater emphasis on nonproliferation in the case of Pakistan (which soured the U.S.-Pakistani bilateral relationship)—seemed to open the way for this new Soviet strategy. These U.S. policies conveyed the impression to the moderate states in the area that the United States was withdrawing west of Suez, following the earlier British exodus.

The fall of the shah in Iran was another blow to the U.S. position. While it did not increase Soviet influence there, it reduced U.S. regional presence, having a net effect favorable to Moscow.

The Soviet invasion of Afghanistan, however, catalyzed a reversal of the trends. It generated a political consensus in the United States to back a reassertion of U.S. influence, including military presence in the region. In a short time, Arab states, the PRC, and the United States were cooperating in support of the Afghan resistance to the Soviet military presence. The events in Ethiopia and South Yemen have not been smooth for the Soviet Union, and Moscow has paid the price of retaining control over these client states. Chaos in Lebanon, Israeli military losses in Lebanon, the Iraq-Iran war, and the drift in U.S. diplomacy on the peace process would seem to have reopened opportunities for great Soviet influence, but Moscow was not able to exploit them.

The 1980s, therefore, have witnessed a large shift in favor of U.S. influence and a reversal of some of the Soviet gains in the late 1970s. Moreover, the apparent U.S. victory in the global East-West competition has effectively yielded a victory for U.S. influence in this region as well. The fruits of that victory, however, are not proving sweet. Let us, therefore, examine what they may be.

The Post–Cold War Era and the Iraqi Crisis

The U.S.–Soviet competition in the Middle East, as well as in other regions, provided a considerable degree of stability. Neither side was inclined to let its clients draw it into a war that could expand and upset the overall strategic military balance. The demise of that competition, therefore, loosens the constraints on regional powers.

One can argue that, had the Cold War not ended, Moscow would never have permitted Iraq to invade Kuwait. Whether Soviet influence was really that great is questionable, but it remains a serious argument.[70] What is indisputable, however, is that, had the Cold War still been active when Iraq invaded Kuwait, the dangers of escalation into a world war would have been immeasurably greater. Among Pentagon war games, one of the few scenarios that has reliably pushed players for both the United States and the Soviet Union to direct hostilities has included an Iraqi invasion of Kuwait. The United States players cannot accept it, and the Soviet players cannot abandon their client. Although war games cannot be trusted as wholly valid projections of how states will behave, they have a fairly impressive record of revealing the structure of choices and consequences. In this case, the scenario suggests that we are extremely fortunate that the invasion occurred after the Cold War. The other argument remains, however, that the end of the Cold War made the war possible. In either event, we are left with the conclusion that the decline of U.S.–Soviet competition has increased the volatility in the region.

The U.S. response to the Saudi request for military forces was in line with the Carter doctrine and the Reagan administration's reconfirmation of it. While the Carter doctrine was aimed primarily against an external military threat to the region, it implied preventing any regional power from upsetting the regional balance of power. The Reagan administration, by defending Kuwaiti shipping in the Persian Gulf, was preventing Iran from winning the war with Iraq and from throwing the regional balance into question. Henceforth, that implied feature of the Carter doctrine would be explicit. Thus President Bush's dispatch of large forces to Saudi Arabia falls within the Carter doctrine. It would have been an abrupt reversal of ten years of U.S. policy for him to have refused the Saudi request.

Bush's action has, however, more fully shifted the focus of the Carter doctrine onto the maintenance of the internal regional balance of power. Although the UN Security Council fully backed the U.S. actions, the reality is that the United States now has the primary responsibility for the balance. Other states may help or they may not. That is the major consequence of the end of the Cold War: new burdens with uncertain help from allies in carrying them.

The Soviet Union cannot be counted out of the region. Unless Moscow effectively lets the republics in the Caucasus and Central Asia secede from the union, disengaging from its domestic problems with

Muslim minorities, it will inevitably be forced to have concerns about the Middle East and Southwest Asia. Its concerns, of course, are already greatly changed. As opposed to expanding influence and acquiring new client states, the primary Soviet worry is with the possible meddling by states of this region in the civil wars in Muslim areas of the Soviet Union. As Soviet military and academic circles review the military security concerns for the USSR in the post–Cold War era, they are devoting considerable attention to the "threat from the south,"[71] and saying little about the "opportunities" to the south.

Another factor that will keep the Soviet Union concerned with the region is its improving relations with Israel and the surge of Soviet Jewish emigration to Israel. In turn, Israel is likely to see Moscow as an ally against the Muslim world. Thus the Soviet Union, far from withdrawing from the region, is in a chaotic process of altering dramatically its involvement. Moscow remained in the UN coalition against Iraq, but that cannot be taken as the final turn in the new Soviet strategy, and Moscow's eleventh-hour effort to obtain a cease-fire before the ground war with Iraq is evidence of the ambivalence in Soviet strategy. Additional turns are probable, and not all of them will be inexorably favorable to the United States. It is simply too early to judge how the new configuration of Soviet influence will settle out, but it is also difficult to imagine that it will not be greatly reduced.

An equally unsettling turn came with the Saudi decision to invite U.S. forces onto Arab territory. Traditional Saudi security policy included weakly compatible components. On the one hand, the Saudis paid for security by large fiscal donations to the radical Arabs—that is, blackmail money. On the other hand, they kept the U.S. security tie but insisted that the U.S. presence remain "over the horizon" so that charges of being lackeys of U.S. imperialism were more difficult to make. Bringing U.S. forces into Saudi Arabia has essentially destroyed that old security strategy. Not surprisingly, Saddam Hussein has leveled charges against Saudi Arabia about the American connection and has called on the spirit of pan-Arabism to mobilize all the publics in moderate Arab states against their governments for supporting this Saudi action.

It seems unlikely that Saudi Arabia and the smaller Gulf states could have moved back to the status quo ante, even if Iraq had withdrawn peacefully from all of Kuwait. The ruling circles in all of these states would be vulnerable to both internal and external political forces seeking revenge. And these forces could likely acquire considerable military means, especially if the Iraqi armed forces had remained intact.

As we observed earlier, U.S. strategy toward the region changed fundamentally from the Carter and Reagan approach when President Bush decided to build up U.S. forces beyond the level needed to defend Saudi Arabia. That change led inexorably to the war with Iraq, the liberation of Kuwait, and the destruction of the better part of the Iraqi military forces. In what sense was this really a change?

Throughout the 1980s, maintaining a regional balance of power had been the priority strategic objective, the primary U.S. interest. It took priority over U.S. interests in Iraq's human rights record, support of terrorism, and acquisition of chemical weapons. It took priority over punishing Iraq for having invaded Iran without provocation in 1980. It took priority over Kuwaiti attempts to play off the United States against the Soviet Union in reflagging Kuwaiti ships in 1987–88. In all of these cases, higher principle was subordinated to larger strategic purpose: no significant shifts of power, no expanded role of outside powers, no decisive military victory for either Iraq or Iran.

In destroying Iraqi forces in Kuwait and in carrying the air war to the whole of Iraqi territory, devastating the economy and the communications infrastructure, U.S. actions have upset the regional balance of power. The Iraqi regime, once counterbalancing Iran and Syria and holding together a socially, ethnically, and religiously fragmented population, is now enormously weakened. While it is too early to say with confidence what the pattern of destabilization in this part of the region will be, it is not too early to say that destabilization is highly probable. Let us consider some very tentative scenarios that it could take. They must be tentative because the new uncertainties created by the stunning military victory of the coalition forces probably have ramifications that will eventually surprise the best students of the region.

Iraq could fragment into three new states—one Shiite state in the south, a Kurdish state in the north, and a residual piece in the center, predominately Sunni in its religious makeup. Why would this be destabilizing for the region? First, the Shiite state in the south could be theocratic and a client of Iran. Such an outcome would be as big a gain for Iran as it could have hoped to achieve from victory in the Iran-Iraq War. United States strategy prevented that outcome during the war. Now U.S. strategy has made it conceivable.

Second, the Kurdish state in the north would create immense new problems for Turkey and Iran. Both would be inclined to interfere with its internal and external policies because of the large Kurdish populations in Turkey and Iran.

Third, Syria is unlikely to stand by, ignoring these developments. Its policies would certainly be directed to prevent the reemergence of a strong government in Baghdad.

The first of these developments, Iranian influence in southern Iraq, would threaten the security of Kuwait, Saudi Arabia, and the sheikdoms. Iran harbors no goodwill for the Saudi royal family or any of the other ruling families on the southern littoral of the Persian Gulf. Iranian policy toward these rulers will be a major problem in the best of outcomes, and a client state or population in southern Iraq would make it a severe problem, beyond the means of the other Gulf states to solve without assistance.

Iraq may not fragment. As of this writing, Saddam Hussein's future is uncertain, but he remains in power. He could survive and hold Iraq together with the Baathist party, or possibly a military successor to him could do the same. In either event, postwar Iraq would be weak and subject to meddling by Iran, Syria, and Turkey. Eventually, if it survives as a state, Iraq will begin selling oil, reconstruct its economy, and probably rearm its military forces. Its foreign policy, under Saddam or a successor, will hardly be devoted to maintaining regional stability. Revenge against the Saudi royal family and the sheiks is likely to be its primary goal. Since direct military action for many years will be out of the question, the new Iraq will probably attempt to use radical Arab organizations to achieve this goal.

Yet another scenario might be turmoil somewhat like that in Lebanon throughout the 1980s. In that event, all the problems of a fragmented Iraq would exist as well as additional ones caused by periodic fighting and social deprivations.

In all of these scenarios, internal war would be extensive. Even a consolidated Iraq under Saddam or a successor will continue to face some of the resistance that has erupted in the first weeks after the Gulf War. Moreover, Iran and other outside parties are likely to encourage it, especially if Saddam survives. U.S. assistance to Kurdish refugees in the north of Iraq could lead to a long-term U.S. presence there; withdrawal can hardly contribute to stability except through a reassertion of Saddam's dictatorship.

Beyond Iraq, instability is likely in Kuwait. Perhaps the emir and his family will reassert control and achieve something like the status quo ante. Alternatively, the Kuwaiti resistance groups who have demanded wider political participation could succeed in overthrowing the Saba family. Or a compromise might be reached, retaining the emir's rulership but with a more inclusive political system. In other words, there could be a struggle to create a democratic system, something that would inevitably bring periods of instability. The role of foreign workers could become a problem as well. In all of these eventualities except a full reversion to the status quo there is likely to be instability, and with it internal war.

Saudi Arabia and the sheikdoms may not go untouched by the impact of the Gulf War. The foreign military presence brought, for example, the spectacle of Western female military personnel without traditional dress performing jobs forbidden to Saudi women. As a result, a push occurred among some Saudi groups to raise the prospect of allowing Saudi women to drive automobiles. Satellite TV antennas became more numerous, allowing Saudis to see Western programs previously forbidden. Several other such disturbing things probably occurred which increased social and political demands on the regime.

The impact of the war on Jordan has been great, but its likely political consequences are difficult to anticipate. Greater anti-Americanism, however, has been visibly expressed. Egypt, Morocco, Tunisia, and Algeria all have survived public protests against the U.S.–led military coalition remarkably well. Yet the spectacle of high-technology foreign armies and air forces killing thousands of Arabs will probably remain indelibly etched on the minds of those publics. In the right times and circumstances, opposition political activists may well successfully evoke that image to create disorders. Conceivably, internal war could be the result.

In sum, the regional balance of power in the Persian Gulf area has been upset, and the prospects for internal wars have increased. Accordingly, the United States' larger strategic interest in the regional balance of power is threatened. The question for this analysis, of course, is whether the United States is more likely now to become involved in maintaining internal stability in any of these states and concomitantly to become involved in internal wars.

At this early stage after the war, the spring of 1991, it is too early to venture an answer. Possibly internal wars will be avoided or abbreviated. Perhaps the one now in progress in Iraq will be quickly ended. Possibly it will not, and possibly others will break out.

In any event, the United States will have to plan to deal with such contingencies. The most likely early decision it will face is the kind and level of forces to leave in Saudi Arabia and possibly in Kuwait. In the best event, residual U.S. forces could lower the prospects of an internal war, standing as insurance for the incumbent regime as it deals effectively with the pressures generated by the Gulf War. In the worst event, they could find themselves inexorably drawn into an internal war. If all ground forces are withdrawn and no scheme for frequent deployments made, U.S. influence on the internal stability of its allies will be nil, and the probability of hostile successor governments will increase.

The range of uncertainties is so great in the aftermath of the Gulf War that all of the foregoing speculation could prove wide of the mark. The level of regional instability could rise dramatically, change little at all, or decline. From the vantage point of the spring of 1991, however, it is difficult to see how it could decline and easy to see how it could rise. Thus, at this point, the betting would have to be on a decline of political stability, greater likelihood of internal wars, and greater chances that the United States will be involved in them.

In the event the United States does become involved, it may or may not be disposed to insist on democratic development. Possibly the American public and the Congress could accept the view that traditional Arab societies have their own values and political customs which the United States should respect rather than try to change. And, to be sure, a few Americans would see the involvement as an amoral matter of realpolitik, actually opposing efforts at democratic development. Concern for oil supplies is likely to be shared by all parties to the U.S. debate. There are precedents for this kind of patience with client states. South Korea, for example, has been very slow in making progress toward democracy, and Taiwan, long dependent on the United States for military security, has only lately shown signs of expanding the political franchise to include broader parts of the society.

The issue of expanding political participation is more likely to come up early in these Arab states than it is in the American public concern. These regimes have long been repressing forces of change that would lead to greater demand for political participation. Modernization of their economies, both to produce oil and to spend the earnings, has brought social mobilization and clashes between traditional Islamic and Western values. Moreover, a U.S. military presence is bound to increase both mobilization and conflict. Any way we look at it, therefore, the issue of democratic political development will have to be faced sooner or later.

The Prospects for Political Development

We can get some idea of the nature of the challenge confronting Saudi Arabia, Kuwait, and the sheikdoms merely by applying cursorily some of the concepts used in the case studies of the Central American states. For example, we can consider to what degree the preconditions for democracy are present.

Economic. Wealth is not a problem for these states, except that they perhaps have too much of it. How they use it is another matter, but among Third World states they stand apart as wealthy giants. For years to come, they can count on large oil revenues.

If there is a connection between economic development and democracy, then we ought to see the wealth, to the degree it becomes more diffuse in these states, as generating classes and groups who demand a greater political role. Thus, the availability of wealth is no impediment to democracy in these states, but its distribution could be.

Social. Traditional feudal, religious, and tribal institutions are the mainstays of these states. The concept of the state is patrimonial and jealously guarded as such. The nomadic tribesmen have been encouraged to keep their traditional life style and herding practices, even paid off to do so. The quid pro quo is that they remain politically quiescent. Slowly a class of indigenous intelligentsia and bureaucrats has emerged, increasingly displacing the foreign experts who have long played a role as surrogates for this class. Additionally, the size of the foreign labor population is quite large and wholly excluded from political participation. The society in Saudi Arabia is thus both bifurcated and fragmented: bifurcated between a small privileged ruling elite and miniscule intelligentsia on the one hand and the indigenous tribesmen and foreign workers on the other; fragmented along tribal lines and between foreigners and indigenous population.

The state institutions have both strengths and weaknesses, and neither are conducive to democracy. Oil wealth has contributed to this predicament. As Chaudhry explains in her study of Saudi Arabian responses to inflows of oil revenues, "The primary structural impact . . . is the dismantling of extractive institutions." The state bureaucracy is busy with handling the inflows of capital. Yet, as she argues, "Extractive institutions are the basis of administration, without which regulation and redistribution are impossible."[72] When the sharp decline in oil revenues occurred in 1983, the state bureaucracy proved virtually incapable of shifting to the task of devising economic austerity policies. Privileged business cliques were able to constrain the bureaucracy, and the absence of local private organizations to protect the interests of the lower economic stratum and foreign workers left those groups vulnerable to the bureaucracy's discretion.

The point here is threefold. First, while there are private business groups, they, like their Central American counterparts, are part of the statist economy. They are not outside the state and participating in a political process to influence it. Thus they do not contribute to democratic political development but rather impede it. Second, the groups which otherwise might play a political participatory role are traditional tribal and kinship groups, not modern interest-aggregating institutions. Third, the state's local administration is weak in its capacity to monitor and regulate local economic activity and collect taxes. This applies both the Saudi subjects and to foreign businesses and workers. According to Chaudhry, the state bureaucracy cannot even gather adequate statistics to follow such activities, much less regulate them.

The police and security forces are another matter. All of these regimes have placed great emphasis on the instruments for repressing antigovernment activity. Saudi Arabia in particular, because it must host the annual pilgrimages to the Islamic holy places, has developed an impressive capacity for crowd and population control.

The situation probably varies among the smaller sheikdoms but not in its larger contours. The social structure and institutions essential for a stable democratic system simply do not exist. Instead, we find fragile bureaucracies, practiced at distributing inflows of foreign capital but largely incompetent at other kinds of administration. Parallel to this development we find a strong police and security system, one wholly intolerant of the kind of organizational activity required for moving toward democracy.

External. The Ottoman Empire long ruled this region. When it collapsed, British and French influence prevailed. The British had backed Arab insurgents against the Ottomans. The impact of the British, however, was small compared with the private oil companies that developed the peninsula's major oil fields. Because American companies played the primary role, American influence has been large. Since the collapse of the Ottoman Empire and especially with the growth of oil wealth, these states have scrupulously tried to control and limit the impact of external influences on the indigenous populace. And to a large degree they have succeeded. Traditional Islamic customs and practices have survived behind the barriers contrived to limit Western commercial and cultural influences. Perhaps the presence of foreign laborers in large numbers is affecting these societies, but we know little about it.

External factors certainly cannot be said to have promoted democratic values. The rather numerous American and large degree of other Western business influences in the post-World War II decades have merely brought a clash between modern bureaucratic organizations and the traditional society—a clash that is far from resolved and that must result in an inevitable showdown, however long it is consciously postponed by the leadership.

Cultural. Two kinds of cultural attributes in these states work against democratic development. First, both the rulers themselves and the tribesmen at the bottom of society hold dear the feudal traditions and ways of life. The rulers show little inclination to change this situation voluntarily. How the tribesmen feel is difficult to know, but they certainly have not been effective in expressing demands for change.

Second, the culture is Islamic, and, as Huntington notes, Islamic societies have proven highly resistant to democracy. Moreover, pan-Arabism, with its Islamic cultural base and its concept of political loyalties, is a force against the modern secular and democratic state.

Building democracy in these cultural conditions is hardly promising. Given the experiences of Turkey and Pakistan, two Islamic cultures that have tried with mixed results, one cannot expect a rapid and successful move to democracy in any of these Persian Gulf states. Recently liberated Kuwait may try. As long as returning members of the emir's family remain determined to reimpose as much of the old order as possible, conflict and repression are more probable than democracy. An enlightened Kuwaiti leadership, however, might make that country an exception. The Gulf War has caused a discontinuity in the Kuwaiti political system, which could change it fundamentally.

Of the four preconditions, then, only one—economic growth—can be said to favor evolution toward democracy in these states. Moreover, the character of economic development is unique in that it is not built on a large private market sector. Rather the economies are better described as highly statist with the bulk of the economic resources in the hands of the state and its bureaucracy. A private commercial sector is not developing on a scale that could equal the government-owned oil production in economic importance. Given these special characteristics of economic development, it is fair to say that perhaps all four preconditions for democracy are missing.

Instead of the preconditions for democracy, it might be more accurately observed that the preconditions for praetorianism and internal wars prevail. That is the conclusion one would be inclined to reach if political development theory is a reliable guide to the dynamics of change in these states.

To be sure, a close empirical examination, especially of Saudi Arabia, might reveal factors that promise more optimistic outcomes. The fragility of these states has long been noted by Western political scientists and policymakers, and some worried that they might fall much earlier in the face of internal upheavals. Yet they have managed, albeit with some highly repressive measures of rule.

The combination of massive wealth and wise political leaders might well allow these states to remain stable and to develop along a unique political path, adapting traditional values and institutions to the requirements for modern institutionalization. Even in this event, authoritarian rule would seem to be required for many years. An abrupt move to a broad-based electoral political system would surely release sharply destabilizing forces, which would come not only from the indigenous population but also from the large number of foreign laborers.

Implications for U.S. Involvement

Before August 1990, the U.S. strategy of maintaining a regional balance of power did not run significant risks of involvement in domestic political development and internal wars. It did, of course, risk involvement in regional interstate war, but that has always been the risk required to implement the balance of power strategy.

When the United States responded to the Saudi request for military forces in early August and as it secured UN–backed economic sanctions against Iraq, the risks changed only marginally for the United States. Keeping U.S. military forces in Saudi Arabia, certainly at much reduced levels after several divisions of weapons and equipment had been brought to Saudi Arabia and stored so that a quick regeneration of large ground and air forces was possible, would have added to the pressures within Saudi society for political development and wider participation.

Some specialists in Arab politics would probably argue that this small military presence would sooner or later have caused domestic political instability in Saudi Arabia. Perhaps, but it would have been only a small cause among many others. Alternatively, it might have spurred progressive political development that increased stability. The U.S. presence could have reassured the regime, serving as a kind of security safety net and allowing it to be more venturesome in political reform. Political instability is probably coming to the small traditional monarchies on the Gulf littoral in any event. A U.S. military presence, in that event, could limit the degree of radicalization by successor regimes. Whatever its outcome, the deployment of U.S. forces there marked the crossing of a boundary between virtually no U.S. involvement and significant involvement in local political development.

That boundary, however, pales by comparison with the implications of the next boundary that was crossed. Subordinating the Carter-Reagan strategic aim, a regional balance of power, to the liberation of Kuwait, a matter of high principle, required military action that has destroyed the most significant parts of the Iraqi military, unleashed new political forces in Kuwait and Iraq, thrown the future territorial integrity of Iraq into question, created an opening for Iranian influence in southern Iraq, left the Kurdish region of Iraq in chaos, and probably set in motion several other destabilizing developments.

The United States could try to reestablish the regional balance by sponsoring political stability in Iraq and Kuwait, or only in Kuwait. This would be an enormous expansion of commitments, and the risk of involvement in internal wars would be very high. The temporary U.S. presence in northern Iraq to help Kurdish refugees could be the first step onto this slippery path.

Alternatively, the United States could retire to its prewar posture in Saudi Arabia and ignore the instabilities in Iraq, Kuwait, and elsewhere. This would require Saudi cooperation which may not be forthcoming now that Iraq's military is weak. Eventually, if the instabilities portended growing threats to Saudi security, standing aside might not be a viable approach. Again, the risk of involvement in an internal war is high.

The crux of the matter lies in the change in U.S. strategy. Deploying forces to Saudi Arabia marginally increased the longer term risk of involvement in an internal war, mainly in Saudi Arabia or in the sheikdoms. Going to war with Iraq, by contrast, virtually ensures U.S. involvement in several internal wars unless Washington is willing to stand aside and let the unleashed forces travel their course unchecked.

In other words, by shifting from a strategy of balance of power to a strategy of regional dominance by military power, the United States has made its involvement in internal wars much more probable. Shifting back to a balance of power strategy may be attempted and may succeed, but it does not look easy at this point. And involvement in internal wars looks almost certain unless the shift is successfully and quickly made.

Case Assessments Conclusion

Our three cases were selected because they are countries with internal wars in regions and locations of strategic significance to the United States. Other parts of the Third World also have strategic significance, but three—Central America, the oil-producing parts of Southwest Asia and the Middle East, and the Philippines—stand out as having a clear claim on a higher strategic priority. The United States could readjust its international commitments and reduce even these areas to lesser significance—the Philippines in particular and perhaps even the Southwest Asian region—but the present U.S. strategic posture in the world depends on significant American influence in these regions. This means that if we choose to walk away from any of the three case study states, we do so at certain risks. Although we may want to consider that option for analytical purposes, in drawing conclusions, we should be clear that these are not involvements of marginal consequence over a decade or so. In the short run, adverse consequences might not be great, but in time the costs to the United States could be considerable.

Internal War versus External War

All three cases make abundantly clear that these countries not only are immersed in internal wars but also have complex external coalitions backing each side in the internal conflict. The FMLN and the URNG have been receiving critical support from Nicaragua, Cuba, and the Soviet Union. Some other countries may actually be involved. (North Koreans, East Germans, and Bulgarians were found in the Soviet embassy in Grenada, for example, when the U.S. invaded. Similar surprises probably await exposure in Nicaragua and Cuba, perhaps even with the leadership of the FMLN and the URNG.)

The U.S. participation is at the invitation of the host government. It is entirely within the limits of international law. Cuban and Nicaraguan involvement, and indirectly Soviet involvement, has violated international law. Here the United States finds itself with a handicap that comes from its strong tradition of viewing war as primarily an interstate phenomenon. Nicaragua and Cuba are not formally at war with El Salvador or with Guatemala. Therefore, the United States accepts that formality as a limitation on its own geographical scope of operations.

It can be immediately objected that the United States has not respected Nicaragua's territory because it has supported the Contra insurgency against the Sandinistas. That is indeed true, but it is also true that U.S. support for the Contras could not be maintained in the face of deeply seated American attitudes about participating in such internal wars. In other words, traditional views of interstate and internal warfare prevailed over a U.S. attempt to compete in the conflict on a transnational basis as the Soviet Union and its allies do. The Contra campaign proves precisely the point that the United States adheres in general to international legal traditions on warfare. Much genuine public opinion and key political opinion in the United States has made its case on a legal basis. International law has not been the only issue, to be sure. Contra and Sandinista human rights violations, elections, freedom of the press, and many other related issues have been central in the debate. Nicaraguan and Cuban public diplomacy and covert action have exploited these issues to the fullest extent, and in some instances the result has been very hurtful for U.S. policy. On the whole, the Nicaraguan and Cuban approach has been to play on the American traditional views of sovereignty and international law and the belief that the United States has historically abused those norms in Central

America. Against this apparently deplorable record, many Americans are persuaded that we should restrict our role in these states today. Perhaps it oversimplifies complex public opinion in the case of the Contras, but one is encouraged to infer that many Americans believe we can right past wrongs in our international behavior if we now respect Nicaragua's sovereignty and borders no matter how the Sandinistas behaved toward their neighbors. To be sure, the new regime in Nicaragua makes this case more a matter of history, but the analytical point still stands.

It might also be objected that U.S. aid to the Afghan insurgency and to Savimbi in Angola are examples to the contrary, examples proving that international legal norms are really not very important in U.S. policy. But do they? A political consensus for support to Savimbi was never very strong, and the Reagan administration probably was able to provide it without drawing criticism because the Contras and other problems gave the detractors so many better political targets that they simply did not have time to make a big issue of Savimbi. Afghanistan is another matter. It is indeed an exception, a major exception and a most instructive one. Why were we able to keep up the consensus for that support? Clearly the Soviet invasion—a clear and brutal violation of Afghan sovereignty—inflamed public opinion. It was easy to keep up the public belief that the Soviet invasion morally justified our support. It may, however, turn out that the NPA, the FMLN, and the URNG, if any or all prevail in their struggle for power or as they continue their hostilities for a few more years, perpetrate no fewer inhumanities than those committed during the Soviet occupation of Afghanistan. Yet the way they execute these brutalities is designed, to the degree possible, to leave no basis for a popular American consensus for employing our power to stop the external contributions to these internal wars. In reality they are in considerable part foreign invasions, although not in their outward appearance.

Law, both domestic and international, presumably is meant to provide norms of just conduct that can regulate behavior, notwithstanding the varying levels of moral indignation that violations prompt. If we fall back on the argument that we can participate in internal wars on an illegal transnational basis when the U.S. public is sufficiently outraged to sustain such action, are we really sure that this is an adequate basis for our foreign and military policies? Certainly moral outrage is a critically important factor in our policy. To try to ignore it would be to overlook an important factor in the objective equation of the international balance of power. Moral outrage must be part of any so-called realpolitik calculation.

Some students and practitioners of balance of power policy, such as George Kennan and Henry Kissinger, may disagree, as they frequently have, by insisting that passion in public opinion should have no role in realpolitik. If they do, they have forgotten Clausewitz, who started his rational analysis of war with the recognition that the "passion of the nation" provides the energy for war. The cabinet and the general staff should try to give it purposeful direction, but they would be without power to conduct a war if the nation were not impassioned to destroy the opponent by violent means.

One does not have to give up the importance of the moral factor to argue that standards of international practice ought to have a more solid basis than the winds of public indignation stirred up by the hot breath of the media. The media is quite capable of overlooking great crimes abroad—atrocities, violations of international law, and the like. The UN Charter and the tendency to place primary value on "peace" at the expense of "justice" in defining when it is proper to resort to war have made it exceptionally difficult to handle the Central American cases within a legal context. Cuba, the Soviet Union, and Nicaragua have provided more than adequate objective behavior to serve as a casus belli. Yet the presumption of the law seems to be strongly on the side of not recognizing a casus belli in the Central American cases.

There would seem to be no reason why the United States could not develop an equally legal basis for supporting Pakistan in its aid to the Afghan insurgency. After all, the Soviet forces invaded. The same is true in Cambodia and in a number of other states. The United States might choose not to try to use international law in such a way. We might decide that we do not have adequate resources or security interests for all such wars. The main point is that the Leninist transnational concept of interclass conflict need not have a free ride in exploiting international law to constrain the exercise of U.S. power in protecting and furthering its foreign policy interests, in particular the fostering of the development of democracy.

Understanding the external dimensions of internal wars and trying to adapt the norms of international law better to support justice in such conflicts will provide no panacea for U.S. policy in competing with the Soviet Union, Cuba, and other Marxist-Leninist states in these wars.

Such efforts, however, could make it easier for the United States to apply its power in more effective ways in such struggles.

The Sandinista loss of the elections in Nicaragua could be seen as invalidating much of this argument. It might be asserted that to have acted on the basis of Nicaraguan support to the FMLN and URNG as a casus belli would have preempted the developments of the spring of 1990 and that the results would have been much less desirable. That may well have turned out to be true, but the free elections in Nicaragua did not arise from a Sandinista change of ideology and purpose. They came as the result of a successful set of actions by the United States and Central American governments. The Arias plan in fact placed considerable emphasis on the "external" aspects of the "internal" wars in Central America. And that is the crux of the argument here: recognizing and taking into account the external connections.

Far more critical for the change of leadership in Nicaragua was the U.S. diplomatic action with the Soviet Union. Throughout 1989, the Department of State put considerable pressure on Moscow to stop its support for the Central American insurgencies. In the fall, U.S. intelligence detected several cases of a step-up in supply of weapons, including the introduction through Nicaragua of SA-7 air defense missiles (hand-held small missile launchers that can hit low-flying aircraft, particularly helicopters). President Bush confronted General Secretary Gorbachev directly on these actions during the Malta summit on December 2, 1989, demanding that they stop. It seems he made Gorbachev realize that U.S.–Soviet cooperation would not become what Gorbachev wanted without a significant change in Soviet support for these insurgencies. The Soviet response was detected on December 7, when a Soviet ship carrying helicopters to Nicaragua was ordered to return to port in the USSR.[73]

The change in Soviet policy clearly undercut the staying power of the Sandinistas on their old policy course. Denied both materiel and diplomatic support from Moscow, they had to devise a new one, and it led to their electoral defeat.

This episode demonstrates the efficacy of attacking the external connections. As we have suggested earlier, diplomacy and media attention should by all means be used before a resort to military force. In this particular case, U.S. leverage with the Soviet Union was remarkably high given Gorbachev's policies on other aspects of East-West relations, an exception to the rule. It may have been higher in the past than

U.S. policymakers believed, but they seldom have staked enough on the U.S.–Soviet relationship to determine if it was higher than conventional wisdom suggested.

The game is not yet over in Central America, however, because the Soviet Union is not the only external factor in the internal wars there. Cuba still shows little enthusiasm for Gorbachev's perestroika, and international organizations can still provide a modicum of financial and political support to radical insurgent movements in the region.

Political Development and Praetorianism

In all three of our case studies, we have seen vivid examples of what Huntington defined as praetorianism, not simply military intervention in politics—although it includes that—but a struggle by a dictator or oligarchy to resist with force the expansion of political participation. In all three of the cases, praetorianism has for the moment been abandoned in a formal sense for democratic governmental forms. Guatemala, which has been trying democracy in the past five years, has virtually no experience with anything but praetorianism since the end of Spanish colonial rule. The same is true for El Salvador, although the oligarchy kept the army out of power until quite late, 1932. In both states, however, social mobilization without sufficient institutional development to permit political participation placed great stress on the regime. In its own particular fashion, each resorted to repression rather than expanded participation. Repression, of course, required growing dependence on the military. That allowed the military to share, at times monopolize, the power.

The Philippine case looks somewhat different because American rule for forty years imposed democratic forms, even some democratic traditions, on top of the Spanish colonial patterns. The institutionalization for democracy—a free press, professional and labor organizations, political parties, and the like—appears better developed in the Philippines. In particular, the military officer corps is schooled in the view that the military should stay out of politics, something not true in Central America at all. The Marcos period, however, showed how easily the old Spanish patterns could reemerge. The landed oligarchy held power but was seriously challenged by the déclassé Marcos. His system of patron-client vertical integration actual undercut the traditional patterns of power in the Philippines, much as the peasant uprisings in

El Salvador allowed the army to undercut the traditional pattern and force the oligarchy to share power.

In none of the three cases has the urban sector created a political challenge of critical importance to the ruling elite. Although all three states have urban sectors that have grown dramatically since World War II, they are far from what Huntington calls the "urban breakthrough" which makes the transition to democracy more likely. The effort in both El Salvador and Guatemala to introduce a democratic system naturally opens the door for a greater political role by the urban sector of society, but in both cases it is highly polarized. The business and commercial concerns are more interested in preventing the sharing of power with the labor unions and other groups than they are with instituting democratic legal norms. The leftist sectors of urban society are similarly less concerned with political reform than with preserving their power. The Christian Democrats in El Salvador, and to a lesser degree in Guatemala, have tried to play a positive role in support of democracy; but the legal front organizations for the guerrillas, some of the labor leadership, and a faction of the clergy have given up on democracy, if they were ever for it.

The same is true in the Philippines, but the experience of overthrowing Marcos has had a temporarily moderating impact on politics in Manila. The urban elites, including the clergy and the military, played key roles in making Aquino's election possible. The urban elites in El Salvador and Guatemala have not enjoyed this kind of exercise of power. It rests on delicate roots even in the Philippines because the political parties simply have no serious regional and local organization to allow urban-based political groups to enjoy a broader coalition including rural and regional support.

The first key unresolved problem in all three cases is the presence of a politically and economically powerful landowning elite which stubbornly resists land reform and genuine democratic political development. This social and economic condition—feudal in character, colonial in origin—stands as a major obstacle to progress in building democracy in all three countries. It blocks both economic development and the diffusion of economic power that is necessary for what Dahl calls "contestation" for moving to democracy. Landless peasants cannot participate effectively with virtually no hold on economic resources; neither can trade unions and other urban groups.

In many cases, particularly in Latin America, the regimes insist that they have a market economy based on private property. In some regards, this is true, but in others it is highly misleading. We have noticed in the case studies that the business and agricultural oligarchs dominate the government, often as incumbents. Protectionism and subsidies are extensive. The local economy is shielded from many market forces, especially those that would cause inefficient local enterprises to fail and allow new entrepreneurs a better chance to enter the economic competition. A number of observers have focused on this antimarket pattern, and it has been called "statism" by some. Indeed, it is.

While statism differs from the command administrative systems of the Soviet Union and Eastern Europe (until lately), it shares commonalities. State monopoly and subsidy in command economic systems beget inefficient allocations of capital. Statism creates some of the same inefficiencies. It does not throttle the petty shopkeeper and artisan the way East European systems have, but it does prevent the emergence of a private commercial and industrial sector responsive both to domestic and international "relative scarcities" in pricing and investment.

The large landowners, dependent on landless peasants as cheap labor, may have to be responsive to international commodity prices, but domestically they share much in common with the chiefs of the collective farm bureaucracies in Eastern Europe. Collective farmers are landless peasants. Both the Soviet and (to a lesser degree) the East European agricultural sectors need land reform as badly as the three states in the case studies. Here it is important to be more specific about what kind of reform. Because of the varying crops and types of agriculture in all of these states, a uniform pattern does not necessarily make sense. In all cases, however, private property based on individual ownership should be the aim. Other kinds of land reform—leasing or cooperative ownership—are unlikely to put resources directly into the hands of individuals and make them responsible for their use—not just economic use but also political use for contestation and political participation.

Breaking up large landholdings may well lead to a drop in overall agricultural production. The political and social gains, however, make it a drop worth taking. If small holdings are too inefficient for market conditions, the small holders can sell their land and seek other employment. In the aftermath of a major land reform, reaggregation into large holdings through sale and purchase probably will and should occur under market forces in some places. The important aspect of land reform is the diffusion of economic power away from state or statist control, creating a distribution of private economic power that can make a democratic political process truly competitive.

A second and parallel problem is the dominant role of the military in all three countries. In Guatemala, the military's dominance is long established and deeply rooted. In El Salvador, it is a twentieth-century phenomenon; nonetheless, it is deeply instilled. Reformist sentiments occasionally develop among the younger officers. Coming from lower social levels, the senior military should yield an occasional fanatic populist reformer. That has yet to happen in El Salvador or Guatemala. In the Philippines, although the military senior ranks became quite corrupt under Marcos, signs of a populist reform movement in the military were apparent. Moreover, West Point–educated General Ramos remained above corruption to help bring the military to Aquino's side in the struggle to overthrow Marcos. Whether Aquino can encourage and exploit reformist officers is a key question for her government's longevity and efficacy.

Two tendencies afflict the role of the military in all three countries. First, the insurgencies make it imperative that the military be strong, active, and successful in counterinsurgency operations. The military cannot be kept out of politics simply by taking away its resources and basis of power. Any ruler requires strong military power to survive in the internal war. Second, the insurgency gives the army a military mission that tends to pull it away from politics to the degree it takes that mission seriously. That has occurred in all three countries, first in El Salvador, next in Guatemala, and finally, since Marcos's fall, in the Philippines. This trend, however, cannot be taken for granted, and it is a modest trend to date. The more successful the military is, the less tolerant it is likely to be of the bickering and compromising that politics in the democratic structures require. The military could easily reassert itself to throttle democracy as counterproductive during an internal war.

Of these two problems—economic reform and the political influence of the military—the landed oligarchy's resistance to land reform is the most critical. With land reform, the insurgents in all three states would suffer a dramatic setback, probably irreversible in the near future. Removing the statist character of the industrial and commercial sectors must also be done. The second problem, how the military shares and uses political power, is only slightly less a problem for all three regimes.

The Philippine military tradition is more favorable in this respect, but it may be inadequate if the NPA begins to show capabilities of conducting large-unit operations and challenging the army successfully in pitched battles. The army might collapse for the lack of professional cohesion, or it might blame the civil government and decide that the only alternative is to take the political power in its own hands.

In the case of the two Central American armies, it is difficult to see how they can win the wars unless they play a larger but different political role—particularly a reforming role that includes imposing land reform. At the same time, neither has such a tradition beyond proclaiming support for reform and shortly abandoning all efforts to carry it through.

While all three regimes are experimenting with democracy, it is difficult to imagine that they will not have to fall back on some form of praetorianism as the insurgencies gain strength. The preconditions for democracy—economic, social, external, and cultural—are weak at best and highly adverse in most cases for all three countries. Other countries with more favorable preconditions have tried and failed at democracy. Still others, which have succeeded, required many decades for their leaders to make what Dankwart Rustow calls the "conscious political choice" to institute democratic decision making and many more decades for that decision to become fully internalized in the political system. In light of most of the findings in political development studies, therefore, viable and thriving democracies in El Salvador and Guatemala would indeed be a surprising outcome in the near future. The same is only slightly less true for the Philippines.

There is a possible exit from this seeming dead end for democracy in these states. Again it comes back to land reform. The creation of a fairly large class of small farmers through a sweeping land reform not only would be a blow to the insurgents but also would break the lock of the landowning oligarchs on the political system, and it would provide the diffusion of economic power that would permit effective political participation by this farming class in a democratic system. In the five patterns described for how democracies come to exist, let us recall Dahl's "free farmer society," the condition that he suggests explains in part the emergence of democracy in the United States, Norway, New Zealand, and a few other cases. He expresses doubt that this pattern has contemporary relevance today because of the compressed time schedule the modern world forces on political development. But if land reform created a class of free farmers in the three cases we have examined, why should they not be able to provide a basis for a preurban democracy? They would have to own their land, farm it for whatever return they could get in the private market, or sell it if they could not make an adequate income.

Overcoming statism in the industrial and commercial sectors of the economy is also important, and it should be no lower in priority than land reform. There is, however, an important difference. All parts of the world are not going to industrialize at the same rate, and many states will not be able to attract adequate capital for that purpose even with the best market conditions and free trade opportunities. Capital in many Third World states will not be attracted by market forces alone. In the 1970s large amounts of capital were transferred to Latin America not so much because of the market "pull" as because of the bankers' "push" to statist oligarchs and bureaucrats. Land reform is an option for all of these countries. Successful industrialization may not be.

The shift in political power which such an economic and social transformation through land reform and the destruction of statism would bring should also make it possible for modern political institutions to develop more effectively in the urban areas. At the same time, if economic development does not come rapidly, the small free-farming former peasant could resort to subsistence production and probably enjoy a better standard of living than he has today. The path to democracy through a society of free farmers may not, as Dahl believes, have lost its relevance to the Third World today. It is probably the best hope in some cases.

To put the predicament of these regimes in the context of the five political development goals, the sine qua non for the other four is stability, the maintenance of law and order. But these regimes cannot provide it for large parts of the population. It is not even clear that they try very hard. Economic growth for a time in the 1960s and the 1970s looked promising, but in retrospect it is clear that several forces would eventually slow it or even stop it. First, protectionism for local industry meant inefficient use of what scarce capital was available. Second, the easy availability of capital after the 1972 oil embargo, when the commercial banks undertook to recycle the large dollar accounts of the oil-wealthy Middle East states, allowed large numbers of ill-advised investments. Today, all three countries are suffering the foreign debt consequences of that development. Added to this structural predicament in the economies of all three states is direct foreign economic assistance. As Mancur Olson has pointed out, some economists have long known that government-to-government aid seldom has a significant positive impact on economic growth.[74]

Autonomy has been maintained by all three regimes, but to a significant degree El Salvador has had to yield some of its autonomy to U.S. advice. The Philippines stands second to Guatemala, which is the most autonomous vis-à-vis the U.S. The degree of autonomy is inversely related to the level of direct U.S. aid. The greater the aid, the greater the U.S. ability to play colonialist by ventriloquy. The insurgent control of some parts of the countries also marks a loss of regime autonomy. This is most advanced in the Philippines, least advanced in Guatemala. El Salvador stands somewhere between.

Social equity does not seem to be a serious aim of any of the three regimes, although perhaps Aquino's rhetoric and genuine sentiments are an exception. The one major step all three could take, one that would make the greatest contribution to social equity, would be massive land reform. It does not require foreign aid. It merely requires the political power to force through the reallocations. None of the three governments shows serious intentions or capabilities of carrying through on land reform. None of the regimes has the will or the power to displace the feudal landowning elites from their privileged grip on the economy and the society.

Finally, democracy in the form of competitive elections and legal opposition has been instituted formally in all cases. But the institutionalization necessary to give a large part of the frustrated public a meaningful participatory role simply does not exist. Democracy, therefore, is far from firmly rooted, and it is far from offering serious political competition to the insurgents. Elections have certainly caught the insurgent leader off balance and disoriented them temporarily, but the political parties in all cases have had only minimal institutional coherence and interelection organizational vitality. Their roots in the rural areas are extremely shallow; thus they are not yet serious competition for the insurgents in asserting influence over the electorate.

One of the most discouraging aspects of these cases is that the more aid a country seems to receive, the less well it does against the insurgents. Guatemala has received by far the least amount of foreign help; yet it has fought the insurgents most effectively. Aid, of course, is not the only variable in this outcome. The Guatemalan insurgents are the least integrated, the least unified on strategy and tactics; they are also farther from direct support—that is, from Nicaragua and Cuba. El Salvador's insurgents are much easier to supply directly from Nicaragua.

A similar correlation for economic performance appears to be true. El Salvador, the largest recipient per capita of direct economic assistance, is in the worst economic condition with the worst forecast. Guatemala and the Philippines, of course, do not enjoy rosy economic forecasts, but they have less intractable problems of population pressures, insurgent damage to the economy, and squandering of fiscal aid. The difference among the cases, to be sure, is small. Perhaps we should not draw final conclusions from it, but the implication is unmistakable: direct economic assistance does not help. It may even hurt. Foreign aid easily becomes a substitute for local taxation. Government expenditures can be covered with aid monies as taxes are evaded, stolen through corruption, or simply not collected because the insurgents keep the tax collectors away while levying their own taxes.

We do have evidence from another case that buttresses the argument about the perverse effects of direct aid. Chaudhry's study of Saudi Arabia and Yemen compares the different effects of the way capital flowed into those states. The oil revenues in the Saudi case are analogous to U.S. direct aid to El Salvador because they come through the Saudi government, which has full discretion on how they are distributed. The impact on local administration of the boom years, 1973 to 1983, for Saudi oil revenues was devastating. In the austerity years, 1983 to 1987, the Saudi "extractive apparatus" was unable to reassert itself. Chaudhry observes that "setting up an extractive apparatus is the most 'intrusive' and first economic act of the state, involving the centralization of the fiscal apparatus, territorial control, political and economic decisions about target groups, the acquisition of information, and the design and implementation of collection mechanisms and enforcement procedures." It is the core of governing. As she further observes, "Institutions for taxation spin off related agencies, leading to a diversification of the tools available to decision-makers." [75]

We also have the results of Lewis Snider's analysis of fifty-eight Third World debtor states.[76] Political capacity to tax, especially to levy direct taxes, was the best predictor of their likelihood of making foreign debt service payments, much better than lenders' judgments about the debtors' economic potential and economic management capabilities. The delinquent debtor is more inclined to borrow precisely because it can neither tax effectively nor limit political constituencies that treat public sector spending like an entitlement. Again, the evidence suggests that direct fiscal aid to governments is more politically harmful than helpful.

Admittedly, comparing the Salvadoran and Guatemalan cases without an extensive examination of how the aid monies are used in El Salvador leaves us with a circumstantial case. Chaudhry's close empirical study of the Saudi experience, however, and Snider's analysis of the political capacity of debtor states should give us greater confidence in the circumstantial evidence. Moreover, the author's own personal observations of the impact of aid in Vietnam drove him to the same conclusion. Senior leaders in the U.S. country team there were frustrated at the lack of administrative efficacy of government at local levels, but they were not at all receptive to the evidence that it might be the result of massive foreign assistance. Perhaps the most instructive evidence came from a former Viet Minh guerrilla who had joined the government's pacification effort at the village level. He wrote a long account of how a tenfold increase of revenue from the central government, given to support local security forces, had virtually destroyed the village administration and its control over local affairs. His conclusion about both the government in Saigon and in the provinces was simple and direct: a government which does not raise its own revenues is not the real government.

Transnational private capital need not have the same adverse impact on government. Chaudhry's study of the different ways in which capital flowed into Yemen is as instructive for the private sector as it is for the public sector in Saudi Arabia. In Yemen, the government stood apart from the inflows, which went directly into private hands. That wealth contributed to the growth of local institutions and taxation which redounded to the government's advantage in strengthening its local administrative capacity. How wealth comes into a country, therefore, makes a big difference. Where banks and companies come in and assess profitability in making their investments, and where they oversee them, the impact of foreign capital is positive for growth. This was true until the late 1970s in all three cases. The statist nature of their economies undoubtedly limited benefits to some extent, but the growth rates in all cases were quite good. The surge of petrodollars and irresponsible bank lending policies to the Third World, however, created quite another effect in the late 1970s and throughout the 1980s. And the sharp fall in international commodity prices is yet another factor that impacts heavily on all three cases, explaining in part their recent poor economic performance.

These two factors—excessive and ill-advised borrowing and the collapse of commodity prices—make the three cases exceptional. In different international economic circumstances, they might well have performed more effectively. They had done so previously. The effect of the large petrodollar loans on the economies in the 1980s, therefore, should perhaps be seen as exceptional, not as the rule. Major debt relief by the commercial banks could do a great deal to help the present situation, probably more than vast sums of government aid. No less important, of course, is the disentangling of commercial and banking sectors from excessive government influence.

However one looks at them, all three cases give little cause for optimism. There are no reforming Atatürks to save these systems from their own statist elites and the insurgents; nor is democracy providing participatory channels for enough of the population rapidly enough to build countervailing political forces to balance and eventually eliminate the dominant role of the oligarchs and the military. The urban sector in the Philippines is perhaps large enough to do this, but it is not politically organized in a fashion that would permit it to do so. If the new urban middle classes use the next year or so to build party organizations in the countryside, they might have a chance, but the evidence that they are trying, or that they even understand the importance of making the effort, is not encouraging.

The single most encouraging factor on the side of the governments in all three states is the relative incompetence of the insurgents. The Guatemalan insurgents are the weakest, the most fragmented, and the least challenging to the regime. In El Salvador, they have proven extremely tough and resilient when defeated and driven into the remote safe areas. Nonetheless, they have not worked effectively to build rural institutions, and they have at times committed awful political and military errors which the government forces exploited. In the Philippines, the insurgent forces are scattered and weak in many places, but their strategy and means of support are far more threatening to the government than those of the insurgencies in the other two countries. With or without foreign support, they can fight the government for a long time. The internal war in the Philippines is only beginning to expand its external dimensions.

Insurgent Ideology and Policies

Let us suppose that the insurgent movements in these three countries win the internal war and take power. Granted, the apparent withdrawal of Soviet support makes their victory improbable in the near future, but that is not the point here. Rather, for purely analytical purposes, let us assume the improbable. What would the consequences be for political and economic development? We have a considerable number of practical cases from which to infer the likely consequences. East Europe, China, Cuba, Vietnam, Cambodia, Laos, Ethiopia, South Yemen, and Nicaragua (until recently) are such examples.

In every case, Soviet-type institutions have been established. The number of landless peasants has been increased by the expansion of collective farming. The state bureaucracy has become all powerful. Economic development has been poor, and after an initial period, it has stagnated. Political mobilization has been expanded within a vast network of institutions and organizational devices to ensure that it can be controlled and directed but denied appreciable influence on policy-making.

In El Salvador and Guatemala, victorious insurgents would certainly destroy the old landowning elites. They would indeed cause a break with the old traditions of a feudal aristocracy. But the change would be less one of substance than form. The old elites would be replaced by a new oligarchy of party bureaucrats directing collectivized agriculture. The old latifundia are in effect precisely the same system in that they allow the oligarchs to extract wealth from the agrarian sector and reallocate it according to their own preferences.

In the urban and industrial sector, state planning would replace inchoate private enterprise. But it might not differ greatly from the old oligarchs' system of "import substitution"—that is, protected industry which is incapable of competing in world markets and which creates a drag on further industrial progress, and numerous other state mechanisms which protect business and industry from market forces.

The old militaries would be destroyed, but in their place new military elites would arise. If Nicaragua in the 1980s is an example of what to expect, then the military would expand enormously. The Nicaraguan armed forces have tanks, helicopters, artillery, and armored personnel carriers in significant numbers, making the Nicaraguan army qualitatively much more advanced than any other military in Central America. Tanks are nonexistent in the other armies. Artillery on a limited scale first appeared in the Honduran Army in 1983. Before that time, 60-mm mortars were the largest indirect fire weapon available. Even with U.S. aid, the El Salvadoran army has not come close to matching the armaments buildup in Nicaragua. In fact, the Nicaraguan military has fundamentally changed the military balance on the Central American isthmus.

Political freedoms would be no greater under ruling communist parties than at present in El Salvador and Guatemala, and their restriction would be more methodical and complete. The regimes in those countries today are unable to control the countryside and much of the urban society to the extent that communist regimes would. Death squads and terror by the present regimes are manifestations of weakness in control. Such terror would soon disappear under new regimes after initial destruction of the old elites and would be replaced by a more comprehensive and less visible spiritual terror. In many respects, the transition to communist systems would be more culturally congruent for these societies than would a transition to democracy in that the new regime would be so like the old—absolutist, dictatorial, and uncompromising in matters of politics and ideology.

Finally, war in the region would not cease. Victory in two more countries would only encourage further spread of internal war to Honduras, Costa Rica, Panama, and eventually Mexico.

What difference does it make for this forecast that communism is an admitted failure in the USSR, East Europe, and China? Does not the Gorbachev phenomenon mean that the insurgents will have to take on board some of the reformist tendencies in the Soviet Union?

The answer to this question is not easy, and two or three answers can be cogently offered. First, to all appearances, it looks as though Gorbachev himself has abandoned the "international class struggle" in his revised definition of "peaceful coexistence." [77] While he did not wholly disavow the "class approach," it was certainly given a back seat to all other Soviet policy concerns. Moreover, former Foreign Minister Shevardnadze had emphasized the new strategy and the new priority in Soviet foreign policy repeatedly in 1988 and 1989. Far more impressive than this change in policy pronouncements, however, has been Moscow's abandonment of the ruling parties in Eastern Europe: it has done nothing to prevent their collapse and has sometimes apparently encouraged their demise. It can be argued, nonetheless, that the events in Eastern Europe simply escaped Moscow's control, that they were not intended but merely accepted in light of the imperatives of Soviet internal politics combined with the aim of developing good relations with the West. To have supported them against mass resistance would have cost Moscow all of the good will that Gorbachev had worked so hard to build in the previous four years. The result, nonetheless, has been effective abandonment of the international class struggle.

As we learn more about what Gorbachev thought was possible through perestroika in 1985–88, it seems that he and several of his collaborators believed that a revitalization of the Soviet and East European political systems was possible without collapse or systemic change. Gorbachev has admitted that he misunderstood the extent of the economic problems in the Soviet "command administrative" system; he has confessed the same misestimate of the nationality problem within the USSR.[78] It might be a mistake, therefore, to assume that what has happened to the "international class struggle" was entirely intended by Gorbachev when he redefined "peaceful coexistence." Events have overtaken him in a way that makes it possible to misinterpret his initial ideological revisions.

A second kind of answer to the question of the impact of the failure of Soviet communism can be based on what we know of the official party line that Moscow was sending to Third World communist parties. Soviet strategy appears to have been aimed at lowering its material commitments to its clients, reducing the level of competition, consolidating influence in a smaller set of states, and altering the tactics of class struggle. As a former member of the Central Committee's International Department has reported in detail, foreign parties were being told to keep their political controls in place through well-trained party cadres while becoming less visible and less strident. Materiel support from Moscow would be minimal. These foreign parties were to find new ways of obtaining resources, including direct appeal to Western states for aid.[79] This guidance has been primarily for ruling parties, but the same general line has been given the nonruling parties. In other words, the insurgents have been told that they must find ways to extract resources on a larger scale from foreign capitalist societies and from societies where they are fighting for power. A general shift in this direction, of course, was already evident in the mid- and late 1970s.

This answer, of course, could be accurate about Soviet policy intentions but wrong about the Soviet capacity to make it work, just as seems to have been the case with domestic policies where intentions and consequences have diverged dramatically. The cascading events of perestroika have overtaken these policy guidelines of the mid- and late 1980s. It should be remembered, however, that considerable direct military assistance was still flowing to Nicaragua as late as December 1989. Notwithstanding Shevardnadze's proclamations in 1988, assistance to insurgencies at some level was continuing.[80]

A third possibility is that Gorbachev is trying to end the Third World competition, but he will not be able to make the new policy stick. Eventually perestroika will fizzle; the reformers will be unable to deliver anything that captures either mass or party support; and the conservative party bureaucrats will belatedly try to restore control, perhaps over a territorially reduced Soviet Union, and reaffirm a commitment to the international class struggle, albeit at considerably reduced levels of support. The reassertion of conservative party attitudes at the Twenty-eighth Party Congress in July 1990 is evidence that Gorbachev's ideological revisions have not been wholly internalized, particularly on the issue of international class struggle. However, the conservatives have been unable to sustain their political comeback of the fall and winter of 1990–91, so the probability of this scenario is very low.

It is unlikely that Moscow could bring the insurgencies in Central America to a halt unless it throttles Cuba in the process. What Gorbachev may lack in enthusiasm for the international class struggle, Castro stands ready to make up for with his own fervor and commitment. To a large extent, these insurgencies have developed with only belated Soviet support, actually almost none in the 1970s. In the Philippine case, the NPA policy has been to remain independent of foreign support—not to reject it entirely but not to become dependent on it. In this respect, it is like the Maoist party in China from the late 1920s onward. Marxist-Leninist in much of its ideology and strategy, it nonetheless developed its own variant of tactics and its own resource base.

In the Central American cases, the Soviet-Cuban connection has allowed significant direct control of the leading cadres. As our analysis of the Soviet approach to spreading revolution revealed, this technique of a coup within the leadership of a movement is what the Soviets are best at doing. They have no good record of actually leading insurgencies. Their prospects for such leadership control in Central America, of course, depend on Cuban cooperation, but, with Cuba's dependency on Soviet material assistance, Moscow can probably hold some lever-age over the insurgent leadership. In the Philippines this seems much less likely. The NPA has reportedly turned down direct Soviet offers of support. As the struggle proceeds, however, the NPA could change its mind, and Soviet techniques for seizing the leadership could prevail. Whether Soviet control would prove more effective than it did over the Chinese Communist party or the Vietnamese is doubtful, but in the international arena the NPA and Moscow might find a strong common interest in reducing U.S. influence in the region.

A significant part of the structure now in place to provide the exter-nal dimension of support for these internal wars is likely to be able to survive and operate for the indefinite future. In other words, it is built for long wars—years and decades. U.S. diplomacy toward Moscow in 1989, especially at the Malta Summit, and U.S. success in forcing the Sandinistas to accept free elections have certainly dealt the external dimension a serious blow. It is probably too early, however, to declare a clear-cut U.S. victory. The insurgents have not lost all their cards.

In its approach to the competition, the Soviet Union has not antici-pated these opportunities in Central America by farsighted calculation. In fact, Moscow fell in behind the insurgents belatedly. The build-ing of cadres and infrastructure, however, goes back for decades. The source of Marxism in Central American politics can be traced to the Comintern (1919–43). The Cuban revolution gave it new energy, new support. The indigenous political systems stubbornly resisted demo-cratic political development, and the United States did not push them until recently with any serious pressure. When Soviet officials say they do not export revolution—which Gorbachev said during his visit to Cuba—they are technically correct: the conditions for conflict are in-digenous. They have exported cadres, resources, and tactics, and thus played a significant role in these insurgencies. But changing domestic politics suggests the role is declining sharply. If the insurgents win, however, the Soviet model will provide the institutional patterns for governing.

The appeal of these patterns need not be wholly ideological. Practical considerations play perhaps a stronger role. Ruling these fragmented and poorly developed societies would be a challenge for anyone, and the Soviet model offers techniques for imposing stability against the strongest kinds of centrifugal and fragmenting political and economic forces. Stability, of course, is a key political development goal. Without it, the others cannot be pursued successfully. The Soviet model has a good record of stability in the early post-revolutionary stage. That is its practical appeal. The insurgents have little choice but to accept it if they expect to keep the power they have won.

This understanding of the nature of Soviet influence is important as an antidote to wishful thinking about possible democratic evolution after a fitful try at revolutionary dictatorship by victorious Marxist-Leninist insurgents. The events of 1989 in Eastern Europe do not change this judgment. Those regimes resisted systemic reform for more than forty years and yielded to it only on direction from Moscow. Soviet control over victorious insurgents in Central America would be inadequate to achieve the same results in the event Soviet leaders tried to assert it. The major change in El Salvador, Guatemala, and the Philippines, if these insurgents were to win the power, would be a mere rotation of elites—much bloodletting, as occurs frequently in such violent changes of power, followed by the installation of a much more stable dictatorship and a long period of economic stagnation and poverty. The social structure would not change significantly. Landless peasants would continue to be the majority. The military would retain its central role, and an oligarchy of new elites would hold the power.

The United States and Its Policies

The reputation of fostering neocolonialism, of supporting right-wing dictatorships, and of perpetrating massive injustices on the impoverished masses of the people in these three cases is not wholly deserved by the United States. Certainly its indifference in the past has not been above reproach, but, since the Carter administration and throughout the Reagan administration, the United States has been the strongest proponent of democracy in all these countries. This is not to undervalue the seriousness of Duarte and Aquino as democratic leaders; it is to judge the means they have at their disposal. Duarte would have never been elected without U.S. demands for free elections, and the U.S. role in the transfer of power from Marcos to Aquino was not trivial. Cerezo Arévalo in Guatemala probably would not have come to power if the United States had not withheld most of its aid from the country before it introduced democratic government.

The United States has exerted its power in favor of democracy in each case with considerable effect. While all human rights violations

have not disappeared, the number has dropped in response to U.S. pressures. These positive achievements look temporary at best, however,
not likely to survive the day when massive U.S. aid no longer pays the
local elites to play by our democratic rules. The Philippines may be an
exception in this regard, but not the other two. In fact, much of U.S.
assistance is undercutting U.S. goals.

Let us first consider military assistance. Where the United States has
been most deeply engaged, the insurgents have done quite well. After
suffering large reverses in the early and mid-1980s in El Salvador, they
are recovering. The large U.S. military aid program has bought some
time; that is all.[81] The El Salvadoran military still operates by its own
rules behind the appearances of taking U.S. advice on command lines,
operational techniques, and tactics. The rural population does not feel
safer. Until the change of regimes in Nicaragua, the war could not be
said to be going in favor of the government. El Salvadoran military
operations have only marginally affected the supply of aid to the insurgents from other external sources. Security violations and disclosures
about U.S. intelligence support have permitted the insurgents to improve their security over time. As time grinds on, it does not seem to be
grinding in the United States' favor. President Bush's success in forcing
the Soviet Union to withhold assistance, to be sure, could bring us to
change this judgment, and indeed it may lead to the eventual winding
down of the internal war, perhaps a victory for the government. That
outcome, however, would not be evidence of the effectiveness of U.S.
military assistance programs in support of the counterinsurgency. It
would be evidence for the effectiveness of a strategy that defeats the
external sources of support to the insurgents.

The story is different in Guatemala largely in that the amount of
military assistance has been much, much smaller, and curiously, with
somewhat better results. With only limited tutorial advice from U.S.
military advisors, the Guatemalan army does at least as well as the
Salvadoran armed forces.

In the Philippines, a U.S. military assistance group has long been in
place, but its advisory role has been limited, denying it anything like
the role of the U.S. assistance group in El Salvador. Large U.S. fiscal
aid goes directly to the government as payment for the U.S. bases there.
Marcos gave the Philippine military very little material support. He discounted intelligence reports about the extent of the insurgency. And he
kept an incompetent senior command structure which further reduced

the effectiveness of the counterinsurgency effort. The degree to which Aquino will be able to turn this state of military affairs around is still unknown. Initial improvements will be easy, but thereafter things will not come easily.

The United States could probably drop all of its military assistance without any appreciable difference in the internal wars except in El Salvador. Even there it is far from certain that things would go much worse for the army. This is a rather shocking conclusion to reach in light of all the enthusiasm within the U.S. military establishment for "low-intensity conflict." It means that the standard U.S. approach to military assistance in internal wars, counterinsurgencies, has little impact on the outcomes of such wars. This has been true in the one case where the U.S. military was up against a Maoist-type insurgency: Vietnam. As the internal wars drag on in El Salvador and Guatemala, the insurgents are moving away from the standard foco-type strategy to more emphasis on organizational and political work. That means a convergence toward the Maoist model. United States success in getting the Soviet Union, and perhaps eventually Cuba, to cease assisting these insurgencies may well drive the insurgents to adopt more fully the Maoist strategy.

The United States can keep the guerrillas from winning, but the annual costs are large—security and economic assistance programs and a steady loss of human life. If the time gained does not really promise stable governments—democratic in form, responsive to popular political demands for justice and participation, and able to provide law and order on their own—then how can the expenditures make sense by any measure?

We could take a wholly different approach in how we use our military power. Let us consider some outrageous options, purely as an analytical excursion, not as serious policies. We know that the two Central American insurgencies throughout the 1980s have depended heavily on outside support, first from Cuba and Nicaragua and second from a network of international organizations and fronts. If these two bases of support had been attacked directly, and if the attack had been at all successful, the insurgencies would have been reduced to minor proportions, posing no serious threat to either regime. The same is less true for the NPA in the Philippines. It would depend on a rather successful exposure and neutralization of the international support network, and even then the NPA would survive on internal resources. It is a much tougher target.

Put in the sharpest terms, if all the military effort going into El Salvador and Guatemala had been concentrated in an invasion of Managua, causing the Sandinistas to flee to the countryside and installing a new regime, the FMLN and the URNG would have declined to insignificance. Cuba would soon find alternative supply routes, but if that action were answered by punitive military action directly against Cuban assets—ships, aircraft, ports, and the like—Cuban policy would likely change radically. Had such military actions been carried out in the early 1980s not long after Grenada, not only would the United States have avoided dependency on the Contra rebel army, but the level of violence and casualties in El Salvador and Guatemala during the remainder of the 1980s would probably have been much lower than it has been in fact.

A parallel approach to the Philippines is difficult to work out. The foreign sources of aid are not focused in one or two countries, and the insurgents are far less dependent on external support. A vigorous *sunshine* publicity policy, creating wide international awareness of the networks of international support combined with much attention to NPA atrocities, might cause the CPP and the NPA a setback, but it would hardly be a fatal blow. Only the Philippine armed forces and police can deliver that kind of stroke.

There is not, of course, even the beginning of a political consensus for such a military policy for Central America. Moreover, its consequences for overall U.S. foreign policy toward Latin America could prove enormously adverse, and they would undoubtedly include negative reactions from other parts of the world—not just the Third World but also from our European allies. Since we are not recommending this military policy, but rather considering it only hypothetically for dealing with insurgencies, these objections to it are beside the point. The analytical point is that the United States could pursue its present counterinsurgency policy for years without decisive results, eventually reaching a level of military costs equal to or exceeding the military costs of implementing this alternative strategy much earlier and with decisive results. Perhaps in the context of overall U.S. foreign policy, a case can be made for bearing the heavier costs without the desired results, but it is instructive to think through the alternatives. Such a military and media strategy promises to break the insurgents' external sources of support and leave them too weak to sustain more than marginal operations, probably no operations at all.

If that conclusion is fairly clear, then the United States would seem to have two sensible choices for using military power: (1) direct military operations against the external supporters of the FMLN and the URNG and (2) early withdrawal, wherein the United States provides no military assistance but simply lets both client regimes struggle with their own fate.

In the Philippine case, only the second would be relevant, but let us consider the consequences of both alternatives for Central America. First, if the United States had destroyed the regime in Nicaragua and had intimidated Cuba and the Soviet Union so they ceased supporting the insurgencies, the client governments in both cases would easily survive. But would they become democratic? That seems unlikely in the short run, even in the fairly long run. The United States might well have devised an expansion of the self-defense statute in the UN Charter to make war against Nicaragua and Cuba legal by international legal standards, but what would have been the prize of this military victory? The survival of the entrenched oligarchs and corrupt military elites? The maintenance of a large landless peasantry? Almost certainly yes.

The direct attack military policy has appeal, but the likely internal political consequences do not. (And this is not even to consider the external consequences for U.S. foreign policy in Latin America and elsewhere.) There is, however, a way out of this dilemma, but not an easy one. The U.S. could cease its old game of colonialism by ventriloquy and assert direct colonial rule along the lines of our former rule in the Philippines. It could disenfranchise the old landed oligarchs by fiat, and it could throw out the indigenous officer corps, replacing it with U.S. officers commanding local troops. The United States could cease throwing its military voices to local commanders and simply put U.S. officers in charge. It could do the same thing in key civil service positions, in the courts, in local government, and elsewhere. After installing democratic forms, it could slowly reduce U.S. presence, yielding to local officials. This kind of commitment would be necessary for several decades, and it would require strong U.S. domestic political support. Neither of these necessities has the remotest chance of materializing. Nor am I recommending such a policy. It is merely an analytical excursion. Moreover, serious doubts could be raised about the United States' capacity to administer direct rule of this kind without bureaucratic corruption and abuses of power, or to train cadres for eventual independence and effective democracy. The task would differ considerably from military government in Germany, Italy, and Japan after World War II. While it would be more like the present situation in Panama, Panama differs in having a fairly large and literate urban middle class that makes the prospects for liberal democracy better than those in the Central American states with serious insurgencies.

Considering this patently unacceptable option, however, does force us to see more clearly what is at stake if we are determined to expand democracy in Central America. It also shows how contradictory most criticism of present U.S. policies has been, particularly that by critics who insist they support democracy. Forcing the United States to withdraw, yielding the field to the insurgents, hardly helps democracy. It is less defensible than Chamberlain's decision at Munich because he did not really know for certain what Hitler would do. We know what the insurgents will do if they seize power. If today's critics truly wanted to see democracy in Central America in our lifetime, then they would consider a combination of military attack directly against external supporters of the insurgencies and direct U.S. rule of the states in the region for the purposes of implementing massive land reform, effective law and order, democratic forms, and other measures the present elites refuse to carry out.

Another analytical excursion is helpful for a fuller appreciation of the range of military choices and consequences. We could conclude that insufficient political support for active and effective resistance to Marxist-Leninist influence in Central America makes it wiser to withdraw, leaving these regimes to their fates. As Mark Twain said, there is nothing like the prospect of being hanged to focus the mind. The local regimes might well focus sufficiently to defeat an insurgency, but more likely they would not. If they fell and became Soviet-Cuban client states (assuming the Soviet Union does not wholly drop out of the competition), it could create in American public opinion a sense of genuine threat to U.S. security, particularly if Mexico fell into the hands of radical leaders hostile to U.S. interests and diplomatically aligned with Cuba and the Soviet Union. The melting of the Cold War alignments makes this most improbable, but it retains value as a scenario for analysis. The U.S. public would then likely provide the kind of political consensus necessary for major military actions in the region. Having conquered most of the isthmus from Marxist-Leninist regimes, the United States could install military governments which would try to impose democracy on these states.

The prospects of success would be greater for two reasons. First, the Marxist-Leninist regimes would destroy the old elites who now obstruct progress toward democracy. Second, direct U.S. rule would prevent another attempt at colonialism by ventriloquy. The costs to the U.S. in military losses, of course, would be large, probably very large. This is not even to consider the impact on U.S. foreign policy elsewhere in the world as well as on U.S. domestic politics over time, and it is to assume an administrative capacity to carry through a long period of tutelage rule. Again, this is not to recommend such a policy course but rather to explore the full range of military alternatives.

Let us consider U.S. economic policies in support of these three case study countries. They seem to be no less feckless than the military policies. Large amounts of U.S. aid do not seem to correlate with improved economic conditions or with better security conditions. Although large amounts of U.S. aid go to El Salvador, nearly $3 billion since 1980, it remains an economic basket case. Through payment for bases and other programs, the United States is now dispensing nearly $450 million annually to the Philippines. The relation of this aid to economic performance is difficult to establish, and the argument that it is positive is far from compelling.

Per capita foreign economic assistance to El Salvador is $83. For Guatemala it is $27. For the Philippines it is $14.30. These are not trivial capital flows. Yet in every case, we see a disturbing economic situation—low international commodity prices—not one wholly of the country's own making but one the country has not made appreciably better through investment of foreign assistance.

Mancur Olson has argued that direct economic assistance in principle is not a productive or efficient way to allocate capital for enhancing growth in developing countries: "Government planning, nationalized industries, and public regulation will . . . usually work less well in developing than in developed countries. Whatever the optimal role of government may be in developed nations, it is smaller in developing countries."[82] Our case studies show not so much a large role in terms of central government expenditures but a dramatically large role for the oligarchs and military elites, who interfere with market forces. In all three countries, the ruling elites have to some degree permitted the market a significant role, particularly in the 1960s and 1970s. They nonetheless protected local industries, spent money on big infrastructure projects primarily for urban advantage, and left the landowning elites in a virtual monopoly position vis-à-vis the labor force and the use of capital for economic development.

Olson further observes that "law and order are needed for economic progress under any system of economic organization. It is evident that at least in rural areas some governments of underdeveloped countries find it difficult to provide even this elemental service." [83] The most important thing that the governments under study could do for economic growth is to provide law and order. This they do very poorly in the rural areas and not all that well in urban areas. No amount of economic aid is likely to improve the situation. On the contrary, it tends to make things worse because it lessens the sense of crisis and urgency within ruling circles.

The two economic policies that could make the greatest impact do not require any U.S. direct aid. First, debt relief could add several points to the GNP of each country with the stroke of several bankers' pens (El Salvador 2.9%, Guatemala 4.4%, and the Philippines 7.0%).[84] Some of this relief is, in fact, being granted quietly by bankers who realize their debtors cannot pay. An explicit U.S. policy with this aim, however, could also lead to debt relief by other countries who have loaned excessively to these Third World states. Second, land reform would break the old coalition of oligarchs and their grip on economic development, giving the urban sector a new opening and relieving a lot of the pressure on the economy and the political system that now prevents both economic growth and the maintenance of law and order. By and large, direct foreign assistance tends to let these governments avoid facing squarely the land reform and security problems, and it permits a trickle of debt service, reducing the foreign bankers' incentives to write off the debt as a bad one.

The ironies in some aspects of U.S. economic assistance policies are sometimes quite deep. For example, it would probably benefit several of the Central American states, including El Salvador and Guatemala, if the United States ceased protecting its own domestic sugar cane farmers. Not only would Americans pay less for sugar but the economies of these debt-ridden states would gain. Those are not the only gains. Environmentalists in the United States have complained bitterly about the damage sugar cane farming is doing to the Everglades in Florida. Central American sugar farmers, if allowed to enter the U.S. market on a free trade basis, would soon put the sugar cane farms in the Everglades out of business and contribute to the protection of the fragile ecological balance there. Removing U.S. tariffs and sugar import quotas with a mere stroke of the legislative pen, the United States could improve the economy in El Salvador and Guatemala, the standard of living of Americans, and the environment in Florida. Further examination of other such linkages might well reveal additional no-cost gains through a simple change in policy. At the same time, the cost of U.S. direct economic assistance could be cut, either shifting the savings to other countries or giving them back to the taxpayer.

Our economic assistance programs, it seems, are as poorly designed as our military assistance programs to get the outcomes we want. We are spending several billions in economic aid and encouraging similar sums to be provided by the World Bank and the IMF. Yet the consequences of these funds are working against our own policy interests as well as the larger interests of the recipient states.

What if we cut off all direct assistance? How would these regimes fare? Guatemala was subjected to a near complete cutoff for several years. The government not only failed to collapse but became more serious about defeating the insurgency. It also managed to obtain some foreign aid elsewhere—from Israel, Germany, and Belgium. A cutoff of foreign economic aid might force the regimes to disallow rampant tax evasion, something that plagues all three countries, especially the Philippines. To do so, they would have to build more effective civil administrations, enhancing their capacity to rule and maintain stability.

A cutoff would also leave these regimes with access to capital only through the private sector. In order to attract it, they would have to provide conditions conducive to sucessful investment. That would mean, first of all, defeating the insurgents and maintaining law and order. The burden of overseeing productive and efficient use of the capital would fall more heavily on private lenders and entrepreneurs, not on U.S. civil servants and embassy staffs. Where statist economies permit governments to undercut market uses of foreign capital, it would be more difficult to attract.

As our review of the political development literature pointed out, contrary to "dependency theory," private capital does not undercut the autonomy of a developing country's government; it enhances it, although not always in the best interests of economic development and local administration. The same cannot be said for direct aid from the U.S. government. Especially in the El Salvador case, U.S. governmental aid does have the effect of undercutting local autonomy. The United

States has essentially paid the El Salvadoran elites to implement a form of government that it otherwise would not have promoted, at least not on the same early schedule and to the same degree. If there is a case for dependency theory, it may be most cogent where direct economic assistance is concerned, not in cases of private capital. Again, drawing on Olson's arguments, foreign investment capital is not in a position to coerce the local regime. It is only in a position to offer choices for economic gain.[85] This is much less true for direct government assistance. Strings are usually attached, and the local government is partially absolved of responsibility for the outcome if it is poor.

Finally, let us consider the political component of U.S. strategy. As we have argued earlier, where the United States has decided to become involved in internal wars, where it takes on some of the responsibility for the conflict, it will find that it must make democracy its goal. There may be exceptions, but they will be just that, exceptions—where other strategic factors are sufficiently compelling to give democracy a low priority. Egypt, for example, has been an exception since the Camp David Accords, which brought peace between Israel and Egypt. In this example, however, the United States is not engaged in an internal war. The Iraqi crisis has created a whole new range of potential involvements in internal conflicts where democracy cannot reasonably be a short-term goal. How the American public debate will tilt in such cases is anybody's guess, but the democracy issue is bound to be a central one. Were the United States to become involved in such a struggle in Egypt, the democracy issue would certainly be raised in the American domestic debate about the involvement.

In the Central American cases, it would seem quite practical and sensible to much of the American electorate if the case had been made that the greater danger to the goal of democracy has come from the radical left and that the United States has to make temporary alliances with the right in order to defeat that challenge. At the same time, the United States would remain committed to turn against the right once the insurgents were defeated. The problem with this strategy, of course, is that U.S. policy would lose its leverage when the insurgents were defeated. In practice, therefore, it has been essential to pursue a political offensive on both fronts, the left and the right, simultaneously.

The Carter administration initially made its main effort against the rightist governments, giving too little attention to the problem from the radical left. When the Reagan administration came into office, the impression was created—an inaccurate one—that U.S. policy would be reversed, shifting all of the resources against the insurgents. President Reagan's spokesmen were not very successful in removing the misimpression, but, in fact, U.S. policy in support of democracy against right-wing regimes continued unabated. In the Philippines, President Reagan was reluctant to withdraw support for President Marcos, but the evidence of Marcos's antidemocratic behavior in the elections against Cory Aquino was too great, and he shifted his position. His change, of course, was critical for Aquino's victory.

Free elections alone, however, do not ensure a stable and thriving democracy, and U.S. policy has been left with freely elected client regimes that do not seem wholly committed to building democracy. Here is the rub for U.S. political strategy. How is it to deal with this problem?

There obviously is no panacea, no easy answer, but our examination of political development theory suggests some ways to sort out the difference between false choices and practical ones. The starting point should be the five political development goals. Prioritization and sequence for their attainment should be the first business for determining how best to get to democracy. Where the client state is involved in an internal war, stability has to receive highest priority. Social equity must also be given fairly central concern in winning government support in the war effort. At the same time, it cannot be mandated in a way that obstructs longer term economic growth. Breaking down the statist character of the urban industrial and commercial sector combined with land reform based on individual holdings offers the double advantage of contributing to the social equity goal and the economic development goal. Political autonomy is also an important goal, one that large, direct U.S. economic assistance undercuts. There is no reason that it cannot be among those goals given early and strong emphasis.

This leaves the goal of democracy rather low on the priority list. There are several reasons for leaving it there in the early stages of political development. First, many of the policy decisions essential to attain stability and social equity are virtually impossible for elected legislatures and presidents to make. We have noted the notorious record of parliaments in dealing with land reform, and the record is probably no better for dealing with statist economic policies.

There is much to be said for a period of authoritarianism in sponsoring the preconditions for democracy. Not only was that the case in many of the older democracies today, but we are seeing some contemporary examples in Taiwan, South Korea, and perhaps even Chile. It is too early to know how the statist tendencies in the East Asian cases will play out, but they have managed remarkable economic growth which has in turn generated pressures for democracy. Modern institutions—labor unions, professional groups, and political parties—have been permitted a modicum of liberty to form and participate. In other words, the authoritarian regimes in these cases have not pursued a simple praetorianism. They have built modern administrative capacities and then given way to the pressures for participation as the diffusion of economic power has permitted such groups to compete effectively. The point remains: a strong state came first.

In light of these cases where authoritarian regimes have sponsored market economic success and then given way to pressures for democracy, one is forced to wonder if the U.S. policy of demanding free elections and democratic government in El Salvador has been well advised. Has the U.S. strategy implicitly stumbled into the wrong prioritization of the political development goals? Has it created circumstances that make building an effective state administrative capacity more difficult?

The events in the Soviet Union and Eastern Europe are giving us yet another case to test this line of analysis. We have observed that there are several commonalities between our three case study countries and the Soviet and East European cases: large landless peasantries and state control of the industrial and commercial sectors.

In several of the East European cases—Poland, Czechoslovakia, and Hungary—democratization has preceded the making of the tough decisions about land reform and privatization of the economy. In the Soviet Union, while democratization has not gone as far, it has preceded economic reform. Gorbachev tried to proceed with economic reform ahead of democratization but failed to overcome the resistance of the economic and party bureaucracies. To break their resistance, he shifted his strategy to democratization in order to break their power. In so doing, he has mobilized much of the population to demand a participatory role in policy-making. That in turn has created new obstacles to economic reform. In the Soviet case, the most serious devolution of power has been to the republics. Their demand for sovereignty has forced Gorbachev to choose between maintaining the empire or pursuing liberal reform. As of early 1991, he was siding with the empire. In doing so, he has to put aside reform. The Soviet example differs fundamentally from most in Eastern Europe because of the national minority problem. Unless several nationalities are allowed to assert their self-determination, it seems unlikely that liberal political development has a chance in any part of the Soviet Union.

A unique sequence in Poland has permitted the making of some of the tough economic policy choices, but whether the democratic regime can carry them through in face of public discontent is an open question. Hungary and Czechoslovakia, as of this writing in early 1991, are trying to make up their minds about how to proceed with economic reform.

On the whole, the events in Eastern Europe and the Soviet Union suggest that giving the democracy goal first priority may not be the wisest strategy for achieving the outcomes they seek. They are further evidence for the wisdom of the sequence followed in South Korea, Taiwan, and Chile. They suggest that privatization and land reform need strong governments to implement.

It should be possible to take a particular case and sort out a sensible strategy of sequence and priority for the five development goals. It would require a thorough and accurate analysis of the particular conditions of the country in question, but it should be feasible. Different countries, to be sure, would have to follow different patterns, depending on their special circumstances.

The political component of U.S. strategy, therefore, should start with this kind of analysis, and it should take an empirically based and realistic view of conditions of the state it seeks to assist. This approach to the political component naturally fits easily with the economic and military components, and to be sure, it should come first and be the basis for those components. While the focus of this study has been entirely on states with internal wars, this approach is just as valid for devising a strategy of assistance to Third World states without such wars but anxious to expedite political and economic development.

While all this analysis may seem quite rational and sensible, its utility finally depends on the character of the political leadership of the Third World state being assisted. Praetorian leaders, by definition, would find such U.S. advice uncongenial. They do not want development. They seek to maintain the status quo except where they benefit by changing economic arrangements.

We are brought back to the "political" in political development and internal wars. Poor leaders or leaders who do not want political development leading to stable democracy either cannot or will not accept a promising strategy offered by a U.S. embassy's country team. Nor are they likely to develop such a strategy on their own.

Veteran U.S. policymakers from the 1950s experience in the Philippines who were involved in Vietnam often said that the real solution was finding a Vietnamese Magsaysay. They recognized the role of local political leadership, but they had no good ideas about how to find it. In truth, there are few rules or insights that can solve this problem. The answer will have to come from within the local political system, and it may not come when it is most needed.

Political development literature has paid some attention to this problem, especially where it has concerned the role of the military in modernization.[86] Sometimes the consolidation occurs if a military elite is committed to modernization and political development, leading to a military takeover followed by a program of authoritarian reform. Atatürk's rule in Turkey is the most notable example. Curiously, the militaries in the three case studies show little propensity to follow this line of development. The traditions and socialization of the officer corps in El Salvador seem to make it virtually impossible. In Guatemala, Arbenz Guzmán followed the reformer military leader pattern but in doing so he turned to another political base and did not keep the army with him. That led to his undoing. Ríos Montt in the mid-1980s gave a similar, much shorter lived impression. His evangelist Protestant religious faith seems to explain his break with the traditional pattern of military leadership. Like Arbenz, he was unable to keep the solid support of the military. The Philippine military shows more potential for such a development. The traditions of the Philippine Military Academy and its imitation of West Point are exceptional in the Third World, but it has yet to produce an effective reforming clique.

The policy implication for U.S. strategy should be obvious. Attention to the socialization of the militaries of client states involved in internal wars is critical. Whether U.S. policy can affect it positively in more than a marginal way is open to question, but it remains an important point for concern. The military ranks are the most likely source of authoritarian reformers. Only they have at their disposal a reasonably disciplined institution for taking power and using it for systemic reform. A civilian authoritarian reformer would have to win military support unless he or she can build an alternative institution with adequate discipline and commitment—most unlikely within the confines of a praetorian political system.

A Marxist-Leninist political party, of course, is designed precisely for this purpose—to take the power and to use it for systemic change. A counterpart authoritarian party dedicated to systemic change toward democracy, however, has yet to be developed either in theory or practice. In the meanwhile, armies have occasionally filled the gap.

U.S. political development strategy can, in the final analysis, only offer guidance and insight for clients who want to accept them. To the extent that economic and military assistance are used to compel them to accept such advice against their genuine desires, it is not likely to be effective. At the same time, that kind of leverage tends to undercut one of the development goals, political autonomy. Leaders become vulnerable to the charge of being merely American puppets, a charge with some validity. Short of assuming direct rule, a politically infeasible option for U.S. strategy, American policymakers will have to accept whatever leadership the client state produces. This is not to say that they should be passive vis-à-vis a client state, but it to say that they should be realistic about what they are buying with support to a client.

Finally, working out a political development strategy must be the primary task. Only when U.S. policymakers have done this, or are in the process of doing it, can supportive economic and military components of an overall strategy be devised that are truly mutually supporting.

In sum, the U.S. strategy for competing in internal wars in our three cases not only is costly but also has poor prospects for success. In most regards, it unavoidably perpetuates the ineffective social, economic, and political structure. One can point to the Korean case as an exception. Genuine democracy shows signs of catching on there, but it is far from deeply rooted. The cost to the United States, however, has been enormous, and the commitment is nearly forty years old. An equal time in the Philippines under a tutelage system of democracy did not achieve as much.

There are more effective alternative strategies for winning the internal wars. They call for recognizing the external component of those wars and directing U.S. military action at the external sources. They do not, however, offer much promise for fostering democracy in the states where the internal contest is occurring. That would require another parallel policy of direct rule for a considerable period, not only a costly policy but one wholly at odds with American values and concepts of national sovereignty and self-determination. Alternatively, success in fostering democracy would require good luck in finding an indigenous set of leaders capable of following and willing to follow a strategy eventually leading to democracy.

VII

What Is To Be Done?

....

In light of our analysis, one can make a strong case that the answer to "what is to be done?" should be "less and less." We should eschew involvement in internal wars entirely. In practice, however, neither is the Bush administration giving that answer nor is any significant political opposition faction pressing it with the public or Congress. Global engagement, therefore, appears to be the thrust of U.S. foreign policy in the 1990s. While Europe and East Asia are likely to remain the primary pillars in U.S. global engagement, involvement in the Third World will also be a critical part of it. The answer to "what is to be done?," therefore, cannot be "nothing." It has to describe "how and where" we can be more effectively involved.

If the U.S. strategy for involvement in Third World internal wars is to be improved, it must be modified in some fairly dramatic ways. Some traditional notions for "causation" must be abandoned and replaced by new ones. This is especially true in the economic and political development components of the strategy. The military component can only be designed effectively in the context of these changes, not as a thing apart. Although no panacea strategy is possible, there are a number of basic changes that could greatly improve U.S. prospects for success.

Choosing the places to compete is the first order of business for any strategy. To be sure, the United States has been selective. It has not competed equally everywhere, but choices have sometimes been by default or forced by short-term political considerations. Choosing those parts of the Third World that are of most strategic significance is critical—not only for conserving and concentrating our resources, but also for building and sustaining a popular political consensus for commitments to Third World states.

Second, a careful and thorough political analysis of the societies confronting an internal war is imperative. It is possible to learn enough about a political system to know whether it has any genuine prospects for democracy and what the major obstacles are. It is also possible to reach some cogent judgments about development goals—which ones ought to be given priority and which can be delayed. And it is possible to judge the likelihood that the incumbent rulers will do the things necessary to foster effective political development for achieving the goal of stability. Until that kind of insight is fully developed, a U.S. commitment to support a government in an internal war is unwise. Jumping in on the side that is destined for defeat cannot be prudent, even if short-term political considerations make it seem so.

Third, economic assistance strategy cannot be developed in isolation from the private sector. If world market forces will not make an economy grow, it makes little sense to provide direct capital assistance on the unspoken assumption that we can make it grow in spite of market forces. This was an error in its Cold War strategy that the United States should not continue. Some Third World areas will not grow rapidly. Others will. U.S. strategy must take that reality into account. Most U.S. direct economic assistance works against market forces, either by allocating capital investment irrationally or by allowing the local authorities to foster protectionism ("import substitution" is a common example), to engage in capital flight, and to squander money on government salaries and feckless programs. As a general rule, there should be no direct assistance. Exceptions should require strong justifications and frequent rejustifications.

Fourth, the military component of the strategy should not be focused primarily on the "internal" aspect of the war. It should take far greater account of the "external" aspects, even to the point in some cases of the direct use of U.S. forces against external bases and sources of support for insurgents. The internal aspect should be left almost wholly to local military and police. The intelligence side of military operations is critical. Determining the "order of battle," that is, the forces on the enemy's side, must not be limited only to counting the insurgents. It must include the complex network of transnational organizations and cooperative relationships that create the resource base for the insurgents. Political intelligence is just as essential for the order of battle in this regard as is military intelligence. The two blend together, and, unless we understand the blending, an effective military campaign against the adversary is not possible. Taking this view of the military component will lead to a quite different requirement for military forces and capabilities than is now recognized.

Fifth, the integration of political, economic, and military strategies is imperative. The traditional approach, pouring in economic aid, often hurts the counterinsurgency campaign by making more resources accessible to the insurgents. The military assistance scheme for "winning the hearts and minds" tends to be a substitute for development of adequate political institutions for coping with social mobilization. Our approach to tutelage democracy gets ahead of the displacement of the antidemocratic elites, particularly the landowning oligarchies. Making the political, economic, and military components of a strategy mutually supporting will require dramatic changes in the traditional approach to all three.

Each of these points needs elaboration for more specificity about what needs to be done.

Areas of Strategic Significance

Our review of U.S. strategic interests did not start with a blank slate. It took present U.S. commitments as given, but it went further and identified reasons why two major regions of the Third World have a much higher priority for national security.

Central America is not Vietnam. The consequences of ignoring internal wars in this region will not be favorable, even neutral, for U.S. security. The geographic, economic, and demographic factors impinge directly on the continental territory of the United States. The United States can deal with the security problems now, or it can wait until they are too great to ignore. Either way, the dilemmas and costs are great. The way we choose will depend greatly on public attitudes, the Congress, and the skill of the executive branch in articulating U.S. interests and the threat to them.

The Middle East–Southwest Asian region has vital U.S. interests which can be neglected only at great peril to the international security order, including our alliances in Europe and East Asia. The economies of these areas depend more heavily on Middle East oil than does the U.S. economy, but the U.S. economy would be affected by a cutoff of oil from that region. Unlike the situation in Central America and other Third World regions, a U.S.–Soviet confrontation has been quite conceivable in the Middle East or Southwest Asia until recently, and, while it will remain unlikely in the next few years, it should not be wholly discounted. That gives U.S. security requirements there a wholly different dimension from those for other regions. This region is also different in that neither the preconditions for democracy nor U.S. power to sponsor democracy are very encouraging in any but a few states. This means that U.S. demands for democratic political development must be more limited, not because Americans do not favor democracy but because their power to support it is extremely limited. The U.S. military defeat of Iraq and the liberation of Kuwait has opened a new chapter of U.S. involvement in this region. It is far too early to judge the basic outlines of the future, but the prospects for a long, complicated military involvement are high.

The Philippines has strategic significance for the United States, particularly its role in providing military bases. This is important for our support to ASEAN. Of the three areas, however, the Philippines is much the least important. Other basing, not as desirable but adequate, could be found. The bases, therefore, should not be the cornerstone of U.S. policy toward the Philippines. A stable, democratic, non-Marxist regime is much more important.

The United States has a formal defense commitment to another country in Southeast Asia: Thailand. Thailand is not a serious problem at present although it has long dealt with an internal war. Our study has not addressed it, and, therefore, no conclusions about it have been offered. It could be included, however, and many of the points of this study apply there as well.

Economic Assistance Strategy

Our analysis suggests that direct economic assistance, now a central aspect of U.S. strategy toward internal wars in the Third World, is not only wasted but actually counterproductive. It was not a significant factor in the successes in Greece and the Philippines in the 1950s, and it may have been hurtful there in the longer run. The case of South Korea may be an exception, but the amount of aid was so large over such a long time that such a strategy is not an option for many other cases, if any. And economists of Mancur Olson's viewpoint would raise questions about the real sources of economic development in Korea. Perhaps U.S. economic aid was not so critical.

In the course of an internal war, economic assistance tends to become an alternative source of revenue for the local regime, allowing it to neglect its domestic tax base and thus to leave it to the insurgents to exploit. This is not to suggest that regimes facing an internal war ought to tax their populations more heavily, but it is to say that, in order to tax the countryside and the urban sectors, they have to rule those sectors. If they rule them, the insurgents do not. Fiscal maintenance of the public sector, therefore, requires that the local regime be more effective in maintaining public law and order—that is, that it deal more effectively with the insurgency.

In the three case studies, it is clear that the most effective economic measure that these regimes could take would be extensive and rapid land reform. While it might initally lower commodity exports by breaking up relatively efficient large holdings, it would allow a large part of its population to enjoy a higher standard of subsistence irrespective of international commodity prices. Land reform might delay industrial development, but the gain in social equity would make the government's task of maintaining stability and dealing with the insurgents much easier.

While the case studies did not explore in detail the role of transnational private capital, we did take note of the findings of political development studies that conclude that such sources of capital strengthen the local regimes. We also noted that efficient use of capital is much more likely through this approach to economic development than through direct aid. How the recipient state allows the capital to come in also affects the efficiency of its use. Highlighting this point makes it clearer that debt relief is critical for many Third World states. The great influx of foreign loans from petrodollars in the 1970s brought an inefficient application of capital, and the debtor governments are now left with the devastating economic and political consequences. Until the foreign debt problem is alleviated for countries involved in internal wars, their prospects of dealing with economic problems are extremely dim. Debt relief is far more critical than any other form of immediate aid. Only after this problem has abated is there any genuine prospect of getting foreign capital to help once again with economic development in these states.

This conclusion about economic aid was not foreseen when this study was begun. The focus was on the military dimension of internal war and political development. The evidence, however, was too strong to ignore. The insight is not necessarily new. Economists have had doubts about direct economic assistance for a long time, and other students of the problem of development have more recently been struck by the fecklessness of U.S. direct assistance. The implications for internal war and the tendency of U.S. assistance monies to become a de facto alternative tax base, however, do seem to be an aspect of the problem that has received little or no attention. U.S. policy-making shows virtually no recognition of it in the cases analyzed in this study.

Political Development and Democracy

The cases studied demonstrate that it is possible to take greater advantage of political development theory as it has matured in the past couple of decades to understand whether democracy has genuine prospects in the near future in Third World states. It can sharpen our understanding of the conflicts in development goals and help us to judge what priority each should be given during an internal war. It can lead to an understanding of the structure of political power that is either blocking or facilitating greater institutionalization of political participation, the sine qua non for stability and victory in internal wars.

Such analysis can also make U.S. policymakers much more aware of the impact of U.S. programs in client states with internal wars. It may yield some very unhappy insights about the prospects of success for present strategy in assisting besieged client states, but the pain of recognition now will be less than the pain of continuing to pursue a strategy that cannot succeed and may even hurt the prospects of the local regime.

U.S. strategy may have to be made with a less optimistic view about what is possible in the course of a few years of support to an embattled ally. A military regime headed by social reformers may be preferable to a democratic regime that is too weak to implement reforms that are necessary to have any prospect of winning against an insurgency. A military regime that will not move beyond praetorianism, however, is not a good alternative. In other words, there are military regimes and military regimes. They are not all the same. Knowing how to choose among them is important. Of the case studies, clearly only the Philippines now shows some signs of having deeply rooted reform sentiments in its military ranks, but the senior officers are less likely to support dramatic policies such as land reform. In El Salvador and Guatemala, the military leadership is far from facing up to such tasks. Only in desperation was the Guatemalan military willing to permit a relatively free election and the taking of office by the winner. In El Salvador, this has happened only under the threat of withdrawal of U.S. aid. The policy implication is critical. Rather than positive incentives through aid, denial of aid would seem to offer better prospects of forcing a regime to reform. Aid allows an oligarchic regime to have it both ways, giving the appearances of reform while retaining the political disposition of power that prevents effective political and economic development.

The major instrumentality available to U.S. policy for encouraging reform-minded officers is the education of foreign officers in U.S. military schools. In the United States they are exposed to democracy. They may or may not take democratic values home with them, but they are unlikely to acquire them more rapidly without the experiences of living in the United States for a time and witnessing democracy in practice. Ironically, during the Carter administration, several Latin America dictatorships were cut off from the military education program (International Military Education and Training—IMET), and the costs of the program were placed on the country sending students. As a general officer from one of these countries told the author, he was the last of the several officers in his army who had been trained in a U.S. military school. His preference for democracy had been acquired during a year in a U.S. Army school, and he declared that other older officers with a similar experience had realized the importance of moving their country toward democracy. The younger generation of officers, wholly without such exposure, has a hostile attitude toward democracy. He made his point tellingly by saying, "The Soviet Union wants to train our officers and make communists of them. Why do you refuse to train them and make democrats of them so they will subvert our dictatorship?"

The U.S. IMET program may not be a panacea, but it has been undervalued. One clear conclusion of this study is that IMET deserves great emphasis. A relatively inexpensive program, its potential for spreading democratic values is great. Third World states relying on praetorianism and facing insurgencies desperately need military elites who understand practical democracy. IMET can provide a few, and even a few can occasionally make all the difference. General Ramos in the Philippines is a case in point. General Zia in Pakistan, twice an IMET visiting military student, did not take home a great commitment to democracy, but he took back a great admiration for the United States and proved willing to resist advice in 1980 not to turn to the U.S. for aid and foreign policy alignment. Moreover, he eventually introduced the election process that brought Benazir Bhutto to power through free elections.

Michael Shafer's study of the U.S. counterinsurgency effort condemns the naive approach of the United States to the political development of its clients, and perhaps he is correct in assessing the assumptions about what would produce democracy in Greece, the Philippines, and Vietnam. He is remarkably wrong, however, about the relevance of political science and what it has to offer to the understanding of the politics of such states. Condemning Huntington's analysis, he points out the importance of the military in Greece and the Philippines. Huntington's analysis *Political Order in Changing Societies*, properly understood, would have anticipated the role the military came to play. The same is true for a number of Shafer's other charges against the political development theorists. Many of his valid points lead him to no sensible policy conclusions, and one is encouraged to reach the inference that he has no objections to seeing Marxist-Leninist insurgencies succeed, even where U.S. interests are clearly at stake. Some other political scientists fall in the same category, especially those focusing on Latin America. Dependency theorists and those who develop such a deep hostility for incumbent Third World dictatorship that they let their analysis become dedicated to justification of the Marxist-Leninist insurgent victories are not very helpful to our understanding of how to foster democracy. Their work, however, may be useful in focusing attention on the varieties of influence that transnational capital can have on both economic development and political autonomy in Third World states. They should also be encouraged to look at the other side of the dependency coin and see that in some regards it is *interdependency*, both for economics and the spread of democracy.

U.S. Military Capabilities for Dealing with Internal Wars

The present enthusiasm for new means of engaging in so-called low intensity conflicts leads to precisely the wrong emphasis in the use of U.S. military capabilities. It encourages colonialism by ventriloquy and military campaigns that leave the adversary's external bases of support more or less out of the equation in a net assessment of the adversary's order of battle. It encourages a limited military technical approach, a tendency to look for technologies and weapons to surmount what are essentially political problems.

One of the least understood and most counterproductive features of this approach is the tendency to compensate for the local military's poor intelligence capabilities with U.S. intelligence capabilities. The local military either uses the U.S. intelligence poorly, usually hurting U.S. collection by security violations and disclosures, or does not make an effort to improve its own intelligence. It becomes dependent on U.S. intelligence, much as the government becomes dependent on U.S. economic aid.

Both U.S. military means and intelligence means would better be directed to the external aspects of the internal war. In the first instance, such intelligence is more relevant. It is critical for uncovering the increasingly complex systems for providing insurgents with external support. It must take a much larger view than direct supply of military aid and also investigate the indirect international organizational linkages that distance patron states from direct support to internal wars. The Western press can also contribute to this effort, but a comprehensive U.S. intelligence effort is required to learn the full dimensions of many of the indirect support linkages.

The first component of a U.S. strategy in attacking the external connection need not be military. It more often should be a "sunshine" attack, putting as much public light on the clandestine links as possible. Here the media can play a key role. Public understanding of the external versus the internal dimensions of an insurgency is critical for a sustained U.S. policy of opposing the insurgency.

The next component should be concerned with how to break the external links through means beyond exposure of them. If direct military action looks promising, it must have political support. If such support cannot be built, then the alternative of a limited focus on counterinsurgency assistance to the besieged regime is not likely to be successful unless the regime is indeed a democracy or has good prospects for becoming one. If it is, it probably will not need our military advice and assistance through a relatively large and visible advisory presence.

While it would be wrong to conclude that the U.S. military needs no military assistance capabilities for advising and tutoring a local military on counterinsurgency, one is forced to conclude that such cases are likely to be very small in number—considerably smaller than the size of the present U.S. Army special operations forces devoted to this task. The same observation may well hold for the navy's special operations forces. A much better approach in developing these kinds of forces is to keep them small and to place greater emphasis on quality, especially in language and area studies. The expansion of these forces in the 1980s has probably diluted an already inadequate concentration of language and related skills. In 1990, there were signs, particularly in the U.S. Army, of an effort to regain some lost ground in the quality of selection and training.

Military assistance for other than counterinsurgency support, such as is the case in most Middle East and Southwest Asian states, requires a different kind of military expertise, but it demands language and area knowledge. Again, quality is preferable to quantity in these cases as it is in the counterinsurgency cases.

There has always been another side to the Special Forces mission. In fact, counterinsurgency was not their original purpose before Vietnam. They were intended to support insurgencies in the enemy's own territory during wartime. Because the U.S. occasionally finds it important to support insurgencies in peacetime, why are these forces not used for this mission? The answer is found in policy decisions about what agency in the U.S. government will execute "covert action" in peacetime. The mission falls to the CIA under the direction of the director of central intelligence (DCI). The DCI could be given use of the Department of Defense (DOD) forces in peacetime if the President so decides, but they would be under the DCI's control. In light of the CIA's disposition not to give the highest quality attention to paramilitary covert action capabilities, and the lack of a strong understanding and experience in the command and control of military operations in the CIA, including insurgent operations, a strong case can be made that the DOD special operations forces ought to be the resources used by the DCI in covert actions involving paramilitary activities. Such forces can be given and are given wartime contingency missions, but that is another issue, not related to Third World competition between the U.S. and Marxist-Leninist states.

Left to their present orientation and given their constituency in Congress, DOD special operations forces will enjoy greater resources while pursuing missions that are not only unpromising but often counterproductive in the Third World.

In some of our analytical excursions, thinking through the implications of the external dimension of insurgencies, we suggested that direct military action against supporting states might well be more effective than U.S. counterinsurgency assistance to the local military and police. Admittedly, this use carries sensitive political implications, and the occasions when it would be possible and advisable politically are few. As we think through the force capabilities needed by the DOD to meet all contingencies, such operations have to be considered in principle. The actions against Grenada and Panama are examples of actual cases. In other words, this approach is not wholly academic. There may arise occasions when the political circumstances permit and encourage direct military operations by U.S. forces. The requirements in these cases are not mainly "special operations" in nature, although the intelligence and reconnaissance means used in their support need some special capabilities beyond traditional intelligence means. This was the case in the Iran rescue mission. The CIA is unlikely ever to take this mission seriously. This is not a criticism; it is merely a recognition that the CIA has many other much higher priorities to which it must give greater resources. Military intelligence services could give the mission high priority if the DCI encouraged and supported them. The effort need not be large, but it needs to be of very high quality. The present large emphasis on "low intensity conflict" does not encourage attention to such an intelligence capability. It actually detracts from it.

The military forces for Third World contingencies, therefore, need to be focused in the three critical areas—Central America, the Middle East, and Southeast Asia—and tailored to the most probable actions conceivable there. This should compel a cooperative approach because no single service has adequate or ideal assets for all aspects of such missions. Joint operations have been a perennial problem for the DOD structure ever since it was created in 1947. Dealing with that problem transcends the limits of this study, but it must be recognized as a persisting one as it affects special operations and Third World military contingencies.

We have mainly discussed the special nature of operations needed for dealing with insurgencies by military means. This, of course, leaves out the Middle East–Southwest Asian region. What kinds of military operations beyond major force deployments are conceivable there?

The Iraqi invasion of Kuwait has altered dramatically the character of U.S. military involvement in the Middle East but not in a wholly unforeseen way. The idea of a "rapid deployment force" (RDF) for such a contingency goes back to the first year of the Carter administration when it was called for in Presidential Directive 18. Slow to start, RDF began to take on serious military substance by late 1979 and throughout 1980, becoming the new Central Command which now controls operations in the region. Designed in the first instance to deal with an external military force entering the region, namely the Soviet military, it was also meant to help maintain the regional balance of power. With the changed Soviet policy toward the region, that has become its primary mission.

The point in dwelling briefly here on the Central Command is that the Iraqi crisis underscores a new reality about Third World conflicts. Much of the sales pitch for "low intensity" forces has been based on the belief that Third World conflicts will be of "low intensity," presumably meaning little use of highly lethal modern conventional weaponry. The Iraqi military hardly fits this definition of military capabilities. The diffusion of the most modern military weaponry to the Third World means that interstate wars in most places will be "high intensity," at least until the available stocks of weaponry are exhausted.

Potential U.S. involvement in such conflicts means that our force structure must include fairly large heavy forces and the lift capacity to move them to the Middle East—the most demanding contingency of all regions of the world—in a fairly short time. The U.S. ground force level in the Gulf appears to have reached at least nine heavy division equivalents. That indeed is a large force for a Third World contingency.

What lesser and different kinds of military contingencies are conceivable in this region? Before the Iraqi crisis, the answer would have been only coups and sudden upheavals within moderate Arab states that promise to change the regional political balance in a way unfavorable to the West—that is, the kind of coup that occurred with the fall of the shah of Iran. Such an afflicted regime might well ask for U.S. assistance in the future.

In such cases, time would be critical. Moving large forces for the operation would be impractical. A small force, a battalion or more, if moved swiftly, might well reverse the situation. If it could arrive before a coup was well established and while confusion still surrounded the crisis, a small force purposefully directed would have a larger impact than its size suggests. A battalion arriving in a few hours would be worth more than a division arriving in several days or weeks.

The presence of large U.S. forces in Saudi Arabia creates uncertainties for moderate Arab leaders in several other states. Thus the wisdom of having such a small special operations contingency force is all the greater after the Iraqi crisis. Admittedly, the political circumstances would have to be conducive to its use—and they seldom will be—but in military planning remote contingencies must be considered. Such a force might also be useful in hostage rescues and terrorist contingencies of other sorts in the region. In the realm of special operations forces, therefore, this kind of small and ready capability makes a lot of sense for the Middle East.

The Gulf War crisis, as we have suggested earlier, also raises a broad range of additional contingencies for internal wars. The best advice would be to stay out of them if at all possible, but they could occur in countries like Saudi Arabia, Jordan, and Oman, where avoiding them would be virtually impossible. As of this writing, the spring of 1991, internal war has broken out in Iraq. The United States has taken an ambiguous stand toward it, avowing no involvement but being marginally involved de facto through its protection of the Kurds in the northern part of Iraq. Political developments in Kuwait also portend internal struggles. The United States may avoid deeper involvement in both countries. These internal conflicts could see a rapid resolution. Or they could be protracted. At this point, one simply cannot offer a cogent prognosis.

Lacking the actual cases, we can only guess at what kinds of U.S. military forces would be most appropriate, and we would probably be wrong. Perhaps the Algerian civil war offers some idea of the kind of military operations that would occur. Certainly they would be different from the insurgencies in Central America and the Philippines. Oil fields, to be sure, would be a special security problem, but not a new one for Saudi Arabia.

One point does seem clear. The prospects for dealing with internal wars in Saudi Arabia, Kuwait, and the smaller Persian Gulf littoral states—including Oman—are much better than elsewhere as long as some U.S. ground forces remain on the Arabian peninsula. A U.S. occupation of Kuwait and even part of Iraq could produce much more troublesome internal conflicts. Iran has already encouraged insurgents in Iraq, and Syria and perhaps other states might well support insurgents there if a postwar settlement is not to their liking and if all U.S. forces do not leave soon—which is most improbable. It would be more difficult for Syria or Iran to support internal wars in the central and southern parts of the Arabian peninsula. South Yemen, of course, could become a base for insurgents in the southern parts.

Perhaps things will work out favorably, and there will be no such contingencies. Perhaps the region can get back to something approximating the status quo ante. All we can do is to speculate broadly for military planning purposes. Even so, it is difficult to be specific. Conventional forces and extensive intelligence capabilities will surely be needed. Beyond that, it is impossible to specify all of the kinds of special operations forces that will be required.

One other kind of special operations capability must be mentioned: counterterrorism forces. They are prudent to have, and they exist. There is a danger, however, in putting too much emphasis on them. It tends to play into the terrorists' hands. Terrorism is a painful nuisance, a personal tragedy for the victims and their families, but it cannot play a major strategic role in the regional balance of power. We have seen the consequences for two American presidents who made hostages a high priority issue. And we have seen presidents ignore them in Iraq with positive results. Trotting out the terrorism threat to justify larger "low intensity conflict" forces is not wise.

The implications of our analysis for military force structure, put succinctly in summary form, are

1. narrowing the contingency regions and states for potential operations;
2. reducing the size of counterinsurgency and military advisory forces while improving their skills and overall quality;
3. much greater attention to the external dimensions of internal wars in friendly states, including consideration of conventional military intervention against bases of external support;
4. expansion of the definition of the legal concept of self-defense in international law to make it easier to justify such military interventions;
5. the use of DOD Special Forces by the DCI when paramilitary covert action is approved by the president and Congress;
6. a small rescue and countercoup force for contingencies in the Middle East and Southwest Asia;
7. contingency planning for new internal wars resulting from the Gulf War.

Integration of the Political, Economic, and
Military Components of a Strategy

It is easy to call for integration of political, economic, and military factors, and we often insist that we are doing so. A major point of this study has been to demonstrate that we do not. In each of the components, specialists understand the confused causal assumptions that beset U.S. strategy. Yet they seldom consider the implications across the components. The problem is compounded by the way the executive branch is organized. Different agencies have different responsibilities which they try to carry out somewhat independently. Interagency coordination is not easy.

The staffing necessary for integration is not available at the places and times it is required. The single place where it could support decision making with adequate authority to implement a truly integrated strategy is at the National Security Council (NSC) level. Yet staffing at this level for operations is not appropriate. NSC can provide general policy guidance, but the staff work to support operations has to be done in the agencies—Defense, State, CIA, USIA, Treasury, Commerce, and a number of others. It is always tempting to propose new organizational solutions, and in some instances they may be appropriate. But this is not the solution suggested here.

More important is that the staffs in the agencies as well as the agency heads come to understand the deficiencies of present policies and the importance of changing them. With that consciousness and conviction that a change in overall U.S. strategy is essential, more effective interagency coordination will be possible, and the agency heads will be more demanding of it. They may well conclude that some reorganization is needed, but until they see clearly what needs to be done, it makes little sense to begin reorganizing the government.

The same is true for Congress, which plays a very large role in U.S. strategy. What kinds of economic assistance monies are needed is a key question for congressional action. The same is true for all the other instrumentalities needed for an effective strategy. Proceeding from some poorly developed notions about the requirements for special operations forces, Congress has forced the Defense Department to give it resources and structures that are largely counterproductive. In the economic area, there seems to be growing awareness in Congress that traditional direct economic assistance does not yield the desired results.

A reconceptualized understanding of U.S.–Soviet competition in the Third World as explicated in this study could provide a basis for quite different congressional action on economic assistance. The same is true for gaining congressional support for any U.S. role in internal wars in the Third World. The deadlock in Congress in the 1980s over our Central American policy reflects the absence of a consensus on how best to support democratic development there. All sides bring flawed assumptions about both the ways to deal with the challenges and the prospects for success of any strategy. And all sides have valid criticisms of their opponents.

Even if reconceptualization is accepted and an effective effort at devising a strategy that integrates all three components is achieved, the U.S. will face some extremely ambiguous situations where the more promising approach is not obvious. An internal war might be won only to leave a praetorian regime in place unopposed and better able to prevent democratic development. Is it better to let the insurgents win and impose another form of oppression? Or is it better to become more deeply involved in tutelage democracy and direct colonial rule? Or is it acceptable to let the praetorian dictatorship continue under U.S. protection from a Marxist-Leninist challenge? No new strategy will remove these fundamental political dilemmas. They will remain, perhaps even become sharper in our perceptions, if we understand more fully the nature of internal wars and concomitant political and economic development.

A final consideration must be dealt with in light of changes in the Soviet Union and the prospects for the collapse of our major opponent in the Third World competition. If communism is the "grand failure" Zbigniew Brzezinski has called it, does that not render irrelevant much of the analysis in this study? Is the Cold War not effectively coming to an end and is not the thrust of the study based on the indefinite continuation of the Cold War? Political developments in the Soviet Union certainly appear to be changing the environment in the Third World, eliminating the U.S.–Soviet competition there. Even as the Soviet Union drops out of the competition, however, the problem will not suddenly disappear. The Marxist-Leninist approach to insurgency has been modified and improved by other Marxist-Leninist states—China, Cuba, and Vietnam. Gorbachev has only drawn scorn from Castro over perestroika and de-emphasis of the class struggle in Soviet foreign policy. Radical movements now pursuing insurgent strategies are even less likely than Castro to indulge in emulation of Gorbachev in ideological revision and internal policies. Moreover, the radical movements in Southwest Asia and the Middle East are not driven primarily by Marxism-Leninism. While they derive aid from Moscow, they would hardly drop out of the struggle in the absence of that aid. The competition with antidemocratic forces in the three areas of most strategic importance to the United States, therefore, is not likely to disappear or abate significantly in the 1990s.

Under these circumstances, to the extent that the United States remains committed to the international security order it built after World War II and that it retains a political commitment to the spread of democracy, the challenge in the Third World will continue. Were the Marxist-Leninist threat to disappear entirely, the United States would still be facing dictatorships repressing political development and democratic evolution. As one of our analytical excursions indicated, defeating the threat from the radical left is not enough. We must not leave these societies to praetorianism and exploitive oligarchies. We now have the reputation for having done just that in Central America and South America. Repeating the mistake is surely not in our interests.

Notes

....

I Introduction

1   This judgment is shared by some careful students of the Third World and
    political development. See Foltz, "External Causes," 54–68. See also David,
    "Why the Third World Matters," 50–85.
2   See Harry Eckstein, *Internal War*, especially pp. 1–21, 101–103.
3   Doyle, "Kant, Liberal Legacies, and Foreign Affairs," 205–35, 323–53, explores
    this emerging pattern in international affairs.
4   Milosz, *The Captive Mind*, gives an insight into the spiritual and moral prison
    such regimes can create for the intellectual—a much more powerful repression
    than the physical means used by other types of dictatorships.
5   Huntington, *American Politics*, 249.

II The Two-Camp Struggle

1   See Weiner and Huntington, *Understanding Political Development*, for a survey
    of the works in political/development theory.
2   See Little, *Economic Development*, for a survey of changing theory of economic
    development.
3   See Yarborough, "Counterinsurgency," 102.
4   Ibid., 104.
5   See Secretary of Defense Carlucci's *Annual Report, Fiscal Year 1990*, 177–80,
    and *Annual Report, Fiscal Year 1989*, 225–30.
6   Henkin, "Vietnam," 303–12.
7   See Brierly, *The Law Among the Nations*, for the best summary of the develop-
    ment of international law.
8   Reisman, "Old Wines in New Bottles," 171–98.
9   Rostow, "Right of Self-Defense," 264–319.
10 Reisman and Baker, *Covert Uses*, 91.

11   See Henkin et al., *Right versus Might*, for a recent set of views on this issue and the continuing debate in the aftermath of the World Court's ruling on Nicaragua versus the United States.

12   See Gaddis, *Strategies of Containment.*

13   These works can be found in Tucker, *The Marx-Engels Reader*, 66–220.

14   See Engels, *The German Revolutions.*

15   This voluntarist concept of revolution is most explicit in the early manuscripts, particularly *The German Ideology.* The older Marx of *Das Kapital* has been interpreted as far more determinist. Because Lenin would reintroduce the voluntarist element, the younger Marx is particularly relevant to Soviet ideas about war and revolution.

16   See Marx, *The Civil War in France.*

17   See Lenin, "What Is To Be Done?"

18   See Lenin, "Imperialism."

19   Lenin elaborates this analysis in *Two Tactics of Social Democracy.*

20   See Lenin, "State and Revolution."

21   Lenin never actually used the term "peaceful coexistence." He did speak of "peaceful cohabitation." "Peaceful coexistence" as a slogan only became widely used by Khrushchev who projected it back to Lenin. I use it here because its contemporary usage is derived from the components of the policy developed by Lenin in 1921. Although it has gone through several modifications under Stalin, Khrushchev, and Brezhnev, it has retained its Leninist core until Gorbachev's recent revision.

22   See Borkenau, *World Communism*, for a history of the Comintern.

23   Gorbachev has explicitly renounced this "holy writ." See his *Perestroika*, 144–48. Nuclear weapons created problems for Soviet military theorists in the Clausewitzian view of war, but they, unlike their Western counterparts, adapted their view of nuclear weapons within the Leninist interpretation of Clausewitz. See Colonel B. Byely et al., *Marxism-Leninism*, 10–98.

24   A growing literature on Soviet theory and practice in sponsoring revolution and insurgencies in the Third World, as well as direct military intervention, offers a wealth of insight into how the Soviet Union has actually applied such theory. See MacFarlane, *Superpower Rivalry*, for the best elaboration of the concepts. Kaplan, *The Diplomacy of Power*, and Porter, *The U.S.S.R. in Third World Conflicts*, are excellent volumes on actual practice. Huntington, "Patterns of Intervention," 39–47, offers a concise overview.

25   Gorbachev, *Perestroika.*

26   MacFarlane, *Superpower Rivalry*, elaborates this scheme in great detail.

27   See Borkenau, *World Communism*, on China and Spain in this regard.

28   See Rostow, *The Stages of Economic Growth.*

29   Fukuyama, "The End of History?" 3–18.

30   Kennedy, *The Rise and Fall of the Great Powers.*

31   Nye, *Bound to Lead.*

III The Political and Economic Context for Internal War

1 Shafer, *Deadly Paradigms*.
2 Almond, "The Development of Political Development," 450–51.
3 Huntington, "Will More Countries Become Democratic?" 193–218.
4 Rustow, "Transitions to Democracy."
5 Huntington, "Will More Countries Become Democratic?" 210–11.
6 Dahl, *Polyarchy*, 40–43, 53–56. Dahl offers his own version of all five paths with slight variations but generally approximate to the ones offered here.
7 As I shall argue later, this pattern indeed does have contemporary relevance. Land reform in Taiwan, South Korea, and Japan created a new class of small holders who have been able to prosper with modern farming methods and who have played a significant role in the political development of those states. Land reform broke the hold of the old economic and political elites who were not interested in either political modernization or industrialization. Their wealth gave them the power to resist both. Land reform diffused the power into many private hands in a market economy. Certainly this is not the only variable that explains the political development of these states, but it is an important one. Moreover, it draws attention to the relationship between democracy and market economies, and it encourages us to believe that it may be more "causal" than Dahl seems to believe. When he wrote his book, however, it was still widely believed that successful economic development was still occurring in the centrally planned economies of Eastern Europe and the Soviet Union, the examples he gave to raise doubts about the causal connection. I would argue that the lack of diffusion of economic ownership of capital in Soviet-type states has proven a monumental impediment to economic development as well as to political "contestation" in Dahl's sense, a phenomenon necessary to transform a "hegemonic" polity into a "polyarchy." Numerous Soviet spokesmen today are also making this argument about democracy and market economies.
8 Lipset, *Political Man*, 31.
9 Dahl, *Polyarchy*, p. 71.
10 Olson, *The Rise and Decline of Nations*.
11 Huntington, "Will More Countries Become Democratic?" pp. 207–8.
12 Ibid., pp. 198–209.
13 Hartz, *The Founding of New Societies*.
14 See Huntington, "The Goals of Political Development," 3–32.
15 Huntington, *Political Order in Changing Societies*, 8.
16 Ibid., 1.
17 See LaPalombara's probing and thoughtful essay, "Political Science and the Engineering of National Development," 27–65.
18 Huntington, *Political Order in Changing Societies*, does give it attention. Moore, *Authority and Inequality under Capitalism and Socialism*, is another exception, an effort at comparative analysis. Roeder, "Modernization and Participation," 859–84, offers an important analysis of the later stage of such systems, namely in Gorbachev's Soviet Union. The topic, however, remains underdeveloped.

19 This is not true of those scholars who developed the "totalitarian models" of politics in the 1940s and 1950s. Hannah Arendt and J. Talmon were early contributors to the concept. Friedrich and Brzezinski, in their *Totalitarian Dictatorship and Autocracy*, gave it a more rigorous and comparative explanation. More recently, Howe, *1984 Revisited*, offered a reexamination of the model. Walser, in his chapter in this volume, makes the critical point that the creators of the concept were seriously trying to distinguish what made the political systems of the USSR, Nazi Germany, Fascist Italy, and Japan different from all other types of dictatorships. They were not seeking propaganda tools for the Cold War, as has been often asserted since then. For our analysis here we follow the Friedrich-Brzezinski version of totalitarianism systems as it was particularized by the Soviet leadership.

20 See Seton-Watson, *The East European Revolution*, and Brzezinski, *The Soviet Bloc*, for the record of this borrowing.

21 See Alexander Zinoviev, *The Reality of Communism*, for an insider's view of how collectivism ties up and dominates the life of individuals.

22 Roeder, "Modernization and Participation," 859–84.

23 The Soviet case, of course, is far more complex than the East European cases. Introducing a market economy will cause major economic dislocations. Misallocation of capital through central planning for several decades means that a large portion of Soviet industry will have to close down or go through massive modernization, requiring enormous new investments. Like Eastern Europe, the Soviet Union is now facing many of the political and economic development issues that confront Third World states. Reflecting on Huntington's five goals of political development, one has to wonder if Gorbachev has chosen the proper sequence. Political democratization makes decisions to facilitate economic growth more difficult because the forces in favor of social equity can use the democratic process to block economic growth policies. At the same time, the massive new mobilization and demand for participation creates political instability. South Korea, Taiwan, and more recently Chile have managed economic development under authoritarian rule, gradually giving way to democratization as economic success has occurred. Gorbachev seems bent on trying to give democracy priority over economic development, believing it is a precondition to economic development. In fact, private ownership and a market economy seem more important than mass democracy, at least in the early stages when social frustration and inequities are bound to be strong.

IV The Indigenous Sources of Internal Wars

1 Shafer, *Deadly Paradigms*, makes this point in a number of ways in all three cases.

2 Ibid.

3 The figure is based on a study done for Civil Operations and Rural Development Support/Military Assistance Command Vietnam (CORDS/MACV), where the author served in 1970–71.

4 The author had the task of providing staff comment for MACV on the U.S. Em-

bassy's annual request for grant aid to the GVN in 1970. The request was for $750 million although the embassy analysis defined the need as one billion dollars. It argued that the domestic budget gap and the foreign trade gap were simply too big for the regime to manage, that the U.S. must help, by absorbing not the whole cost but only a "prudent" three quarters of it. The author reviewed previous year requests to find the same argument repeated for several years in succession, each time contending that the GVN needed time to reduce these gaps. Each year, however, the gaps had grown, not narrowed, as the arguments insisted the next year would allow. The author was roundly rebuked for encouraging MACV to refuse to agree with the embassy because its argument was analogous to recommending that "we tell a drunk man to drink more in order to sober up! The only way to narrow the gaps is to cut off all aid."

5   Organski and Kugler, *The War Ledger*, 94–96. The sources for calculating the aggregate figures in this book's chart are difficult to understand; the hypothesis, however, is intriguing and reasonable although not clearly proven.

6   See Evans, "Foreign Capital and the Third World State," 319–52.

7   While it has not been done for this study, an examination of which of the three patterns is more conducive to growth could be highly relevant for U.S. policy toward states it assists. Where the local government becomes a surrogate for the commercial class, it probably encourages "statism" rather than a competitive market. The same is probably true where local government becomes the intermediary. The role of the state and its bureaucrats in this regard can deceive the casual observer about the degree to which free market economics is actually the case in developing countries.

   As the author learned from several Honduran officials in conversations, an example of self-discovery occurred in Honduras during the spring of 1990. The new regime, dedicated to cutting protectionism and state supports for business, was surprised at the degree of statism and nonmarket factors in the indigenous economy. Hidden subsidies, de facto tariffs, and informal transfer payments were far larger than they had estimated, and it took a major investigatory effort to find them. The important point is that regimes which claim to have market economies may in fact be closer to central planning and Soviet-like socialism than they admit or realize.

8   Chaudhry, "The Price of Wealth," 101–46.

9   Ibid., p. 103.

10   Snider, "The Political Performance of Third World Governments," 1263.

11   Ibid., 1268.

12   Ibid., 1266, 1267.

13   Ibid., 1269.

VI   The Record of East-West Competition in the Third World

1   See Seton-Watson, *Revolution in East Europe*, for country-by-country accounts.

2   See MacFarlane, *Superpower Rivalry*.

3   See Katz, *The Third World in Soviet Military Thought*.

4   Montgomery, *Revolution in El Salvador*, 17.

5   Ibid., 30–40.

6   Ibid., 43.

7   Anderson, "Roots of Revolution," 120.

8   Montgomery, *Revolution in El Salvador*, 50–53.

9   Montgomery, Ibid., 55.

10 Eva Loser, *The 1989 El Salvadoran Elections*.

11 Two excellent sources of data on macroeconomic trends for El Salvador are the World Bank, *Development Report 1990*, 178–240; and the International Monetary Fund, *International Financial Statistics Yearbook 1990*, 338–41.

12 See Gurr, *Why Men Rebel*, for an insightful analysis of the concept of "progressive relative deprivation."

13 Useful data that describes numerous components of El Salvador's social and cultural makeup also can be found in *Development Report 1990*, 178–240; and the Central Intelligence Agency, *The World Factbook 1990*, 90–92.

14 Barry and Preusch, *The Central American Fact Book*, 200.

15 Anderson, "Roots of Revolution," 115.

16 Montgomery, *Revolution in El Salvador*, 99.

17 Barry and Preusch, *The Central American Fact Book*, 208ff.

18 Loser, *The 1989 El Salvadoran Elections*, 7.

19 Montgomery, *Revolution in El Salvador*, 36–70.

20 Anderson, "Roots of Revolution," 114.

21 An excellent, detailed overview of external influences on the FMLN and FDR can be found in Shultz, *The Soviet Union and Revolutionary Warfare*, 148–86.

22 See Shultz et al., *Guerrilla Warfare and Counterinsurgency*, for a brief explanation of the foco insurgency.

23 Evans, "Revolutionary Movements in Central America," 167–93.

24 A very useful one-volume history of the government's and insurgents' perspectives on the war as it evolved is Manwaring and Prisk, *El Salvador at War*.

25 The rates of economic growth in these years, however, suggest that the government not only retained autonomy but also derived the increased autonomy that dealing with transnational capital has been found to bring in most other cases.

26 An excellent critical study of U.S. military support to the El Salvadoran counterinsurgency program is Bacevich et al., *American Military Policy in Small Wars*.

27 See Duarte, *Duarte: My Story*, 208–28.

28 For an overview of Guatemala's early history, see Nyrop, *Guatemala*, 3–39.

29 Two excellent sources on this historical development are Wynia, *The Politics of Latin American Development*, esp. 36–134; and Skidmore and Smith, *Modern Latin America*, esp. 15–45; also useful is Munro, *The Five Republics of Central America*.

30 See Johnson, "The Latin American Military," 91–132.

31 Nyrop, *Guatemala*, 20–22.

32 See Schneider, "Guatemala," 516–35; and Black, *Garrison Guatemala*, 11–18.

33 See U.S. Department of Commerce, *Investment Climate Statement: Guatemala*,

1–12; and U.S. Department of Commerce, International Trade Administration, *Marketing Guatemala*, 3–4.

34   See World Bank, *World Bank Development Report 1990*, 178–240.

35   See, for example, the yearly *Country Reports on Human Rights Practices* submitted by the U.S. Department of State to the U.S. Senate Committee on Foreign Relations and the U.S. House of Representatives Committee on Foreign Affairs.

36   See the Inter-American Development Bank, *1988 Report*, 415–20.

37   Central Intelligence Agency, *The World Factbook 1990*, 125–26; and World Bank, *Development Report 1990*, 178–240.

38   For an analysis of the 1990 Guatemalan elections, see Estevez and Loser, *The 1990 Guatemalan Elections*, 11.

39   Ibid., 147–50.

40   Ibid., 153.

41   The number of U.S. firms in Guatemala is, nonetheless, quite large. See Caribbean/Central American Action, *1987 Caribbean and Central American Databook*, 169–170.

42   See Nyrop, *Guatemala*, 41–82.

43   For a discussion of the shift in the Church's policy toward activism following Vatican II and the Medellin Conference of Catholic Bishops in the mid- and late 1960s, see Montgomery, *Revolution in El Salvador*, 97–118.

44   George Black, *Garrison Guatemala*, 106–7.

45   See Collazo-Davila, "The Guatemalan Insurrection," 113; and *New York Times*, June 13, 1971, 16.

46   Collazo-Davila, "The Guatemalan Insurrection," 121–24, 130.

47   See U.S. Department of State, "Revolution Beyond our Borders," esp. 13.

48   See *Latin American Regional Reports*, "Another Coup Attempt Foiled," 7.

49   An excellent single-volume history of America's influence on the Philippines is Karnow, *In Our Image*.

50   For two excellent sources of macroeconomic data on the Philippines, see World Bank, *Development Report 1990*, 178–240; and International Monetary Fund, *International Financial Statistics Yearbook 1990*, 584–89.

51   Lande, *Rebuilding a Nation*, quoted by David Rosenberg, 348.

52   Kessler, "A New Philippine Political System," 371.

53   Ibid., 369–78.

54   Central Intelligence Agency, *The World Factbook 1988*, 190–91.

55   For a detailed examination of the Huk rebellion from the peasant's perspective, see Kerkvliet, *The Huk Rebellion*.

56   Two studies which provide an analytic framework to assess the relative strengths and weaknesses of numerous counterinsurgencies in the postwar period, including those of the Philippines, are the BDM Corporation, *Fourteen Points*, appendix F; and the BDM Corporation, *Strategies of Counterinsurgency*, 56–64.

57   Chapman, *Inside the Philippine Revolution*, esp. 214–33.

58   Niksch, "The Communist Party of the Philippines," 397ff.

59   Ibid.

60 Ibid.

61 Ibid.

62 Two recent, very revealing articles on the transnational nature of the Philippine insurgency, particularly its financial networks, are Clad, "Anatomy of a Revolution," 12–14; and Gordon-Bates, "Inside the Revolution," 20–23.

63 The NPA's tactical shift to strike at American personnel and facilities and increase Filipino nationalist feelings was reflected in the assassination of U.S. Army Colonel Rowe and the destruction of U.S. Navy communications equipment. For an overview of the history surrounding the importance of U.S. military facilities in the Philippines within U.S.–Philippine relations, see Greene, *The Philippine Bases*; and Berry, *U.S. Bases in The Philippines.*

64 Kessler, "A New Philippine Political System," 369–78.

65 *Far Eastern Economic Review*, August 3, 1989, 8.

66 Chaudhry, "The Price of Wealth," 101–45.

67 The evidence for this judgment comes from the author's own observations as a member of the National Security Council staff at the time. Some countries complained bitterly in private to the United States but dared not make their views public in light of expanding Soviet presence in the Indian Ocean.

68 See Porter, *The U.S.S.R. in Third World Conflicts*, for excellent case studies of Soviet interventions in the region.

69 See Katz, *The Third World*, 81–82, for general Soviet views on Third World military versus guerrilla armies as sources of revolution.

70 See Hussein, "Post–Cold War Middle East," 117–19, for Saddam's own analysis of the meaning of the end of the Cold War for the region. In his judgment, the decline of Soviet power leaves the Arabs no alternative but a strong military stand against the United States. In other words, the end of the Cold War makes hot war with the United States imperative for Arab independence.

71 The author heard this concern with the "southern threat" frequently expressed by senior general staff officers and academic specialists during a visit there in the fall of 1990.

72 Chaudhry, "The Price of Wealth," 113.

73 See the account of these events and the related diplomacy in *Time*, June 4, 1990, 28–45.

74 Mancur Olson, interview with author, summer of 1989.

75 Chaudhry, "The Price of Wealth," 114. Chaudhry is not generalizing here only on her study of Saudi Arabia and Yemen. She draws heavily on studies of the development of the governments and economies of Western Europe over the last several centuries. The cross-cultural and cross-regional nature of the generalization, therefore, makes it more compelling for Central America and the Phillipines.

76 Snider, "The Political Performance of Third World Governments."

77 Gorbachev, *Perestroika*, 144–48.

78 See his speech of November 15, 1989, FBIS-SOV–89–220, November 16, 1989, 34–75, on the economy; see his report to the Central Committee Plenum on December 25, 1989, FBIS-SOV–89–246, December 26, 1989, 41–51, esp. 43, on the nationality question.

79 Yevgenii Novikov, in interview with the author, fall of 1989. Novikov was involved in transmitting these instructions to a number of African parties.

80 See *Time*, June 4, 1990, for some public details of the kinds of military assistance to Central American insurgents being followed by U.S. intelligence.

81 For an excellent critical essay on the U.S. military's approach in El Salvador, see Bacevich et al., *American Military Policy in Small Wars*.

82 Olson, "Diseconomies of Scale and Development," 96.

83 Ibid.

84 World Bank, *Development Report 1990*, 224.

85 Ibid.

86 For some examples, see Johnson, *The Role of the Military*; Huntington, *Political Order in Changing Societies*, particularly the chapter on authoritarian reformers; Huntington, *Changing Patterns of Military Intervention*; and Rustow and Ward, *Political Development in Japan and Turkey*.

Bibliography

••••••••••••••••••••••••••••••••••••••

Adams, Jan S. "Incremental Activism in Soviet Third World Policy: The Role of the International Department of the CPSU Central Committee." *Slavic Review* 48 (Winter 1989): 614–30.

Adelman, Jonathan R., and Gibson, Les, eds. *Contemporary Soviet Military Affairs: The Legacy of World War II.* Boston: Unwin Hyman, 1989.

Albright, David E. "The U.S.S.R. and the Third World in the 1980s," *Problems of Communism* 38 (March–June 1989): 50–70.

Alexiev, Alexander A. *Marxism and Resistance in the Third World: Cause and Effect.* Santa Monica, Calif.: The Rand Corporation, 1989.

Almond, Gabriel A. "The Development of Political Development." In *Understanding Political Development.* Edited by Myron Weiner and Samuel P. Huntington, pp. 437–90. Boston: Little, Brown, 1987.

Almond, Gabriel A., and Powell, G. Bingham, Jr. *Comparative Politics: A Developmental Approach.* Boston: Little, Brown, 1966.

Almond, Gabriel A., and Verba, Sidney. *The Civic Culture.* Princeton: Princeton University Press, 1963.

Almond, Gabriel A., and Coleman, James S., eds. *The Politics of Developing Areas.* Princeton: Princeton University Press, 1960.

Anderson, Charles W. "El Salvador: The Army as Reformer." In *Political Systems in Latin America,* edited by Martin C. Needler, pp. 53–72. Princeton: D. Van Nostrand, 1964.

Anderson, Thomas P. "Roots of Revolution in Central America." In *Rift and Revolution,* edited by Howard J. Wiarda, pp. 105–28. Washington, D.C.: American Enterprise Institute, 1984.

Apter, David E. *The Politics of Modernization.* Chicago: University of Chicago Press, 1965.

Arendt, Hannah W. *Economic Development: The History of an Idea.* Chicago: University of Chicago Press, 1987.

Ashby, Timothy. *The Bear in the Back Yard: Moscow's Caribbean Strategy.* Lexington, Mass.: D. C. Heath, 1987.

Bacevich, A. J., et al. *American Military Policy in Small Wars: The Case of El Salvador.* Washington, D.C.: Pergamon-Brassey's, 1988.

Ball, Nicole. *Security and Economy in the Third World.* Princeton: Princeton University Press, 1988.

Bandow, Doug, ed. *U.S. Aid to the Developing World: A Free Market Agenda.* Heritage Foundation Critical Issues Series. Washington, D.C.: The Heritage Foundation, 1985.

Banfield, Edward C. *The Moral Basis of a Backward Society.* Glencoe, Ill.: Free Press, 1958.

Barry, Tom, and Preusch, Deb. *The Central American Fact Book.* New York: Grove Press, 1986.

BDM Corporation. *Fourteen Points: A Framework for the Analysis of Counterinsurgency.* BDM/W-84-0275-TR. McLean, Va.: BDM Corporation, July 31, 1984.

BDM Corporation. *Strategies of Counterinsurgency: An Analytical Aid.* BDM/MCL-86-0778-TR. McLean, Va.: BDM Corporation, October 31, 1986.

Beitz, Charles R. "Democracy in Developing Societies." In *Boundaries: National Autonomy and Its Limits,* edited by Peter G. Brown and Henry Shue, pp. 177–208. Rowman and Littlefield, 1981.

Bernstein, Henry, ed. *Underdevelopment & Development: The Third World Today (Selected Readings).* New York: Penguin Books, 1976.

Berry, William E., Jr. *U.S. Bases in the Philippines: The Evolution of the Special Relationship.* Boulder, Colo.: Westview Press, 1989.

Bialer, Seweryn. " 'New Thinking' in Soviet Foreign Policy." *Survival* 30 (July–August, 1988): 291–309.

Bienen, Henry, ed. *The Military Intervenes: Case Studies in Political Development.* New York: Russell Sage Foundation, 1968.

Binnendijk, Hans. "Authoritarian Regimes in Transition." *Washington Quarterly* 10 (Spring 1987): 153–64.

Black, George, with Jamail, Milton, Chinchilla, and Norma Stoltz. *Garrison Guatemala.* New York: Monthly Review Press, 1984.

Blasier, Cole. *The Giant's Rival: The U.S.S.R. and Latin America.* Pittsburgh, Pa.: University of Pittsburgh Press, 1983.

Borkenau, Franz. *World Communism.* Ann Arbor: University of Michigan Press, 1962.

Breslauer, George W. "Ideology and Learning in Soviet Third World Policy." *World Politics* 39 (April 1987): 429–48.

Brierly, James Leslie. *The Law Among the Nations.* Oxford: University Press, 1963.

Brownlie, Ian. *International Law and the Use of Force by States.* New York: Oxford University Press, 1963.

Brzezinski, Zbigniew K. *The Soviet Bloc: Unity and Conflict.* Cambridge, Mass.: Harvard University Press, 1960.

Burgess, William H., III, ed. *Inside Spetsnaz: Soviet Special Operations, a Critical Analysis.* Novato, Calif.: Presidio Press, 1990.

Burton, Sandra. "Aquino's Philippines: The Center Holds." *Foreign Affairs* 35 (special edition, *America and the World 1986*): 524–37.

Buszynski, Leszek. *Soviet Foreign Policy and Southeast Asia*. New York: St. Martin's Press, 1986.

Byely, Colonel B., et al. *Marxism-Leninism on War and Army*. Moscow: Progress Publishers, 1972.

Campbell, Kurt M. *Soviet Policy towards South Africa*. New York: St. Martin's Press, 1986.

Caribbean/Central American Action. *C/CAA's 1987 Caribbean and Central American Databook*. Washington, D.C.: Caribbean/Central American Action, 1986.

Carlucci, Frank C., Secretary of Defense. *Annual Report to the Congress: Fiscal Year 1989*. Washington, D.C.: Government Printing Office.

Carlucci, Frank C., Secretary of Defense. *Annual Report to the Congress: Fiscal Year 1990*. Washington, D.C.: Government Printing Office.

Central Intelligence Agency. *The World Factbook 1988*. Washington, D.C.: Government Printing Office, 1988.

Central Intelligence Agency. *The World Factbook 1990*. Washington, D.C.: Government Printing Office, 1990.

Chapman, William. *Inside the Philippine Revolution*. New York: Norton, 1987.

Chaudhry, Kiren Aziz. "The Price of Wealth: Business and State in Labor Remittances and Oil Economies." *International Organization* 43 (Winter 1989): 101–46.

Christian, Shirley. *Nicaragua: Revolution in the Family*. New York: Vintage Books, 1986.

Clad, James. "Anatomy of a Red Revolution." *Far Eastern Economic Review* (July 28, 1988): 12–14.

Clawson, Robert W., ed. *East-West Rivalry in the Third World: Security Issues and Regional Perspectives*. Wilmington, Del.: Scholarly Resources, 1986.

Clough, Michael, ed. *Reassessing the Soviet Challenge in Africa*. Policy Papers in International Affairs, no. 25. Berkeley: University of California Institute of International Studies, 1986.

Cobban, Helena. "The PLO and the *Intifada*." *Middle East Journal* 44 (Spring 1990): 207–33.

Cohen, Eliot A. "Constraints on America's Conduct of Small Wars." *International Security* 9 (Fall 1984): 151–81.

Cohen, Eliot A. "Distant Battles: Modern War in the Third World." *International Security* 10 (Spring 1986): 143–71.

Coll, Alberto R. "International Law and U.S. Foreign Policy." *Washington Quarterly* 11 (Autumn 1988): 107–18.

Collazo-Davila, Vincente. "The Guatemalan Insurrection." In *Insurgency in the Modern World*, edited by Bard E. O'Neill, William R. Heaton, and Donald J. Alberts, pp. 109–34. Boulder, Colo.: Westview Press, 1980.

Cornia, Giovanni A.; Jolly, R.; and Stewart, F., eds. *Adjustment with a Human Face: Protecting the Vulnerable and Promoting Growth* (a study by UNICEF). New York: Oxford University Press, 1987.

Cutler, Lloyd N. "The Right to Intervene." *Foreign Affairs* 64 (1985): 96–122.

Dahl, Robert A. *Polyarchy: Participation and Opposition.* New Haven: Yale University Press, 1971.

Dahl, Robert A. *Who Governs?* New Haven: Yale University Press, 1961.

Damrosch, Lori F. "Politics Across Borders: Nonintervention and Nonforcible Influence over Domestic Affairs." *American Journal of International Law* 83 (1989): 1–50.

Damrosch, Lori F. "Multi-lateral Disputes." In *The International Court of Justice at the Crossroads,* edited by Lori Damrosch, pp. 376–400. Dobbs Ferry, N.Y.: Trans-National Publishers, 1987.

David, Steven R. "Soviet Involvement in Third World Coups." *International Security* 11 (Summer 1986): 3–36.

David, Steven R. "Why the Third World Matters." *International Security* 14 (Summer 1989): 50–85.

deSchweinitz, Karl, Jr. "Growth Development and Political Modernization." *World Politics* 22 (July 1970): 518–40.

deSoto, Hernando. *The Other Path: The Invisible Revolution in the Third World.* New York: Harper and Row, 1989.

Deutsch, Karl W. "Social Mobilization and Political Development." *American Political Science Review* 55 (September 1961): 493–513.

Diamond, Larry. "Beyond Authoritarianism and Totalitarianism: Strategies for Democratization." *Washington Quarterly* 12 (Winter 1989): 141–63.

Donaldson, Robert H., ed. *The Soviet Union in the Third World: Successes and Failures.* Boulder, Colo.: Westview Press, 1981.

Doyle, Michael W. "Kant, Liberal Legacies, and Foreign Affairs," parts 1 and 2. *Philosophy and Public Affairs* 12 (1983): 205–353.

Duarte, José Napoleon (with Page, Diana). *Duarte: My Story.* New York: Putnam, 1986.

Duncan, Raymond W., ed. *Soviet Policy in Developing Countries.* Huntington, N.Y.: Robert E. Krieger, 1981.

Eckstein, Harry, ed. *Internal War.* New York: Free Press of Glencoe, 1964.

Emerson, Rupert. *From Empire to Nation.* Cambridge: Harvard University Press, 1960.

Engels, Friedrich. *The German Revolutions.* Chicago: University of Chicago Press, 1967.

Estevez, Frederica, and Loser, Eva. *CSIS Latin American Election Study Series: The 1990 Guatemalan Elections.* Reports 1 and 2. Washington, D.C.: Center for Strategic and International Studies, 1990.

Europa Publications. "Guatemala: Introductory Survey." In *The Europa Year Book 1988: A World Survey,* vol. 1, pt. 2, pp. 1236–39. London: Europa Publications, 1989.

Evans, Peter B. "Foreign Capital and the Third World State." In *Understanding Political Development,* edited by Myron Weiner and Samuel P. Huntington, pp. 319–52. Boston: Little, Brown, 1987.

Feldstein, Martin; de Carmoy, H.; Narusawa, K.; and Krugman, P. R. *Restoring*

Growth in the Debt-Laden Third World (Report to the Trilateral Commission no. 33). New York: Trilateral Commission, 1987.

Foltz, William J. "External Causes." In *Revolution and Political Change in the Third World*, edited by Barry M. Schutz and Robert O. Slater, pp. 54–68. Boulder, Colo.: Lynne Rienner Publishers, 1990.

Franck, Thomas M. "Secret Warfare: Policy Options for a Modern Legal and International Context." Paper delivered at the U.S. Institute of Peace Conference on Policy Alternatives to Deal with Secret Warfare: International Law, March 16–17, 1990.

Franck, Thomas M. "Who Killed Article 2(4)? Or: Changing Norms Governing the Use of Force by States." *American Journal of International Law* 64 (1970): 809–907.

Friedmann, Wolfgang. "Intervention and International Law." *International Spectator* 25 (1971): 40–66.

Friedrich, Carl J. *Man and His Government.* New York: McGraw-Hill, 1963.

Friedrich, Carl J., and Brzezinski, Zbigniew K. *Totalitarian Dictatorship and Autocracy.* New York: Praeger, 1956.

Fukuyama, Francis. "The End of History?" *The National Interest* 16 (Summer 1989): 3–18.

Gaddis, John Lewis. *Strategies of Containment.* New York: Oxford University Press, 1982.

Gardner, Richard N. "Sovereignty and Intervention: A Challenge of Law-Making for the Industrialized Democracies." *Trialogue* no. 35 (Winter 1984): 3–12.

Gardner, Richard N. "Armed Force, Peaceful Settlements, and the United Nations Charter: Are There Alternatives to 'A New International Anarchy?' " In *Proceedings of the Seventy-Seventh Annual Meeting of The American Society of International Law*, pp. 31–51. Washington, D.C.: American Society of International Law, 1985.

Gastil, Raymond D. "The Diffusion of Democracy and Liberal Modernism." In *Freedom in the World: Political Rights and Civil Liberties, 1984–1985*, pp. 257–69. Westport, Conn.: Greenwood Press, 1985.

George, Alexander L., ed. *Managing U.S.–Soviet Rivalry.* Boulder, Colo.: Westview Press, 1983.

Golan, Galia. *The Soviet Union and National Liberation Movements in the Third World.* Boston: Unwin Hyman, 1988.

Gorbachev, Mikhail S. *Perestroika: New Thinking for Our Country and the World.* New York: Harper & Row, 1987.

Gordon-Bates, Kim. "Inside the Revolution." *South* (November 1988): 20–23.

Gott, Richard. *Guerrilla Movements in Latin America.* London: Thomas Nelson and Sons, 1970.

Graham, Gordon. "The Justice of Intervention." *Review of International Studies* 13 (April 1987): 133–46.

Greene, Fred, ed. *The Philippine Bases: Negotiating for the Future.* New York: Council on Foreign Relations, 1988.

Greentree, Todd R. *The United States and the Politics of Conflict in the Developing*

World: A Policy Study. Report for the Foreign Service Institute, Center for the Study of Foreign Affairs, U.S. Department of State, Washington, D.C.: Government Printing Office, 1990.

Grobar, Lisa M., and Porter, Richard C. "Benoit Revisited: Defense Spending and Economic Growth in LDCs." *Journal of Conflict Resolution* 33 (June 1989): 318–45.

Gurr, Ted Robert. *Why Men Rebel.* Princeton: Princeton University Press, 1970.

Gutman, Roy. *Banana Diplomacy: The Making of American Policy in Nicaragua, 1981–1987.* New York: Simon and Schuster, 1988.

Gutteridge, William. *Military Institutions and Power in the New States.* New York: Praeger, 1965.

Hanning, Hugh. *The Peaceful Uses of Military Forces.* New York: Praeger, 1967.

Harries, Owen. " 'Exporting Democracy'—and Getting It Wrong." *The National Interest* (Fall 1988): 3–12.

Harrison, Lawrence E. *Underdevelopment Is a State of Mind: The Latin American Case.* Lanham, Md.: University Press of America, 1985.

Hartz, Louis. *The Founding of New Societies.* New York: Harcourt, Brace, and World, 1964.

Hartz, Louis. *The Liberal Tradition in America.* New York: Harcourt, Brace, and World, 1955.

Henkin, Louis. "Vietnam: The Uncertain Trumpet of Uncertain Law." *How Nations Behave: Law and Foreign Policy.* New York: Columbia University Press, 1979.

Henkin, Louis, et al. *Right versus Might: International Law and the Use of Force.* New York: Council on Foreign Relations Press, 1989.

Hernandez, Carolina G. "Democracy in the Philippines." *Journal of International Affairs* 38 (Winter 1985): 243–58.

Hirschman, Albert O. *The Strategy of Economic Development.* New Haven: Yale University Press, 1958.

Hosmer, Stephen T. *Constraints on U.S. Strategy in Third World Conflicts.* New York: Crane Russak, 1987.

Hough, Jerry F. *The Struggle for the Third World: Soviet Debates and American Options.* Washington, D.C.: The Brookings Institution, 1986.

Howe, Irving, ed. *1984 Revisited: Totalitarianism in Our Country.* New York: Harper & Row, 1983.

Huntington, Samuel P. *American Politics: The Promise of Disharmony.* Cambridge: Harvard University Press, 1981.

Huntington, Samuel P. "The Change to Change: Modernization, Development and Politics." *Comparative Politics* 3 (April 1971): 283–322.

Huntington, Samuel P. *Changing Patterns of Military Intervention.* Glencoe, Ill.: Free Press of Glencoe, 1962.

Huntington, Samuel P. "The Goals of Development." In *Understanding Political Development,* edited by Myron Weiner and Samuel P. Huntington, pp. 3–32. Boston: Little, Brown, 1987.

Huntington, Samuel P. "Patterns of Intervention: Americans and Soviets in the Third World." *The National Interest* (Spring 1987): 39–47.

Huntington, Samuel P. *Political Order in Changing Societies*. New Haven: Yale University Press, 1968.

Huntington, Samuel P. "Will More Countries Become Democratic?" *Political Science Quarterly* 99 (Summer, 1984): 193–218.

Hussein, Saddam. "Saddam Hussein on the Post–Cold War Middle East." *ORBIS* 35 (Winter 1991): 117–19.

Inter-American Development Bank. *Economic and Social Progress in Latin America: 1988 Report*. Washington, D.C.: Inter-American Development Bank, 1988.

International Institute for Strategic Studies. *Strategic Survey, 1988–1989*. London: Brassey's, 1989.

International Monetary Fund. *International Financial Statistics Yearbook 1988*. Washington, D.C.: International Monetary Fund, 1988.

International Monetary Fund. *International Financial Statistics Yearbook 1990*. Washington, D.C.: International Monetary Fund, 1990.

Janowitz, Morris. *The Military in the Political Development of New Nations*. Chicago: University of Chicago Press, 1964.

Johnson, John J. "The Latin American Military as a Politically Competing Group in Transitional Society." In *The Role of the Military in Underdeveloped Countries*, edited by John J. Johnson, pp. 91–132. Princeton: Princeton University Press, 1962.

Johnson, John J., ed. *The Role of the Military in Underdeveloped Countries*. Princeton: Princeton University Press, 1962.

Johnson, Robert H. "Exaggerating America's Stakes in Third World Conflicts." *International Security* 10 (Winter 1985–86): 32–68.

Johnson, Robert H. "Misguided Morality: Ethics and the Reagan Doctrine." *Political Science Quarterly* 103 (1988): 509–29.

Johnson, Robert H. *Rollback Revisited: A Reagan Doctrine for Insurgent Wars?* Washington, D.C.: Overseas Development Council, 1986.

Jones, Gregg R. *Red Revolution: Inside the Philippine Guerrilla Movement*. Boulder, Colo.: Westview Press, 1989.

Jordan, David C. "An Affirmative Strategy for Latin America." *Global Affairs* 3 (Summer 1988): 157–64.

Joyner, Christopher O. "Reflections on the Lawfulness of Invasion." *American Journal of International Law* 78 (1984): 131–44.

Kaplan, Stephen, ed. *The Diplomacy of Power: Soviet Armed Forces as a Political Instrument*. Washington, D.C.: Brookings Institution, 1981.

Karnow, Stanley. *In Our Image: America's Empire in the Philippines*. New York: Random House, 1989.

Katz, Mark N. *The Third World in Soviet Military Thought*. Baltimore, Md.: Johns Hopkins University Press, 1982.

Kennedy, Paul. *The Rise and Fall of the Great Powers: Economic Change and Military Conflict from 1500 to 2000*. New York: Random House, 1987.

Kerkvliet, Benedict J. *The Huk Rebellion: A Study of Peasant Revolt in the Philippines*. Berkeley: University of California Press, 1977.

Kessler, Richard J. "A New Philippine Political System." In *Rebuilding a Nation,* edited by Carl H. Lande, pp. 369–78. Washington, D.C.: Washington Institute Press, 1987.

Killick, Tony, ed. *The Quest for Economic Stabilisation: The IMF and the Third World.* London: Overseas Development Institute, 1984.

Kindelberger, Charles P. *Economic Development.* New York: McGraw-Hill, 1965.

Kirkpatrick, Jeane J. *Dictatorships and Double Standards: Rationalism & Reason in Politics.* New York: American Enterprise Institute and Simon & Schuster, 1982.

Kirkpatrick, Jeane J. *The Reagan Doctrine and U.S. Foreign Policy.* Washington, D.C.: Heritage Foundation, 1985.

Knight, Amy W. *The KGB: Police and Politics in the Soviet Union.* Boston: Unwin Hyman, 1988.

Korbonski, Andrzej, and Fukuyama, Francis, eds. *The Soviet Union and the Third World: The Last Three Decades.* Ithaca: Cornell University Press in association with the RAND/UCLA Center for the Study of Soviet International Behavior, 1987.

Lande, Carl H., ed. *Rebuilding a Nation: Philippine Challenges and American Policy.* Washington, D.C.: Washington Institute Press, 1984.

LaFeber, Walter. *Inevitable Revolutions: The United States in Central America.* Expanded ed. New York: Norton, 1984.

LaPalombara, Joseph. "Political Science and the Engineering of National Development." In *Political Development in Changing Societies,* edited by M. Palmer and L. Stern, pp. 27–65. Lexington, Mass.: Heath Lexington Books, 1971.

LaPalombara, Joseph, ed. *Bureaucracy and Political Development.* Princeton: Princeton University Press, 1963.

LaPalombara, Joseph, and Weiner, Myron, eds. *Political Parties and Political Development.* Princeton: Princeton University Press, 1966.

Latin American Regional Reports: Mexico and Central America. "Another Coup Attempt Foiled." RM–89–05, June 8, 1989.

Leigh, Monroe. "Legal and Political Issues in the Central American Conflict." In *Proceedings of the Seventy-Ninth Annual Meeting of the American Society of International Law,* pp. 40–57. Washington, D.C.: American Society of International Law, 1987.

Leites, Nathan, and Wolf, Charles, Jr. *Rebellion and Authority: Myths and Realities Reconsidered.* Santa Monica, Calif.: Rand Corporation, 1966.

Lenin, Vladimir I. "Imperialism: The Highest Stage of Capitalism." In *The Lenin Anthology,* edited by Robert C. Tucker, pp. 204–74. New York: Norton, 1975.

Lenin, Vladimir I. "State and Revolution." In *The Lenin Anthology,* edited by Robert C. Tucker, pp. 311–98. New York: Norton, 1975.

Lenin, Vladimir I. *Two Tactics of Social Democracy in the Democratic Revolution.* New York: International Publishers, 1935.

Lenin, Vladimir I. "What Is To Be Done?" In *The Lenin Anthology,* edited by Robert C. Tucker, pp. 12–14. New York: Norton, 1975.

Leo Grande, William M. "The Politics of Revolutionary Development: Civil-Military Relations in Cuba, 1959–1976." *Journal of Strategic Studies* 1 (December 1978).

Levy, Marion J., Jr. *Modernization and the Structure of Societies: A Setting for International Affairs.* 2 vols. Princeton: Princeton University Press, 1966.

Lippman, Walter. *The Public Philosophy*. Boston: Little, Brown, 1955.

Lipset, Seymour M. *Political Man*. Garden City, N.Y.: Doubleday, 1960.

Lipset, Seymour M. "Some Social Requisites of Democracy." *American Political Science Review* 53 (1959): 69–105.

Little, Ian M. D. *Economic Development: Theory, Policy, and International Relations*. New York: Basic Books, 1982.

Loser, Eva. *CSIS Latin American Election Study Series: The 1989 El Salvadoran Elections, Pre-Election Report*. Washington, D.C.: Center for Strategic and International Studies, 1989.

MacFarlane, S. Neil. *Superpower Rivalry and Third World Radicalism: The Idea of National Liberation*. Baltimore: Johns Hopkins University Press, 1985.

McNeil, Frank. *War and Peace in Central America*. New York: Charles Scribner's Sons, 1988.

Manwaring, Max G., and Prisk, Court. *El Salvador at War: An Oral History*. Washington, D.C.: National Defense University Press, 1988.

Marsh, Robert M. "Does Democracy Hinder Economic Development in the Latecomer Developing Nations?" *Comparative Social Research* 2 (1979): 215–48.

Marx, Karl. *The Civil War in France*. New York: International Publishers, 1940.

Marx, Karl. "Das Kapital." In *The Marx-Engels Reader*, 2nd edition, edited by Robert C. Tucker, pp. 294–442. New York: Norton, 1978.

Marx, Karl, and Engels, Friedrich. *The German Ideology*. New York: International Publications, 1947.

Meberge, James D. *The Soviet Presence in Latin America*. New York: Crane, Russak in association with the National Strategy Information Center, 1974.

Menon, Rajan. *Soviet Power and the Third World*. New Haven: Yale University Press, 1986.

Milosz, Czeslaw. *The Captive Mind*. Translated by Jane Zielonko. New York: Vintage Books, 1981.

Montgomery, John D. "How Facts Replace Fads: Social Science and Social Development." *Comparative Politics* 22 (January 1990): 237–48.

Montgomery, Tommie Sue. *Revolution in El Salvador*. Boulder, Colo.: Westview Press, 1982.

Moore, Barrington, Jr. *Authority and Inequality Under Capitalism and Socialism*. Oxford: Clarendon Press, 1987.

Moore, Barrington, Jr. *Social Origins of Democracy and Dictatorship*. Boston: Beacon Press, 1966.

Moore, John Norton. "Grenada and the International Double Standard." *American Journal of International Law* 78 (1984): 145–68.

Moore, John Norton. "The Secret War in Central America and the Future of World Order." *American Journal of International Law* 80 (1986): 43–127.

Moore, John Norton, ed. *Law and Civil War in the Modern World*. Baltimore: Johns Hopkins University Press, 1974.

Muller, Edward N.; Seligson, Mitchell A.; Fu, Hung-der; and Midlarsky, Manus I. "Land Inequality and Political Violence." *American Political Science Review* 83 (June 1989): 577–95.

Munro, Dana G. *The Five Republics of Central America*. New York: Russell and

Russell, 1967.

Needler, Martin C. "Political Development and Military Intervention in Latin America." *American Political Science Review* 60 (September 1966): 616–26.

Nelson, Joan M. and contributors. *Fragile Coalitions: The Politics of Economic Adjustment.* Overseas Development Council, U.S.–Third World Policy Perspectives, no. 12. New Brunswick, N.J.: Transaction Books, 1989.

Neubauer, Deane. "Some Conditions of Democracy." *American Political Science Review* 61 (1967): 1002–09.

Newberry, David, and Stern, Nicholas, eds. *The Theory of Taxation for Developing Countries.* World Bank Research Publications. New York: Oxford University Press, 1987.

Niksch, Larry A. "The Communist Party of the Philippines and the Aquino Government." In *Rebuilding a Nation,* edited by Carl H. Lande, pp. 397–416. Washington, D.C.: Washington Institute Press, 1987.

Nordlinger, Eric A. *On the Anatomy of the Democratic State.* Cambridge: Harvard University Press, 1981.

Nye, Joseph S., Jr. *Bound to Lead: The Changing Nature of American Power.* New York: Basic Books, 1990.

Nyrop, Richard F., ed. *Guatemala: A Country Study.* Area Handbook Series prepared for the Department of the Army. Washington, D.C.: Government Printing Office, 1984.

O'Donnell, Guillermo, and Schmitter, Philippe C. *Transitions from Authoritarian Rule: Tentative Conclusions About Uncertain Democracies.* Baltimore: Johns Hopkins University Press, 1986.

O'Donnell, Guillermo; Schmitter, Philippe C.; and Whitehead, Laurence, eds. *Transitions from Authoritarian Rule: Comparative Perspectives.* Baltimore: Johns Hopkins University Press, 1986.

O'Donnell, Guillermo; Schmitter, Philippe C.; and Whitehead, Laurence, eds. *Transitions from Authoritarian Rule: Latin America.* Baltimore: Johns Hopkins University Press, 1986.

Olson, Mancur. "Diseconomies of Scale and Development." *CATO Journal* 7 (Spring–Summer 1987): 77–97.

Olson, Mancur. *The Rise and Decline of Nations.* New Haven: Yale University Press, 1982.

O'Neill, Bard G.; Heaton, William R.; and Alberts, Donald J., eds. *Insurgency in the Modern World.* Boulder, Colo.: Westview Press, 1980.

Organski, A. F. K., and Kugler, Jacek. *The War Ledger.* Chicago: University of Chicago Press, 1980.

Westlake, Melvin, "Out of the Shadows." *South* 115 (May 1990): 12–17.

Palmer, M., and Stern, L., eds. *Political Development in Changing Societies.* Lexington, Mass.: Heath Lexington Books, 1971.

Palmer, Robert R. *The Age of the Democratic Revolution.* 2 vols. Princeton: Princeton University Press, 1959–1964.

Papp, Dr. Daniel S. *Soviet Policies toward the Developing World during the 1980s: The Dilemmas of Power and Presence.* Maxwell Air Force Base, Ala.: Air University Press, 1986.

Parsons, Talcott. *Essays in Sociological Theory.* Rev. ed. Glencoe, Ill.: Free Press, 1954.

Parsons, Talcott. *Structure and Process in Modern Societies.* Glencoe, Ill.: Free Press, 1960.

Perlmutter, Amos. "The Praetorian State and the Praetorian Army: Toward a Taxonomy of Civil-Military Relations in Developing Polities." *Comparative Politics* 1 (April 1969): 382–404.

Perkins, John A. "The Right of Counterrevolution." *Georgia Journal of International & Comparative Law* 17 (1986): 171–227.

Porter, Bruce D. *The U.S.S.R. in Third World Conflicts: Soviet Arms and Diplomacy in Local Wars, 1945–1980.* New York: Cambridge University Press, 1984.

Powell, G. Bingham, Jr. *Contemporary Democracies: Participation, Stability, and Violence.* Cambridge: Harvard University Press, 1982.

Powelson, John P., and Stock, Richard. *The Peasant Betrayed: Agriculture and Land Reform in the Third World.* Washington, D.C.: CATO Institute, 1990.

Price, Robert M. "Military Officers and Political Leadership." *Comparative Politics* 3 (April, 1971): 361–79.

Pye, Lucian W., and Verba, Sidney, eds. *Political Culture and Political Development.* Princeton: Princeton University Press, 1965.

Ra'anan, Uri, et al. *Third World Marxist-Leninist Regimes: Strengths, Vulnerabilities, and U.S. Policy.* Washington, D.C.: Pergamon-Brassey's, 1985.

Rappoport, David C. "The Political Dimensions of Military Usurpation." *Political Science Quarterly* 83 (December 1968): 551–72.

Reisman, W. Michael. "Coercion and Self-Determination: Construing Charter Article 2(4)." *American Journal of International Law* 78 (1984): 642–45.

Reisman, W. Michael. "Old Wines in New Bottles: The Reagan and Brezhnev Doctrines in Contemporary International Law and Practice." *Yale Journal of International Law* 13 (1988): 171–98.

Reisman W. Michael, and Baher, James. "Covert Uses of Coercion Abroad: Practices, Contexts and Policies in International American Law." Paper delivered at the U.S. Institute of Peace Conference on Policy Alternatives to Deal with Secret Warfare: International Law, March 16–17, 1990.

Remmer, Karen L. "The Politics of Economic Stabilization: IMF Standby Programs in Latin America, 1954–1984." *Comparative Politics* 19 (October 1986): 1–24.

Roeder, Philip G. "Modernization and Participation in the Leninist Development Strategy." *American Political Science Review* 83 (September 1980): 859–84.

Rosenau, James N. *The Study of Global Interdependence: Essays on the Transnationalization of World Affairs.* London: Frances Pinter, 1980.

Rostow, Eugene V. "Disputes Involving the Inherent Right of Self-Defense." In *The International Court of Justice at the Crossroads*, edited by Lori Damrosch, pp. 264–319. Dobbs Ferry, N.Y.: Trans-National Publishers, 1987.

Rostow, Nicholas. "Law and the Use of Force by States: The Brezhnev Doctrine." *Yale Journal of World Public Order* 7 (1981): 209–43.

Rostow, Walt W. *The Stages of Economic Growth.* Cambridge: Cambridge University Press, 1960.

Rowles, James P. " 'Secret Wars': Self-Defense and the Charter—A Reply to Professor

Moore." *American Journal of International Law* 80 (1986): 568–83.

Rubenberg, Cheryl A. "Israel and Guatemala: Advice and Counterinsurgency." *Middle East Report* (May–June 1986): 16–44.

Rubenstein, Alvin Z. *Moscow's Third World Strategy.* Princeton: Princeton University Press, 1988.

Rubin, Seymour J. "World Court Jurisdiction and U.S. Foreign Policy in Latin America." In *Proceedings of the Seventy-Eighth Annual Meeting of the American Society of International Law*, pp. 321–37. Washington, D.C.: The American Society of International Law, 1986.

Russett, Bruce M. "Inequality and Instability: The Relation of Land Tenure to Politics." *World Politics* 16 (April 1964): 442–54.

Rustow, Dankwart A. "Transitions to Democracy: Toward a Dynamic Model." *Comparative Politics* 2 (1970): 337–64.

Rustow, Dankwart A. *A World of Nations: Problems of Political Modernization.* Washington, D.C.: Brookings Institution, 1967.

Rustow, Dankwart A., and Ward, Robert. *Political Development in Japan and Turkey.* Princeton: Princeton University Press, 1964.

Sartori, Giovanni. *The Theory of Democracy Revisited.* Chatham, N.J.: Chatham House Publishers, 1987.

Schachter, Oscar. "The Legality of Pro-Democratic Invasion." *American Journal of International Law* 78 (1984): 645–50.

Schachter, Oscar. "Self-Defense and the Rule of Law." *American Journal of International Law* 83 (1989): 259–77.

Schiff, Ze'ev, and Ya'ari, Ehud. *Intifada: The Palestinian Uprising—Israel's Third Front.* Edited and translated by Ina Friedman. New York: Simon and Schuster, 1989.

Schirmer, Daniel B., and Shalom, Stephen Rosskamm, eds. *The Philippines Reader: A History of Colonialism, Neocolonialism, Dictatorship, and Resistance.* Boston: South End Press, 1987.

Schneider, Ronald M. "Guatemala: An Aborted Communist Takeover." In *Studies on the Soviet Union: The Anatomy of Communist Takeovers*, pp. 516–35. Institute for the Study of the U.S.S.R. Vol. 11, no. 4, 1971 [Munich].

Schutz, Barry M., and Slater, Robert O., eds. *Revolution & Political Change in the Third World.* Boulder, Colo.: Lynne Rienner Publishers, 1990.

Seton-Watson, Hugh. *The East European Revolution.* New York: Praeger, 1951.

Seton-Watson, Hugh. *Revolution in East Europe.* New York: Praeger, 1958.

Shafer, D. Michael. *Deadly Paradigms: The Failure of U.S. Counterinsurgency Policy.* Princeton: Princeton University Press, 1988.

Sheehan, Michael A. "Comparative Counterinsurgency Strategies: Guatemala and El Salvador." *Conflict* 9: 127–54.

Shultz, Richard H., Jr. *The Soviet Union and Revolutionary Warfare: Principles, Practices, and Regional Comparisons.* Stanford: Hoover Institution Press, 1988.

Shultz, Richard H., Jr.; Ra'anan, Uri; Pfaltzgraff, Robert L., Jr.; Olson, William J.; and Lukes, Igor. *Guerrilla Warfare and Counterinsurgency: U.S.–Soviet Policy in the Third World.* Lexington, Mass.: D. C. Heath, 1989.

Sigmund, Paul E., Jr., ed. *The Ideologies of Developing Nations*. New York: Praeger, 1963.

Skidmore, Thomas E., and Smith, Peter H. *Modern Latin America*. New York: Oxford University Press, 1984.

Smith, Tony. "The Underdevelopment of Development Literature." *World Politics* 31 (1979): 247–88.

Snider, Lewis W. "The Political Performance of Third World Governments and the Debt Crisis." *American Political Science Review* 84 (December 1990): 1263–80.

Sofaer, Abraham D. "International Law and the Use of Force." *The National Interest* 13 (Fall 1988): 53–64.

Stern, Ellen P., ed. *The Limits of Military Intervention*. Beverly Hills: Sage Publications, 1977.

Streeten, Paul, et al. *First Things First: Meeting Basic Human Needs in Developing Countries*. World Bank Publications. New York: Oxford University Press, 1981.

Sunkel, Osvaldo. "Transnational Capitalism and National Disintegration in Latin America." *Social and Economic Studies* 22 (1973).

Tannenbaum, Frank. "On Political Stability." *Political Science Quarterly* 75 (June 1960): 161–80.

Taubman, William. *Stalin's American Policy: From Entente to Detente to Cold War*. New York: Norton, 1982.

Taylor, George E. *The Philippines and the United States: Problems of Partnership*. New York: Praeger, 1964.

Taylor, Maxwell D. *The Uncertain Trumpet*. New York: Harper & Brothers, 1960.

Thayer, Carlyle A. *War by Other Means: National Liberation and Revolution in Viet-Nam, 1954–60*. Boston: Allen & Unwin, 1989.

Tocqueville, Alexis de. *Democracy in America*. Edited by Phillis Bradley. New York: Knopf, 1955.

Tucker, Robert W., ed. *Intervention and the Reagan Doctrine*. New York: Council on Religion and International Affairs, 1985.

Tucker, Robert W., ed. *The Marx-Engels Reader*. 2d ed. New York: Norton, 1978.

Turner, Robert F. "International Law, the Reagan Doctrine, and World Peace: Going Back to the Future." *Washington Quarterly* 11 (1988): 119–36.

Ulam, Adam B. "Communist Doctrine and Soviet Diplomacy." *Survey* 76 (Summer 1970): 3–16.

Ulam, Adam B. *Expansion and Coexistence: The History of Soviet Foreign Policy 1917–67*. New York: Praeger, 1968.

U.S. Department of Commerce. *Investment Climate Statement: Guatemala*. Washington, D.C.: Government Printing Office, January 30, 1988.

U.S. Department of Commerce. International Trade Administration. *Overseas Business Reports: Marketing Guatemala*. American Embassy, Guatemala, December 1985.

U.S. Department of State. *Country Reports on Human Rights Practices*. Submitted to the U.S. Senate Committee on Foreign Relations and the U.S. House of Representatives Committee on Foreign Affairs. Washington, D.C.: Government Printing Office, yearly.

U.S. Department of State. Bureau of Public Affairs. *Communist Interference in El Salvador.* Special Report, no. 80. Washington, D.C.: Government Printing Office, Feb. 23, 1981.

U.S. Department of State. Bureau of Public Affairs. *Cuba's Renewed Support for Violence in Latin America.* Special Report, no. 90. Washington, D.C.: Government Printing Office, Dec. 14, 1981.

U.S. Department of State. Bureau of Public Affairs. *"Revolution Beyond Our Borders": Sandinista Intervention in Central America.* Special Report, no. 132. Washington, D.C.: Government Printing Office, Sept. 1985.

U.S. General Accounting Office. *The Philippines: Accountability and Control of U.S. Economic Assistance.* GAO/NSIAD-86-108BR. Washington, D.C.: Government Printing Office, May 1986.

USSR Ministry of Foreign Affairs. "The Foreign Policy and Diplomatic Activity of the USSR (April 1985–October 1989)." *International Affairs* (January 1990): 7–111.

Valenta, Jiri, and Cibulka, Frank, eds. *Gorbachev's New Thinking and Third World Conflicts.* New Brunswick, N.J.: Transaction Publishers, 1990.

Valkenier, Elizabeth K. "New Soviet Views on Economic Aid." *Survey* no. 76 (Summer 1970): 17–29.

Valkenier, Elizabeth K. *The Soviet Union and the Third World: an Economic Bind.* New York: Praeger, 1983.

Wallander, Celeste A. "Third-World Conflict in Soviet Military Thought: Does the 'New Thinking' Grow Prematurely Grey?" *World Politics* 42 (October 1989): 31–63.

Walton, John. *Reluctant Rebels: Comparative Studies of Revolution and Underdevelopment.* New York: Columbia University Press, 1984.

Ward, Robert, and Rustow, Dankwart, eds. *Political Development in Japan and Turkey.* Princeton: Princeton University Press, 1964.

Weiner, Myron, and Huntington, Samuel D., eds. *Understanding Political Development.* Boston: Little, Brown, 1987.

Wiarda, Howard J. "Political Culture and National Development." *The Fletcher Forum of World Affairs* 13 (Summer 1989): 193–203.

Wiarda, Howard J., ed. "The Origins of the Crises in Central America." In *Rift and Revolution,* pp. 3–23. Washington, D.C.: American Enterprise Institute, 1984.

Widlanski, Michael, ed. *Can Israel Survive a Palestinian State?* Jerusalem: Institute for Advanced Strategic and Political Studies, 1990.

Wilson, Heather A. *International Law and the Use of Force by National Liberation Movements.* New York: Oxford University Press, 1988.

Wolf, Charles, Jr. *Controlling Small Wars.* Santa Monica, Calif.: Rand Corporation, 1968.

Wolf, Charles, Jr. *United States Policy and the Third World: Problems and Analysis in the Third World.* Lexington, Mass.: D. C. Heath in association with the Rand Corporation, 1987.

Wolf, Charles Jr., and Webb, Katharine Watkins. *Developing Cooperative Forces in the Third World.* Lexington, Mass.: D. C. Heath in association with the Rand Corporation, 1987.

Woods, Alan. *Development and the National Interest: U.S. Economic Assistance into the 21st Century.* Report prepared by the administrator of the Agency for International Development. Washington, D.C.: Government Printing Office, February 17, 1989.

World Bank. *World Development Report 1988.* New York: Oxford University Press, 1988.

World Bank. *World Development Report 1990.* New York: Oxford University Press, 1990.

Wynia, Gary W. *The Politics of Latin American Development.* 2d ed. New York: Cambridge University Press, 1984.

Yarborough, William P. "Counterinsurgency: The U.S. Role—Past, Present, and Future." In *Guerrilla Warfare and Counterinsurgency,* edited by Richard H. Shultz et al., pp. 103–14.

Yin, John. *The Soviet Views on the Use of Force in International Law.* Hong Kong: Asian Research Service, 1980.

Zinoviev, Alexander. *The Reality of Communism.* London: Victor Gollancz, 1984.

Index

Lieutenant General William E. Odom retired from
the army in 1988 after thirty-four years of service. At
present he is Director of National Security Studies at
the Hudson Institute and an Adjunct Professor of
Political Science at Yale University. At the time of
his retirement General Odom was Director of the
National Security Agency. He received his Ph.D.
from Columbia University in 1970.

Library of Congress Cataloging-in-Publication Data
Odom, William E.
On internal war : American and Soviet approaches
to Third World clients and insurgents / by
William E. Odom.
Includes bibliographical references and index.
ISBN 0-8223-1182-8
1. Developing countries—Politics and
government. 2. Insurgency—Developing countries—
History—20th century. 3. World politics—1945– 4.
Developing countries—Foreign relations—Soviet
Union. 5. Soviet Union—Foreign relations—
Developing countries. 3. Developing countries—
Foreign relations—United States. 7. United States—
Foreign relations—Developing countries. I. Title.
D883.O36 1992   91-18572 CIP
909.82—dc20